JACK UBALDI'S
MEAT BOOK

To

Dot Watson

It was a real pleasure
to have had you in class.
I hope it is only a Prelude
to great cooking success.

Best wishes

Sincerely.

Jack Ubaldi.

JACK UBALDI'S MEAT BOOK

A Butcher's Guide to Buying, Cutting, and Cooking Meat

by Jack Ubaldi
and Elizabeth Crossman

ILLUSTRATED BY MARIO PIAZZA

COLLIER BOOKS
Macmillan Publishing Company
New York

Maxwell Macmillan Canada
Toronto

Maxwell Macmillan International
New York   Oxford   Singapore   Sydney

Collier Books   Maxwell Macmillan Canada, Inc.
Macmillan Publishing Company   1200 Eglinton Avenue East
866 Third Avenue   Suite 200
New York, NY 10022   Don Mills, Ontario M3C 3N1

Macmillan Publishing Company is part of the
Maxwell Communication Group of Companies.

Library of Congress Cataloging-in-Publication Data
Ubaldi, Jack.
Jack Ubaldi's meat book:
a butcher's guide to buying, cutting, and cooking meat/
by Jack Ubaldi and Elizabeth Crossman; illustrated by Mario Piazza.
p.   cm.
Reprint. Originally published: New York: Macmillan, ©1987.
Includes index.
ISBN 0-02-007310-0
1. Meat cuts.   2. Meat cutting.   3. Cookery (Meat)
I. Crossman, Elizabeth.   II. Title.   III. Title: Meat book.
[TX373.U23   1991]   91-12750   CIP
641.3'6—dc20

Macmillan books are available at special discounts for bulk purchases
for sales promotions, premiums, fund-raising, or educational use.
For details, contact:

Special Sales Director
Macmillan Publishing Company
866 Third Avenue
New York, NY 10022

First Collier Books Edition 1991

10 9 8 7 6 5 4 3 2 1

Printed in the United States of America

TO
My loyal customers,
who suggested I write this book

and

My wife and children,
who gave me the strength to do it

The authors acknowledge with gratitude and admiration the contribution of John Woodside to this book. His editorial skills and his unflagging enthusiasm have enhanced the book immeasurably.

CONTENTS

INTRODUCTION

I HAD MY BUTCHER SHOP, The Florence Prime Meat Market, on Jones Street in New York City for forty years. It was probably the smallest butcher shop in New York, but I think it was the best. All kinds of people came into my store—young people, old people, good cooks, beginning cooks, and, very often, people of European descent. Jones Street is in Greenwich Village in Manhattan, and many of the residents there in the thirties and forties were recent immigrants. That suited me fine because I was a fairly recent immigrant myself.

We came from Bevagna, a small town in the province of Umbria in northern Italy. In 1917, after my father had been here a few years, he sent for the rest of the family. I was seven. I was a wild kid, and just before the ship was due to sail, I ran into a shovel and cut a gash on my eye and face. I packed it with dirt, but it was so large and ugly-looking that we weren't allowed to go. On the way across, that ship was sunk. When the next ship was ready, our papers were not in order. That ship was sunk also. Finally we got on a ship that was one of seven in a convoy. The first night out, the other six ships went down. Twenty days later we made it to Ellis Island. I have always thought Saint Francis meant me to become an American.

I worked in my father's butcher shop from the time I was ten; later I did butchering for other stores, including Gristede's and Grand Union. In 1930 I opened my own restaurant on Cornelia Street in Greenwich Village. It was small and Italian, and for a while I did a good business serving lunch for the people who made costume jewelry and artificial flowers on the top floor of the factory across the street. I had a chef, a waiter, and a dishwasher; we had a lot of fun. There was a piano in the restaurant, and some of the cast of the Ziegfeld Follies used to come in after the show. We would lock the door of the restaurant and have a party. After we served our last meal at night, we played cards or took bottles of wine and went down to the Bowery to eat scungilli. But the Depression hit the flower and jewelry business, the factory closed, and I lost my customers. I gave up the restaurant in 1934 and went back to butchering. At that time I was making $9 a week; eventually I worked my way up to $18.

I started my store with a partner in March 1936. I had $115 in my pocket and a $200 loan. By September I paid off my partner and was on my own. In the beginning the monthly rent was $30, and I made just enough to pay the bills. It was hard work. I left home at 6 A.M. to go to the market; we kept the store open until seven weeknights, midnight on Saturdays. Eventually I had two men and a boy working for me in that very small store. There was no extra space at all and no time for relaxing. We kept a sandwich beside the scale and took a bite whenever we had a few minutes.

When the Second World War came along, I joined the U.S. Navy. We put a big sign in the window of the store: CLOSED UNTIL THE WAR IS OVER. I worked with sonar in the Navy, and when I returned after the war, I thought about giving up butchering and going to electronics school. I decided I wouldn't have as much fun talking to people if I was a television repairman, so I reopened the store in March 1946. Nearly thirty years later, I sold the store to my assistant and planned to retire. A few months of doing nothing was enough for me, so I started my new career, teaching, when I was sixty-four years old. For the past twelve years, I have been Instructor of Butchering at the New York Restaurant School, teaching professional and cooking classes.

From my experience, most shoppers know the cuts of meat by name, but after that they are in trouble. They rarely know what the meat should look like, what part of the animal it comes from, and what is the best way to use it. The large number of beef cuts and confusion about what cuts are good for what recipes are the reasons I started writing this book seventeen years ago. Customers would come into my store and ask for a piece of brisket, an expensive cut of beef. If I didn't have brisket in the store, I would ask them how they planned to cook the meat and then suggest another, cheaper cut of meat that would do nicely for their recipe. Often one would say, "Oh, no, Jack, the recipe says brisket. I must have brisket." Sometimes they would bring me the piece of "brisket" they had been sold at another butcher shop. Of course, it wasn't brisket at all, but another piece of meat like the one I had originally suggested, and they had paid top price for it.

I hope, by spending some time looking at the drawings and descriptions in this book, you will learn to recognize the shapes and sizes of the cuts of meat. If you keep the book in the kitchen near your shopping list so that you can leaf through it before you go to the store, I think you will find that you buy more wisely at the supermarket, and if you are lucky enough to shop at a prime butcher shop, your butcher will respect your knowledge and make sure you get the best. By learning more, you will feed yourself better and increase your pleasure in cooking and eating.

There have been great changes in meat buying since I first went into business in 1936. At that time, Americans enjoyed the cheapest food prices in the world; if you made a mistake with a piece of meat, you might have a bad meal, but you were not out a lot of money. Today meat prices are at an all-time high, more in proportion to what Europeans pay for meat. Another shift is that 90 percent of the meat sold in the United States today is bought at a supermarket where the meat is precut and plastic-wrapped. Except in a few large cities where there are still prime butcher shops, the neighborhood butcher who knows his customers by name has disappeared.

The third noticeable change is the amount of meat we eat. When I opened the store, it was not unusual for a customer to ask for a two-inch-thick sirloin steak, a six-pound piece of meat, to serve four people. This was astonishing to me, as a European portion of meat is about five ounces per serving. But now we are seeing a trend in this country toward smaller portions. I think this is a healthier way to eat and am not surprised by the forecast that our present portion size of five to six ounces of meat may diminish to three ounces.

You may well wonder what a butcher knows about cooking. Although I have no professional training as a chef, I have always been interested in food. Many of the recipe ideas I have gathered over the years started from conversations in the store. I learned a lot from my customers, and I like to think they learned a lot from me. After the Second World War, I began to travel to Europe. By talking to butchers and chefs in Italy, France, Spain, Portugal, and Belgium, I have been able to expand my own knowledge of butchering and cooking.

Since I started teaching in 1976, I have always served a meal at the end of my classes. I feel students should get some concrete idea of how to use the meat we have been discussing and cutting. I often make a pasta or a vegetable dish to go with the meat, and when there is a little leeway in the budget, we have a glass of wine with our meal. And many, many times, I make bread.

Let me tell you about this bread. Seventeen years ago I was in my home region of Umbria in northern Italy talking to Aldo Olivieri, a fisherman who had become a baker. As bread baked in his ovens, its intense fragrance suddenly brought back memories of my own mother making bread at home before we came to the United States. In all my years of working, I had completely forgotten this bread until I smelled and tasted it again in 1970. I loved it and couldn't wait to make it myself.

When I make bread at school, its good baking smell wafts outside the door of the classroom. By the time we are ready to eat, there is usually a line of hungry students who come by for a piece of bread. If you would like to taste this bread, you have three choices. You can go to Santa Cruz, California, where Aldo features the bread in the seaside restaurant attached to his marina and bait shop, you can take one of my butchering classes, or you can make it yourself.

My Favorite Bread—Focaccia Umbrian Style

This bread is not cooked in a bread pan, it is spread out on a baking sheet. Don't worry if it doesn't rise evenly; it rarely does.

1 package active dry yeast or 1
  ounce yeast
1 tablespoon sugar
1 ½ cups water
4 cups all-purpose flour
1 tablespoon salt

½ teaspoon white pepper
1 teaspoon dried rosemary or
  leaves of 1 rosemary branch
2 tablespoons olive oil,
  approximately
1 cup finely chopped onions

Warm ½ cup of the water to about 110°. Dissolve the yeast and sugar into it for 15 minutes.

Measure out the flour, salt, pepper, and rosemary into the large bowl of an electric mixer with a dough hook attachment. With the machine on low speed, gradually add the watered yeast, and the remaining water (which is still at room temperature) until it is all incorporated. Add ½ tablespoon of the olive oil. Let the machine knead the dough for at least 10 minutes. To knead the dough in a food processor, process with the plastic blade for about 5 minutes, no longer.

Pour a bit of olive oil in the bottom of a large bowl. Gather up the dough into a large bowl and place it in the bowl, rolling it around a bit. Cover with plastic wrap and keep in a warm place until it has doubled in size.

Punch the dough down with your fist, add the onions, and knead for a few minutes. Re-cover with plastic wrap and let rise a second time. The first rising will take a few hours, the second rising about 45 minutes.

When the dough has risen, rub a bit of oil on a cookie sheet and empty the bowl onto it, spreading the dough into a large oval an inch thick with your hands, as if you were making a pizza. Drizzle olive oil onto the top of the dough. Set aside for 15 minutes.

Place the pan on the bottom rack of a preheated 375° oven and bake for 30 minutes. Change the pan to the top rack for 15 more minutes, then remove the pan and place it on a cake rack to cool.

Serve warm, toasted, or for hero sandwiches with sausages, fried onions, and peppers. For extra flavor add ½ cup of minced prosciutto or salami to the dough.

YIELD: 1 FLAT LOAF

IN THE KITCHEN

❧~❧

THE RECIPES IN THIS BOOK are meant to be guidelines for your own cooking. A good cook puts personality into his or her cooking, so it is important for you to taste as you cook and adjust the seasonings for your own palate. I must be on the spicy side because that's the way I like my food, but if you don't, cut down on the seasonings.

People think of Italian cooking as heavily accented with basil, oregano, and tomatoes; you will not find this true in these recipes. Basil never hurt anyone; it is an inoffensive little herb, just as oregano is very powerful, but neither should dominate a cuisine. For that reason, I use thyme and marjoram sparingly because they are strong herbs with strong tastes. To my way of thinking, an herb should not be the highlight of a dish; rather it should help bring everything together and bring out the flavor of the meat.

You may notice I do not use green peppers in my cooking, as their strong taste is not agreeable to me. But don't let my prejudices affect your preferences or your creativity.

Because my background is that of northern Italy, I use butter, light olive oils, and mild cheeses like fontina and Parmesan. Grated Parmesan is perfect on pasta, but I use pecorino romano, a slightly stronger cheese, in some stuffings and in meat loaf. I have specified when olive oil is to be used in a recipe; other oils good for browning are peanut oil, corn oil, and safflower oil.

Cooking Tips

After browning meat in butter and oil, discard the fat and continue the recipe with fresh butter and oil.

When adding wine to a recipe, let it reduce for a few minutes without stirring in order to prevent a slightly offensive aftertaste.

I have noticed that most non-Italians cook tomatoes too fast. If you let tomatoes come to a rolling boil, they burst and become acidic. By simmering tomatoes very slowly, you will not need to add sugar to compensate for their loss of sweetness. Mash canned tomatoes thoroughly with a food mill or food processor before using for a tomato or marinara sauce.

Mushrooms look more appealing in some dishes when they remain white after cooking. When you want this effect, clean the mushrooms by placing them in a bowl of acidulated water (water with the juice of one lemon) for about 10 minutes. Do not leave them in the bath too long, or they will get soggy. Drain and pat dry with a paper towel before using.

When making a pasta such as Pasta with Broccoli, page 78, cook the pasta in the water in which you cooked the broccoli. Add a ladle of this water to the base of the sauce, the garlic browning in oil, to prevent the garlic from burning.

I noticed when I had my restaurant that the chefs always cooked chopped onions, carrots, and celery with roasted meats and birds. The juices of the roast and the juices of the vegetables mingle together to make a fragrant natural sauce, a mirepoix gravy. Just before serving, put the juices and the vegetables through a food mill. See directions for Roast Chicken with Mirepoix Gravy, page 26.

For coating meat or vegetables before frying, grate bread crumbs from dry or stale bread. I keep a piece of bread in a paper bag in the cupboard for up to two weeks, then grate it as needed. Save any extra crumbs in a covered jar. Bouillon cubes are useful back-ups, but your own stock is worlds better. It is so easy to make stock and keep it in the freezer, I hope you will get in the habit of doing so. If you use bouillon cubes, go easy on the salt you add to the recipe.

Since most home stoves are not perfectly calibrated, a meat thermometer is a useful tool. I like the small thermometer shaped like a fountain pen that gives an instant reading of the internal temperature of the meat. Insert it into the meat, away from the bone, remove it and look at the degrees registered. Never leave the thermometer in the meat. Use this chart as a guideline for roasting meat.

INTERNAL TEMPERATURES FOR COOKED MEATS

Chicken, turkey	170° to 180°
Fresh ham	160° to 170°
Loin of pork	160° to 170°
Leg of lamb	120° to 125°—rare
	130° to 135°—medium
Veal	160° to 175°
Prime ribs of beef	125°—rare
	140°—medium
Boneless beef roast	125° to 130°—rare
	140° to 145°—medium
Leg of venison	130° to 135°—rare

Knives

Most good knives today are a combination of approximately 60 percent high-carbon steel, 20 percent nickel, and 20 percent or less chrome.

Chrome does not sharpen well, but it prevents the steel from tarnishing and so helps keep the blade clean and shiny. High-carbon rusts quickly, but its edge will last longer than stainless steel. The quality of the knife depends on the quality of the steel and how it is tempered. German, Swiss, and Swedish knives are usually good-quality knives. I now use high-carbon "no stain" knives that have a small quantity of chrome and nickel.

When you buy a knife, be sure to feel the balance of it in your hand. It is important that it is not too heavy nor too light. You want it to feel just right for you because a good knife should last you for years.

You need knives with a firm blade for meat cutting. (Fish knives, on the other hand, need a flexible blade.)

ESSENTIAL KNIVES AND TOOLS

A 5- to 6-inch boning knife, narrow or wide
A 10- to 12-inch steak knife, preferably of layered tempered steel
A carving knife with a rounded tip
A 10-inch chef's knife
A 4½-inch paring knife
A sharpening steel
An instant meat thermometer

VALUABLE OPTIONAL KNIVES AND TOOLS

An 8-inch chef's knife
A cleaver
A 19-inch meat saw
A pounder
A furrier's needle or similar 6-inch sewing tool
A larding needle
A skinning knife (for hunters)

A meat saw is relatively inexpensive and will last you a lifetime. A good knife will cost you about $50, a small saw only about $20. Pounders are useful to flatten out and widen slices of meat. They are no longer made of solid brass, but you may be able to find an old one in an antique store. Inexpensive stainless steel pounders are available for $4 and up, depending on the weight. Davpol Enterprises, 267 Lafayette Street, New York, N.Y., 10012, (212) 966-4242, as well as many cookware catalogues, carries pounders and small meat grinders.

A curved furrier's needle is very useful for sewing boned roasts, poultry, etc. It is an inexpensive item, about a dollar, and is available at

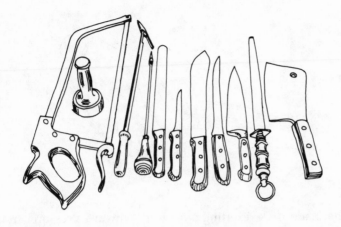

most 5 and 10 cent stores. Larding needles come in two sizes, 6-inch and 12-inch.

KNIFE SKILLS

If you will remember a few commonsense rules, you will rarely have an accident with a knife. The single most important precaution is to work with a sharp knife. A dull knife is of absolutely no value to you. It is dangerous and inefficient and the cause of most knife accidents. Meat cut by dull knives will be ragged. Use the steel every time you use your knife.

Never hide the knife, either with your other arm or hand or under a piece of meat. It should always be visible and easily available, with the knife handle toward you, on your right side if you are right-handed, on your left if you are a southpaw. When you carry a knife, keep the point down; never hold it sticking out.

When you are cutting or boning meat, ALWAYS CUT DOWN toward the table and away from you. Never cut straight up and never in the middle of the air. If you are right-handed, cut toward the table with your left hand holding the meat; if you are left-handed, do the reverse.

Slicing. Use the steak knife for this most basic of cutting operations. Stand in a comfortable position with your feet apart so that your arm, bent at the elbow, can move easily back and forth. To slice cutlets from any piece of solid muscle meat, hold the knife as you would hold a frying pan, with the blade at a 20° angle. Reach slightly forward and place the heel of the blade close to the end of the meat nearest your other hand. Hold that end with your hand absolutely flat. This is the correct approach for all cutting and sawing procedures.

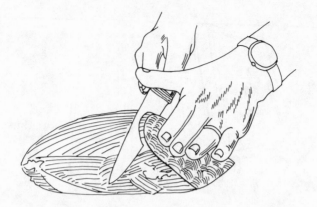

Pull the blade back, exerting a slight downward pressure, from the heel all the way to the tip. Concentrate on keeping the motion of the blade smooth and parallel to your hand; don't worry about speed or exerting force. Return the heel of the blade to the slice you have started and, keeping the blade flat against the surface you have just created, pull the blade back through to the tip again. For this pass you should hold the piece you are slicing between your thumb and forefinger or fingertips so that you can pull the slice away as you cut. Keep pulling the blade back through the meat until you have completed the slice. Never push the blade or saw with it; always pull. With a little practice and a sharp knife, this technique will become very simple for you.

Remember: In any slicing operation—cutting cutlets, slicing between ribs, butterflying—always pull the knife through the meat and use the full length of the blade. To keep your cuts straight and flat, use the surface you have just cut as a guide for the next pull by keeping the blade flat against the just-cut surface.

Pounding. To use a pounder, strike the meat with some force, enough to flatten it noticeably, and then move the pounder, in practically the same motion, to the outer edge of the meat.

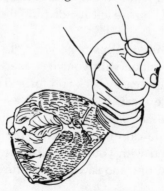

Boning. Hold the boning knife in a comfortable grip as you would hold a frying pan. Most boning involves cutting tendons and nerves away from the joints and then scraping the meat from the length of the bone with the blade perpendicular to the bone. When you need to apply more pressure or when you need the blade to be vertical to cut more conveniently, hold the boning knife as you would an ice pick. When boning, try to keep your position comfortable and be sure never to cut toward the hand with which you are holding the meat. Again, make sure your knife is sharp. Never pick it up without running it down the steel a few times to restore its edge.

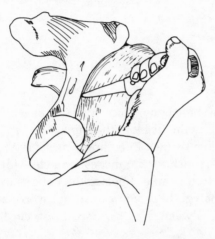

Butterflying. Open up a slice of meat like the leaves of a book or the wings of a butterfly without separating the pieces. Place the knife (usually a steak knife) on the center of the outside edge of the meat. Hold the meat flat with one hand while pulling the blade horizontally through the meat until it is about a half inch from the end. Open up the pieces. To further expand the size of the meat, repeat the process. Cut from the center horizontally to the outer edge; there are now four leaves or wings.

Sawing. Slice the meat through to the bone with a steak knife. Replace the knife with a saw, and saw through the bone by keeping the saw very lightly on the bone. Never press down or the teeth will catch in the bone. Only the forward motion of the saw cuts. The piece of meat should move hardly at all under your hand; if it moves a lot, you are pressing too hard. When you have cut through the bone, finish cutting the meat with the knife.

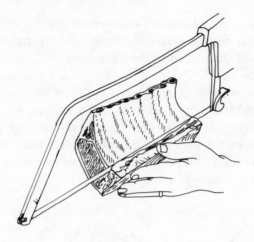

When cutting the chine bone, place your saw at a 90° angle just at the place where the end of the ribs join the chine.

When cutting a loin or rack into chops, measure the width of chop you desire, ½ inch, 1 inch, or 1½ inches, and cut with a steak knife at this point through to the bone. Replace the knife with a saw and saw the bone through as lightly as you can. Don't worry about the ribs. If you happen to cut between the ribs, fine; if not, cut the ribs with the saw.

Cutting Vegetables. When using a chef's knife to cut vegetables, curl the fingers of the hand holding the vegetable so that the blade slides against the last knuckle of your fingertips.

Larding. Inserting strips of salt pork or lard into lean meat to enhance flavor and juiciness. If today's trend toward leaner meat continues, larding will become more and more a necessity. Without a fine marbling of fat, meat becomes dry and flavorless during cooking. To insert strips of salt pork with a larding needle, you sew through the meat, releasing the salt pork in the puncture.

Trussing. To truss a bird for roasting, fold the wings under the back. Lay the string under the wings so you catch a little bit of the neck skin. Bring the ends of the string over the thighs between the breast, then swing to the outside of each leg. Pull up and cross the string under the legs and go around the back. Pull tight and tie.

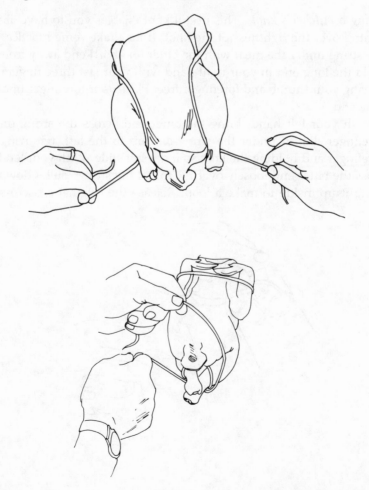

Tying. To tie a piece of meat that will be a portion, like a meat roll (braciole), wrap the string once around the meat lengthwise and tie at one end. Without cutting the string, wind it around the roll three or four times crosswise until you reach the other end. Bring the string back across the roll and tie again at the first knot. To tie a large, solid piece of meat or a roast filled with a stuffing, it is better to tie each ring of string separately so that when you carve, you only need remove one or two strings at a time to keep the roast firm. Start at the thickest part and tie your strings to either end.

Tying a butcher's knot. This useful knot enables you to have absolute control over the tightness of the knot. It may take some practice. Place the string under the meat with the bitter (or short) end away from you. Hold the long end in your right hand with your last three fingers only, leaving your thumb and forefinger free. Place your forefinger under the long end.

With your left hand, bring the bitter end across the string on your forefinger. Pull it under the string and up to the left, removing your forefinger and holding the knot so it doesn't slide. With your left hand, cross the bitter end loosely over the top of the string, pull it down, and bring it up inside to make a loop. Release the original crisscross with

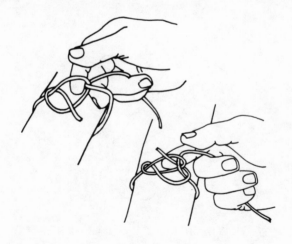

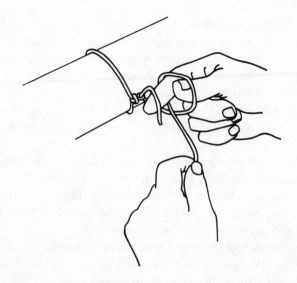

your forefinger and reach down through the loop with it, bringing it back up under the first crisscross. With your left hand, place the bitter end on the tip of your right forefinger and hold it with the thumb of your right hand. Twist the forefinger and thumb, holding the bitter end, back through the loop so your thumb is sticking up through the loop with the bitter end on it. Holding the bitter end with your left hand and the long end with your right hand, tighten the knot. To lock it, make a loop in the long end. Reach back through with your forefinger and thumb, catch the bitter end, and pull through the loop to make a half hitch.

If you are left-handed, reverse the procedure.

Carving. If the meat is boned, carving is a simple matter of slicing, page 11. You will find directions for carving bone-in roasts at the end of recipes for ham, leg of lamb, etc.

Knife maintenance

Sixty years ago butchers and housewives relied on the itinerant knife grinder to sharpen knives. The knife grinder carried a portable grinder on his back and charged 5 or 10 cents a knife. At that time, most knives were made of carbon steel that became stained easily but sharpened quickly and well.

After the itinerant grinder came the horse-drawn wagon rigged up with a motor-driven grinder. Charging 25 cents a knife, $1.50 flat fee for all the knives in a butcher shop, the grinder followed a regular route, replacing his horse and wagon with a truck in the 1930s. After the Second World War, however, the system changed. Grinders preferred to lease knives to butchers (an expensive proposition for the butchers), and service to domestic customers was completely discontinued. Just at this time there was a terrific new interest in fine knives due to the surge in professional and amateur cooking. People were spending a few hundred dollars for a set of knives and needed to know how to take care of them.

Commonsense maintenance will help keep your knives sharp. First, cut only on soft surfaces such as butcher block or composite chopping boards, never on metal or plastic laminate countertops. Store your knives so that the blades are protected; knives jumbled together with other utensils in a drawer are bound to get nicked.

There are two separate steps in keeping knives sharp. The first is to keep a good edge by using a steel as often as you use the knife. The second is to sharpen the knife on an abrasive stone.

Steels. Steels come in many shapes, sizes, and qualities, but basically consist of a long rod usually made of metal fitted into a plastic or wooden handle. Steels do not sharpen the knife; rather they maintain the blade's edge. Correctly passing the knife blade over the steel smooths out microscropic nicks in the blade's surface and realigns the molecules in the cutting edge.

Steels range in price from $5 to $50. I do not recommend the cheapest ones, but you can get a fairly good one in the middle price range. The 12- to 14-inch size is preferable. The best steels are magnetized to help draw the molecules into realignment. You can tell if the steel is magnetized by touching something iron or steel to the very tip. (Steels made of ceramic are not magnetized, but they are also effective for realigning the blade. Since ceramic is smooth, it wears away even less of the knife blade than a regular steel, although it has the drawback of being breakable. You may be surprised to know that ceramic is harder than metal.)

A knife may be steeled in three different ways; in each method the knife is always held to the steel at a 20° angle. Remember you are realigning the blade, not sharpening, so a light touch is important. Hold the steel in your left hand and the knife in your right (reverse if you are left-handed). Begin with the rear part of the knife blade at the point of the steel. Rotate the knife in sort of a quarter circle, drawing the full length of the knife across the full length of the steel. Take one stroke in front of the steel and one stroke in back for about six times on each side.

Or, if you are afraid you may cut your thumb, you can reverse the stroke by starting near the handle of the steel and moving the blade toward the tip. If you are not comfortable with either of these methods, rest the steel point on the table and stroke the knife downward.

Sharpening Stones. No matter how careful you are with your knives, the blades will eventually become dull and will then have to be reground with an abrasive stone or grinding wheel. The stone or wheel will actually grind away metal from the dull blade to make a new, very sharp edge. Depending on how much you use your knives, regrinding is necessary only once or twice a year.

The original sharpening stones were simply natural abrasive stones. Natural stone sharpeners are still used today. They are quarried from high-quality deposits and sawed to proper size. Novaculite, a very hard rock composed of microcrystalline quartz ranging in color from white to black, is a common natural abrasive. Manufactured grinding stones are made from abrasives such as aluminum oxide or silicon carbide that are tumbled with heavy balls of iron, steel, or stone in a drum-shaped grinding mill to the correct particle size and then bonded together.

Sharpening stones come in a variety of grit ranges: coarse, for restoring a badly worn edge; medium, for producing an average edge; fine, for producing a sharper-than-average edge; super-fine and ultra-fine, for precision tools and delicate instruments.

For household use, I recommend an India stone with one coarse-grit side and one fine-grit side. Place the stone on a damp cloth on your work surface to prevent it from slipping while you work. Put a few drops of mineral oil (or a special stone oil) on the coarse side of the stone to prevent the grindings from clogging the pores of the stone, which would ruin the abrasiveness.

Hold the handle of the knife in your right hand and the fingers of your left hand lightly on the flat part of the blade of the knife (reverse if you are left-handed). Holding the knife blade at a 20° angle, stroke right to left in a quarter arc, using the full length of both the knife and the stone. After the first stroke, reverse the procedure and sharpen the other side of the blade. When you have reached the desired sharpness, turn the stone over, oil the fine-grit side, and use it in the same manner. Finally, finish the sharpening process by steeling the knife to complete the realigning.

Wipe off the knife blade, stone, and steel to get rid of any microscopic metal filings. Wipe the stone clean immediately after using and store it, covered, so that dirt and dust doesn't load the pores and reduce its effectiveness. A good way to keep your stone in good condition is to immerse it in a bath of mineral oil when not in use.

Grinding Wheels. An abrasive grinding wheel performs the same function as a sharpening stone. Each side of the knife blade is passed perpendicularly across the rotating wheel to sharpen the whole length of the blade. The knife is held at a 20° angle, and the wheel must be moistened with a few drops of oil or water. The whetstone grinder is usually found on farms to sharpen knives and axes. Farmers can wear out a knife pretty fast.

Diamond Sharpeners. A diamond sharpener is an excellent new tool that combines the functions of a steel and a stone. It has a metal shaft covered with tiny industrial diamonds. Used in the same manner as the conventional steel, the diamond steel hones a keen edge speedily and realigns the blade in the process. Because the diamonds are so sharp, a very light touch is needed. If you use this tool daily for household knives, they will rarely require any other sharpening. There is also a diamond stone for sharpening, also covered with millions of tiny diamonds, that can be used in the same manner as a regular stone.

POULTRY

❧❧

B UYING POULTRY TODAY is a far cry from what it was like when I was a boy. In those days you went to a live chicken market, picked out your chicken, took it home, killed it, and dressed it. The chickens scratched the soil for corn or grain. In Europe you can still buy chickens raised in this manner, although they cost a good deal more than the commercially grown chickens.

In the United States most of the small chicken farmers have disappeared. Today chicken production is big business; chickens are part of a continuous mechanical process from the moment of hatching in the incubator to the moment they are dressed and iced and ready for sale. Their feet never touch the ground, and the amount of food, water, and light they need is all calculated and arranged by computer.

Chickens arrive at the stores in refrigerated trucks, and the customer has the choice of buying a whole chicken or any of its parts. It may seem strange now, but it took a long time to educate customers to accept a dressed chicken.

In the early 1920s my father, mother, and I had a meat market in Greenwich Village. We sold dressed chickens, but many oldtimers wanted live ones, and we were getting a lot of competition from horse-drawn wagons going about the streets filled with coops of live chickens for sale. It was illegal at that time to keep live chickens at a meat market, but my father wanted to make his customers happy. So he put some chickens in a cellar under the store, and to keep their existence a secret, the only entrance to the cellar was through a trapdoor in the floor behind the walk-in refrigerator. There was no stairway down to the cellar, only a folding ladder that was, unfortunately, about two feet short of touching the floor. You had to be agile, but you didn't have to worry too much if you fell—the floor was soft from all the chicken feathers.

Chickens in the Market

When you buy chickens at the supermarket, you need to know what kind of chicken you want for your recipe.

Most of the chickens we buy at the store are White Rocks, known by their white feathers and lack of pinfeathers. The smallest are 1½ pounds, squab broilers. Next come broilers, 2½ to 3 pounds; then fryers, 3 to 4 pounds, which can be broiled, fried, baked, or broiled. They can also be roasted whole. These small chickens can be male or female, but after they grow over 4 pounds, the sex of the bird makes a difference.

Pullets are full-sized young females up to 6 pounds who have not yet begun to lay eggs; they are tender and juicy, for roasting or for soup. A pullet's breast is nicely rounded, its breastbone soft enough so you can bend the tip, and its skin tight and firm. Hens, laying chickens of about 6 pounds good for fricassee or soup, are older birds with crinkly skin, an uneven breast shape, and hard breastbones.

Plymouth Rocks and Rhode Islands Reds, both hen varieties that lay brown eggs, are the best layers for eating; Leghorns, 3½ pounds, are often the best layers, but are stringy and make the poorest eating.

Roasters are 4- to 6-pound males that are excellent for roasting and braising. Capons, desexed males of 6 to 9 pounds, are prized for their delicate, tender meat. A roast capon makes a particularly fine meal. They are highly priced because they are difficult to raise and have a high mortality rate. A capon always has a 1- to 1½-inch scar just above the thigh on the side of the body; if it does not have this mark from the desexing, it is not a capon.

You will seldom see roosters in the market; they are used mostly for canning. They weigh about 6 pounds and have dark, reddish meat that is dry and tough.

More different kinds of domestic poultry and farm-raised game birds are becoming available in the markets today, although you can find some of them only during the winter holiday season. Most can be cooked in a similar fashion to chickens of the same size. See the Game chapter for more recipes.

Cornish Game Hens (a cross between a White Rock chicken and a game hen) are 1 to 2 pounds; and best are the 1-pounders. Guinea hens, newly popular here again after a forty-year period of being out of favor, are about 2½ pounds. They are prized in Europe.

Ducks are about 3 to 5 pounds; the Long Island (Pekin) variety are the most available type in the East. Geese of 8 to 13 pounds are young roasters; you can usually find them during the winter holiday season at prime butcher shops. (See the Game chapter for goose recipes.)

Turkeys come in all sizes and, recently, in parts. The two most common turkey types we see at the store are the Beltsville Small White (BSW) and the Broadbreasted Large White (BBLW). The latter, developed at Cornell University, is a cross between the Broadbreasted Bronze (BBB) from England and the Holland White. The United States Department of Agriculture developed the Beltsville turkey in 1941 in an effort to create a bird that would mature quickly and so produce more meat during the war years.

Smaller turkeys are Beltsvilles: Squab turkeys of 4 pounds are good for broiling, hens run 6 to 9 pounds, and toms go up to 12 pounds. The Broadbreasted Whites run 10 to 14 pounds for hens, a medium turkey, and 18 to 35 pounds for toms, a large turkey.

Tips for Buying, Storing, and Freezing Poultry

It is hard to investigate a chicken thoroughly through the sealed plastic package at the supermarket. You can, however, avoid chickens that have bruises or blood spots on the skin. When you get home, open the package immediately to make sure the bird is fresh and wholesome. If the chicken feels slimy or if the package with the gizzards smells bad, return it to the store for a refund or an exchange. If the little veins under the skin in the neck area have a brownish tint, that is a giveaway that the chicken is too old. (The veins should be red.) The liver in the little package inside the chicken should be firm and a good brown color.

It is better to buy poultry fresh, not frozen. Freezing is, of course, a great convenience and often economical when you can buy poultry on sale, but it does not enhance the flavor or texture of the meat. Do not freeze a fresh turkey in your home freezer. Its frame is too big to freeze quickly and efficiently. Instead buy a frozen turkey and keep it in your own freezer.

Do not refreeze poultry once it has partially or completely thawed. Refreezing does not spoil the meat, but it does cause it to lose some of its flavor and juiciness.

If you plan to keep a chicken for two or three days before you use it, wash it in cold water, pat it dry, and sprinkle it lightly with salt. If it is a whole chicken, salt the interior of the bird also. Place the chicken on waxed paper on a plate in the coldest part of your refrigerator. Cover with another sheet of waxed paper.

If you are having a large party and want to cut up the chickens some time before cooking, here is a trick professional cooks use to prevent the skin from drying out and becoming pockmarked: Wash the chicken pieces and dry them. Place them on a tray and cover with a towel that you have soaked in ice water, then wrung out. Return the chickens to the refrigerator for up to 12 hours. Chicken livers, hearts, and gizzards should be kept in a covered plastic container packed in cracked ice.

A PRECAUTION

All poultry should be washed before using. You should also wash your hands, the knife, and the cutting board after you work with raw poultry before touching or working with other food, like raw vegetables. Use a few drops of vinegar to clean the cutting board.

Chicken Stock

Chicken stock is the basis for soups and sauces. It is easy to make and keeps well in the freezer. To make good chicken stock, use an entire uncooked chicken but add to it any uncooked chicken bones, backs, and necks that you have previously stored in the freezer. They are a good addition to stock and should never be wasted. Or make your stock from 5 pounds of chicken necks and backs, available very cheaply at the supermarket.

Oldtimers say an old hen makes the best soup. It is better not to salt the stock unless you plan to use it immediately.

1 hen, about 5 to 6 pounds, cut
into quarters
Chicken bones, necks, and backs
(optional)
Chicken giblets (gizzard and
heart; do not use the liver)

2 carrots
2 celery stalks, with leaves
1 onion, split in half, with 3
cloves inserted
1 tomato, quartered (optional)
A few peppercorns

Wash the chicken pieces (including the giblets) and place them in a stockpot or any tall pot. Cover with a quantity of cold water (about 6 to 7 quarts) and bring to a boil. Lower the heat and skim off the dark froth that accumulates at the top.

Add the vegetables and peppercorns. Cook gently for a minimum of 3 hours, when the liquid should have reduced to half.

Strain the stock and cool it. Place it in the refrigerator overnight. Scrape off the fat that covers the top of the gelled stock. The stock will keep in the refrigerator for 4 days, or in the freezer indefinitely.

YIELD: 3 QUARTS

Variation: Boiled chicken

A whole boiled chicken is probably the most basic of all poultry dishes. Cooked in this manner, it makes a welcome presentation either hot or cold. The moist meat is perfect for recipes like chicken salad, Chicken Tetrazzini, and chicken croquettes.

The process is exactly the same as the recipe above for stock; once the chicken has cooked in the water, the water becomes stock. Use a whole young chicken or hen; it will be tender in about 1 hour and 30 minutes to 2 hours.

Serve hot with boiled vegetables such as turnips, carrots, and potatoes added to the stock for the last 30 minutes of cooking, or cold with mustard or a vinaigrette sauce.

SERVES 4

Chicken Salad Elisabettiana

I like chicken salad dressed with a strong vinaigrette to give it flavor.

1 boiled chicken, 3½ to 4 pounds
½ cup virgin olive oil
1 tablespoon Dijon mustard
3½ tablespoons balsamic vinegar
Salt, freshly ground pepper
A few lettuce leaves, such as
    radicchio or Bibb

12 to 15 pimiento-stuffed olives
6 to 8 radishes
2 tablespoons capers
1 orange, peeled and cut into
    sections

Let the chicken cool in the stock. Remove all the meat from the bones and cut it into cubes.

Mix the olive oil, mustard, vinegar, salt, and pepper (be generous with the salt and pepper). Place the chicken on the lettuce leaves and arrange the olives, radishes, capers, and orange sections on and around the chicken. Stir the dressing again and dress the chicken lightly.

SERVES 4

Roast Chicken with Mirepoix Gravy

Chopped vegetables that have cooked in the pan with a roasting bird make a tasty gravy. At the end of the cooking time, put them through a food mill with all the juices from the pan. This mirepoix gravy is also excellent with roast meats and game.

1 chicken, about 4 pounds
2 to 3 garlic cloves, unpeeled
A pinch of rosemary and/or
    tarragon
Salt, freshly ground pepper
2 tablespoons butter and/or oil

2 onions, chopped into large
    pieces
2 carrots, peeled and chopped
    into large pieces
2 celery stalks, cut into pieces

Wash the chicken and pat it dry. Season the cavity of the chicken with garlic cloves, rosemary and/or tarragon, salt, and pepper. Rub some of the herb, salt, and pepper on the skin of the bird. Truss it (page 15).

Heat the butter and/or oil in a roasting pan and add the onions, carrots, and celery. (You should have about 2 cups of vegetables.) Cook the vegetables together for a few minutes, then place the chicken on them, breast side up.

Roast the chicken in a preheated 375° oven for about 1 hour and 45 minutes. To test if the chicken is done, prick the thigh with a fork; if the juices come out clear, the chicken is ready. Another easy test is to wiggle the drumstick; when the chicken is cooked, it will move freely.

Remove the chicken from the pan. Spoon the vegetables and the pan juices into a food mill so that the gravy will drip into a bowl or saucepan. (*Note:* Do not use a food processor; the resulting puree will be too thick.) Discard the vegetable residue in the mill and skim off as much fat as possible from the gravy. Reheat it if necessary. If you wish a thicker gravy, add a roux of a small amount of butter and flour or a tablespoon of cornstarch dissolved in ¼ cup of cold water and cook for a few minutes before serving.

SERVES 4

Variation: Stuffed Chicken Grandmère

Chop the heart and liver of the chicken and place them in a bowl with ¼ pound of chopped chicken livers. Soak 2 slices of bread in milk or water and squeeze out the extra moisture; shred the bread into the bowl. Add 6 ounces of chopped salt pork (or use pancetta or fatback), 1 lightly beaten egg, and 1 tablespoon of chopped parsley. Mix well and season lightly with salt and pepper. Fill the cavity of the chicken with the stuffing and close the opening with one or two skewers.

Cook as directed above, browning the chicken a bit with the vegetables before roasting and moistening it with about half a cup of white wine.

Cornish Game Hens in a Casserole

Originally designed for squab, this recipe is perfect for the far less expensive game hens available in supermarkets everywhere. Sage and prosciutto give a lovely flavor to these useful little birds.

4 Cornish Game Hens, about 1 pound each	½ cup dry sherry
	4 lemon slices
Salt, freshly ground pepper	½ cup water
12 sage leaves	A pinch of rosemary
4 thin slices of Italian prosciutto	½ cup Madeira wine
8 slices of bacon	

Rinse the game hens under cold water and dry. Season each interior with salt and pepper, 3 sage leaves, and 1 slice of prosciutto.

In a heavy skillet or flameproof casserole, cook the bacon until well browned and set it aside. Brown the game hens in the hot bacon fat, turning them over so that they become brown on all sides.

Pour out the fat and add the sherry. When it has reduced by half, add the lemon slices, water, and rosemary; cover the pan, lower the heat, and let the birds simmer for about 1 hour and 15 minutes. Turn them several times during the cooking process. If the wings move easily, the game hens are done.

Remove the game hens to a serving platter and keep warm. Remove as much fat as possible from the pan juices. Add the Madeira and cook until it is reduced by half.

Pour the juices over the game hens and top each one with 2 slices of warmed bacon. If the lemon slices have not disintegrated, add 1 to each bird.

SERVES 4

Tarragon Roast Chicken with Roast Potatoes

A perfectly roasted chicken is one of the great dishes of the world. I like the subtle accents and glorious smells of tarragon, rosemary, and garlic with my roast chicken.

1 roaster or capon, 6 to 7 pounds
2 tablespoons butter
Salt, freshly ground pepper
A few fresh tarragon stalks or 1
* teaspoon dried tarragon*
1 teaspoon dried rosemary

3 garlic cloves, unpeeled
12 to 18 small red potatoes or 6
* to 8 white potatoes*
1 large onion, sliced thick
2 to 3 tablespoons oil

Wash the chicken and pat it dry. Rub butter all over the skin and season it with salt and pepper. Put the tarragon, ½ teaspoon of the rosemary, and the garlic into the cavity. Truss the chicken (page 15) and put it in a lightly oiled roasting pan, breast side up.

If you are using small red potatoes, wash and dry them. If the potatoes are larger, peel them and cut them into quarters. Salt and pepper the potatoes and sprinkle them with the remaining rosemary.

Toss them in a bowl or small saucepan with the oil until they are well coated.

Place the potatoes and the onion slices around the chicken. Roast the chicken in a preheated 375° oven for 45 minutes. Turn the chicken over and cook for about another hour and 15 minutes; stir and turn the potatoes occasionally.

At the end of 2 hours the chicken and potatoes should be completely brown and tender.

SERVES 6

Chicken Country Style

1 roaster or capon, 6 to 7 pounds
Salt, freshly ground pepper
1 onion
4 tablespoons butter
2 tablespoons oil
¾ pound fresh mushrooms, sliced and cleaned in acidulated water (page 8)

4 tomatoes, peeled and cut into strips
6 asparagus spears, cut into pieces
12 pimiento-stuffed olives, sliced
½ teaspoon curry powder
½ cup cream

Wash the chicken, pat it dry, and season with salt and pepper; truss it (page 15).

Cut half the onion into thin slices. Heat 2 tablespoons each of the butter and the oil in a large skillet; add the onion slices and cook until they just begin to color. Add the chicken and brown it lightly on all sides. Put the skillet in a preheated 375° oven and cook for about 2 hours, turning and basting the chicken with its own juices several times during the cooking period.

Forty minutes before serving time, chop the other onion half into small pieces and brown in a large skillet in the remaining 2 tablespoons of butter. Add the mushrooms, tomatoes, and asparagus pieces to the onions; season to taste with salt. Cover the pan and cook on low heat for 20 minutes.

Add the olives, curry powder, and cream. Put the cover back on the skillet and cook for another 10 minutes.

When the chicken is cooked, place it on a platter and pour the sauce over it. Or carve the chicken into serving pieces before adding the sauce.

SERVES 6 TO 8

Duck à l'Orange

A domestic duck is a fatty bird. The first time I cooked one, it looked like a swan swimming in a sea of grease. Thanks to Lottie Chisholm, executive chef of New York University's dining room, I have learned how to do it correctly. Here is her recipe.

1 Long Island duck, about 5 pounds	3 tablespoons potato flour
Salt, freshly ground pepper	1 teaspoon tomato paste
4 oranges	1 tablespoon meat extract, such
1 lemon	as Bovril
2 tablespoons butter, softened	1 cup chicken stock or duck or
Ice water	any other game stock
4 mushrooms, chopped	½ cup red wine
	2 tablespoons red currant jelly

Truss the duck (page 15) and season the interior with salt and pepper. Peel and quarter 2 of the oranges and place them in the cavity. Cut the lemon in half and rub it all over the duck; then rub the duck skin with the softened butter.

Place the duck on a rack in a baking pan and cook for 1 hour in a preheated 400° oven. Several times during the cooking, baste the duck with ice water and prick its sides with a skewer or fork.

With a vegetable peeler, cut off the zest of 1 orange and cut the zest pieces into thin slivers. Squeeze the rindless orange and the remaining orange; reserve the juice.

When the duck is nicely browned, remove it to a plate and drain off most of the fat in the pan, leaving about ¼ cup. Add the mushrooms and the orange zest to the hot fat, lower the heat, and cook slowly.

Stir the potato flour into ¼ cup of water until it is dissolved. After the mushrooms have cooked for 6 minutes, remove the pan from the heat and stir in the potato flour mixture, the tomato paste, and the meat extract. When all is well mixed, return the pan to the heat, add the stock, and cook over low heat until it comes to a boil. Add the wine, orange juice, and jelly. Taste the sauce for seasoning and add salt and pepper if necessary.

Carve the duck into serving pieces and put them in the pan with the sauce. Cover the pan and cook slowly over moderate heat for about 1 hour, until the duck is tender.

If at the end of the cooking time the sauce seems too thin to you, remove the duck pieces and boil the sauce until it thickens to your liking.

Serve the duck pieces on a platter with some of the sauce poured over them, the rest of the sauce in a separate bowl. Garnish the platter with orange slices.

SERVES 6

TO SPLIT A CHICKEN FOR BROILING OR THE BARBECUE

When cutting, as a safety precaution, it is wise to cut the bones just to the right of the spine if you are right-handed, or just to the left if you are a lefty. This way you are cutting just the ends of the ribs, not the actual spinal column, where your knife could slip.

To split a chicken, lay it on your workspace breast side down. With a boning knife, cut straight down the back from the tail to neck.

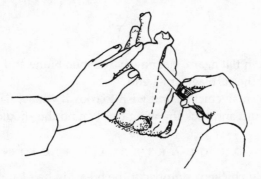

With your left thumb and forefinger, spread the rib bones on the breast area apart; make a *small* cut in the center of the white cartilage.

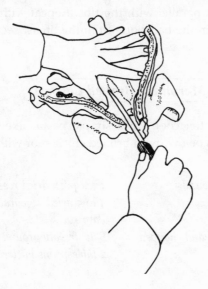

Pick up the breast with both hands (your thumbs on top and your forefingers under the breastbone, also called the keel bone) and push up with your forefingers. The breastbone will pop up.

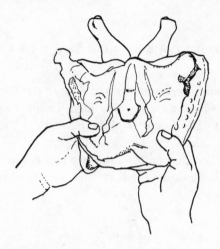

Lay the chicken flat again; clear away the membrane and pull out the breastbone and the cartilage at its end.

If you have a small chicken and wish to cook it whole, flatten it out a bit with your hand and tuck the wing tips behind the shoulder joints.

TO HALVE OR QUARTER A CHICKEN

To halve the split chicken, simply cut the breast in half lengthwise.

To cut the chicken into quarters, separate one breast and wing section from its leg, thigh, and backbone section by cutting across the skin at the end of the breast parallel with the ribs. Repeat with the other half. You may want to trim the backbone from the breast section to which it is attached.

Marinated Broiled Chicken

In my classes I often cook up a simple pasta, like the Pasta with Zucchini and Eggs below, with broiled chicken or with any broiled or roast meat.

1 chicken, 2½ to 3 pounds
½ cup olive oil
1½ lemons
1 garlic clove, peeled and chopped
  (optional)

1 teaspoon dried rosemary
4 to 5 dried sage leaves
Paprika
Salt, freshly ground pepper
2 tablespoons butter

Split the chicken in half or cut it into quarters as desired. Place it in a dish large enough to hold the chicken in one layer.

Mix the olive oil, the juice of 1 lemon, the garlic, rosemary, sage, a few sprinkles of paprika, the salt, and pepper. Pour the mixture over the chicken and let it marinate in the refrigerator for at least 1 hour. You can also start it marinating in the morning for cooking in the evening.

Preheat the broiler. Place the chicken on a rack skin side down so that the cut side is about 5 inches away from the flame. Turn the chicken at least twice; when the skin side is toward the flame, lower the rack. (If the skin gets burned, it will taste bitter.)

The chicken should be done in 20 to 25 minutes. Let the butter melt on both sides of the hot chicken and squeeze the remaining lemon half over it.

SERVES 4

Pasta with Zucchini and Eggs

Penne is a thin tube pasta cut on the diagonal at the ends like a fountain pen; mezzani tubes are cut straight across.

1 pound penne or mezzani	1/4 teaspoon hot red pepper flakes
Salt	1 tablespoon chopped parsley
4 tablespoons olive oil	Freshly ground pepper
1 garlic clove, peeled and minced	2 eggs
1 large onion, sliced thin	4 tablespoons grated pecorino
2 medium zucchini, sliced into	romano cheese
1/4-inch rounds	4 tablespoons butter, cut into
1/2 teaspoon oregano	small pieces

Set a large pot with 8 quarts of water to boil. As soon as the water comes to a full boil, cook the pasta in the boiling, salted water according to directions on the package, usually 12 to 15 minutes.

Heat the oil in a heavy skillet and add the garlic. When it just begins to color, add the onion and cook until translucent. Add the zucchini rounds and continue cooking on fairly high heat for a few minutes.

Stir in the oregano, red pepper flakes, parsley, salt, and pepper. When the zucchini begins to wilt, lower the heat and add a ladle of water from the pasta.

Beat the eggs into a large serving bowl with the cheese and butter.

When the pasta is done, drain it and turn it into the bowl of eggs and cheese and stir. Add the zucchini and toss well. Serve immediately.

SERVES 4

TO CUT A CHICKEN INTO PARTS

Although you can buy chicken already cut into parts at the supermarket, if you know how to do it yourself you will get the pieces exactly as you like them. Also, whole chickens are usually cheaper per pound than cut-up chicken.

Lay the chicken on its side with the legs away from you, the wings toward you. Lift up one wing and put the knife between the body and the wing; cut the skin at the point of the V and pull the wingbone out from the body as you cut the wing away from the socket. Follow the knife down and cut the wing off. Turn the bird over and repeat with the other wing.

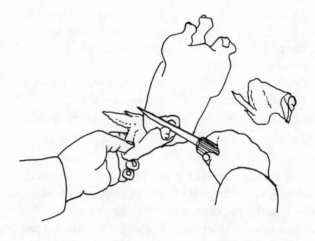

Lift up one leg and slice the skin between the leg and the breast; the knife should be parallel to your workspace.

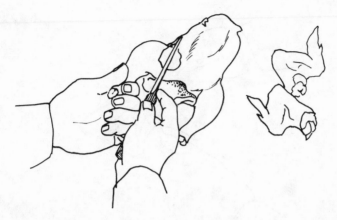

Holding the leg and thigh out from the body, use your fingers from behind to pop the thighbone out of the socket where it is connected to the hipbone; at this point cut off the leg and thigh piece.

Turn the chicken over and cut off the second leg and thigh piece. (If you are not planning to use the backbone, be sure to include the oysters, the little pieces of meat in spoon-shaped cavities on either side of the backbone at the front of the hip socket.)

To separate the thigh from the leg, lay the piece flat on your workspace. You will see a thin line of fat going across the meat. Holding your knife perpendicular to the table, place the knife 1/16 inch toward the drumstick end and cut through—you will go right through the middle of the socket.

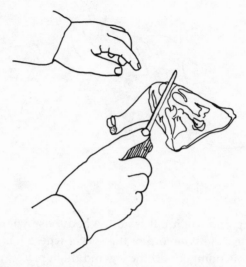

Cut the skin down next to the rib cage and snap the tailbone off with your hand. Cut through the skin where it snapped. Lay the chicken breast side down with the front end toward you. Place your knife just off to the right of the spinal cord and cut down; repeat on the other side. Remove the spine.

Split the backbone in two pieces with a heavy knife. If you are not going to use it for the chicken recipe, save it for stock along with the kidneys and wing tips.

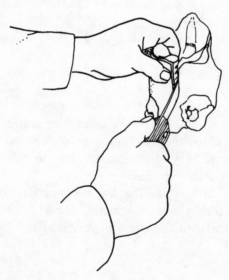

Place the breast skin down with the large end toward you; with your left thumb and your left forefinger, spread the rib bones apart; make a *small* cut in the center of the white cartilage.

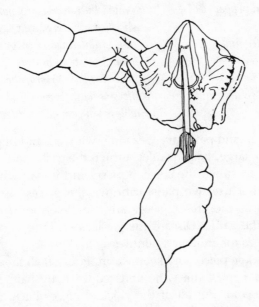

Pick up the breast with both hands, your thumbs on top and push up with your other fingers (your forefingers should be under the breast). The breastbone will pop up. Lay the chicken flat again; clear away the membrane and pull out the keel bone and the cartilage at its end.

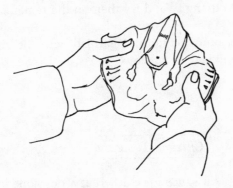

Cut the breast in half; you now have two breast halves suitable for barbecued chicken or recipes like chicken cacciatore.

Chicken Marengo

1 chicken, 3½ to 4 pounds, cut
   into pieces
Salt, freshly ground pepper
¼ cup oil
2 garlic cloves, peeled and
   crushed
1½ cups dry white wine
3 tomatoes, peeled, seeded, and
   cut into cubes

½ teaspoon dried oregano
1 tablespoon meat extract
½ pound button mushrooms,
   sliced or quartered and cleaned
   in acidulated water (page 8)
¼ pound (1 stick) butter
½ pound small shrimp, shelled
8 slices of white bread
1 tablespoon chopped parsley

Wash the chicken and pat it dry. Season it with salt and pepper.

Heat the oil in a large, heavy skillet. Brown the garlic and chicken. You do not want to crowd the chicken pieces in the pan while they are browning; either use two pans or brown the pieces in separate batches. As soon as the breast pieces are completely browned, remove them and the garlic. Discard the garlic. Continue to cook the other chicken pieces for another 5 minutes.

Remove the chicken pieces and keep warm. Pour off all the oil from the skillet. Add 1 cup of the wine and reduce it by half; add the tomatoes and oregano. Put all of the chicken pieces back into one pan, lower the heat, and add the meat extract. Taste for seasoning. Cook on low heat for 25 to 30 minutes.

Meanwhile, in a separate pan, sauté the mushrooms in 2 tablespoons of the butter on fairly high heat. Add them to the chicken just before serving to heat them through.

Cook the shrimp in the remaining ½ cup of wine for 3 to 4 minutes.

Cut the bread into triangles and fry them in the remaining 6 tablespoons of butter.

Place the chicken on a platter and garnish with the shrimp and bread triangles. Sprinkle with parsley.

SERVES 4

Chicken Tuscany

I picked up this piquant sauce for chicken at a pensione in Florence in the mid-1960s. My foot had become infected and I could not walk much, so while it healed, I sat around and found people who liked to talk about food.

1 chicken, 3½ to 4 pounds, cut
    into pieces
4 tablespoons olive oil
2 medium onions, chopped
½ tablespoon flour
Salt, freshly ground pepper
½ cup dry white wine
1 tablespoon tomato paste

1 cup chicken stock
½ cup wine vinegar
2 anchovy fillets, chopped fine
2 to 3 dill gherkins, chopped fine
1 tablespoon capers, chopped
1 tablespoon chopped parsley
1 garlic clove, peeled and chopped

Wash the chicken pieces and pat them dry. Heat the olive oil in a large skillet. Cook the onions in the hot oil for 5 minutes. Add the chicken pieces and brown them on all sides, cooking the breast pieces for about 5 minutes, the other parts for 10 minutes. Sprinkle the flour, salt, and pepper over the chicken.

Add the wine and reduce it by about half. Add the tomato paste and chicken stock. Reduce the heat, cover the pan, and cook for about 1 hour.

Ten minutes before serving time, reduce the vinegar to a third its volume in a small saucepan. Add the chopped anchovies, gherkins, capers, parsley, and garlic and cook for about 5 minutes.

When the chicken pieces are done, the stock and juices in which they have cooked will have reduced to a light coating. Transfer the pieces to a platter and pour the piquant sauce over them.

SERVES 4

Chicken Legs with Lemon, Egg, and Mushrooms

You can, of course, also make this recipe with other parts of the chicken if you wish. If the legs are large, 4 whole legs are ample for 6 people.

8 small whole chicken legs,
    drumsticks and thighs
    connected
Flour
3 tablespoons butter
2 tablespoons oil
1 large onion, chopped
1 teaspoon dried rosemary
2 dried sage leaves

Salt, freshly ground pepper
½ cup white wine
1 cup chicken stock
½ pound mushrooms cleaned in
    acidulated water, page 8
1 egg yolk
Juice of half a lemon
½ cup light cream or milk

Wash the chicken legs and pat them dry. Roll them lightly in flour.

Heat 2 tablespoons each of the butter and the oil in a skillet or flameproof casserole. When it is hot, add the chicken legs and brown them on all sides. Remove them and set aside.

Drain most of the oil from the pan and add the choppped onion. Cook for about 3 minutes, then return the legs to the pan. Add the rosemary, sage, and a bit of salt and pepper. Cook for 5 minutes, add the wine, lower the heat, and reduce it by half. Add the stock, cover the pan, and simmer on low heat for 25 to 30 minutes.

Meanwhile, slice the mushrooms and sauté them quickly in the remaining tablespoon of butter. Add them to the chicken legs before you add the egg, lemon juice, and cream.

Beat the egg yolk with the lemon juice and the cream or milk. When the chicken is cooked, remove the pan from the fire. Stir in the egg mixture and return to the stove. Simmer on a very low flame for about 3 minutes, then serve immediately.

SERVES 4 TO 6

Oven-Baked Chicken Legs

The coating of béchamel sauce on these chicken legs gives them a crunchy crust that is a nice contrast to the tender chicken inside. You can prepare the legs in the morning and cook them in the evening.

8 whole chicken legs, drumsticks
　　and thighs connected
Salt, freshly ground pepper
¼ pound (1 stick) butter
2 heaping tablespoons flour
2 cups hot milk and a little cold
　　milk

½ teaspooon nutmeg
1 egg
Dried bread crumbs
1 tablespoon peanut or corn oil

Cut the chicken legs into thigh and drumstick parts. Wash, pat dry, and sprinkle with salt and pepper.

Make a béchamel sauce: Melt 4 tablespoons of the butter in a saucepan over low heat. Mix in the flour. When it is thoroughly incorporated, add a little of the hot milk and stir hard. Pour in the rest of the hot milk and cook until it thickens, stirring constantly. Season with nutmeg, salt, and pepper. Remove the sauce from the heat and let it cool.

Dip the chicken pieces into the béchamel sauce and place them on a dish. Refrigerate the chicken for at least 2 hours, until the sauce solidifies on the chicken. You can keep the chicken in the refrigerator for 8 to 10 hours.

Just before you are ready to cook the chicken, beat the egg with the cold milk. Dip the chicken pieces in it, then roll them in bread crumbs.

Cover a cookie sheet with aluminum foil and rub it with the oil. Place the chicken pieces on the foil, being careful not to let them touch one another.

Cook the chicken in a preheated 400° oven for 45 minutes.

SERVES 6 TO 8

Chicken Wings with Sausages and Mushrooms

I like to use hot sausages for this recipe because I like the spiciness. You could also use a combination of half hot, half sweet sausages.

2½ pounds chicken wings
3 tablespoons oil
1 garlic clove, peeled and crushed
1 medium onion, chopped fine
1 pound hot Italian sausages
1 cup dry white wine
1 16-ounce can plum tomatoes, drained

Salt, freshly ground pepper
1 pound button mushrooms, sliced and cleaned in acidulated water, page 8
2 tablespoons butter
1 green pepper, cut into strips
1 red pepper, cut into strips

Wash the wings and pat them dry. Cut off the wing tips and save for stock. Cut each wing into two separate parts. If you are feeling energetic, scrape the meat off part of the bone to form drumettes (page 45).

Heat 2 tablespoons of the oil in a skillet, just enough to cover the bottom of the pan. Cook the garlic and onion in the hot oil until they are translucent. Remove them from the pan and reserve. Add the wings and the sausages and brown them on all sides. Pour off most of the oil and return the garlic and onions to the pan.

Add the wine, lower the heat, and reduce the wine by half. Add the tomatoes and salt and pepper to taste. Lower the heat and cook the chicken for 25 to 30 minutes.

In a separate pan, sauté the mushrooms in the butter. Set the mushrooms aside. Add the remaining tablespoon of oil and the pepper strips. Sauté the peppers on high heat for a few minutes so that they remain crunchy.

A few minutes before the chicken wings are cooked, add the mushrooms and peppers to them.

SERVES 4

TO REMOVE BONES FROM CHICKEN AND OTHER POULTRY PARTS

Chicken Breast. Remove the breastbone as directed on pages 31–32. Remove the wishbone: At the front of the breast feel with your fingers for the sharp little bones just under the surface of the meat. One side of the wishbone is a straight, short piece; the wider or "winning" side has a little hook on top. Make a shallow cut down to the bone on the left-hand side; hold it in one hand and with the other scrape the meat down until you can remove the bone. Repeat with the other side of the wishbone on the right side of the breast.

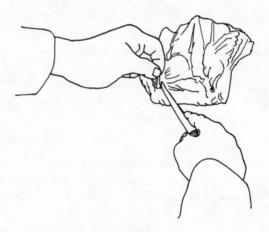

Remove the rib cage: Make a small cut with the knife under the long rib that runs backward parallel to the breastbone. Cut around it so you can hold it up, then continue cutting and scraping toward the back ribs as close as you can to the rib cage. Cut through the white nerve that is attached to the collarbone. Continue scraping the rib cage away from the body until you can remove it. To remove the nerve from the breast meat, hold it with your fingers (wrap a piece of your apron around your fingers to get a good grip) and cut under it; pull it out while you hold the flesh down with the knife. If the breast is small, you can leave it whole, but it is usually separated into two halves.

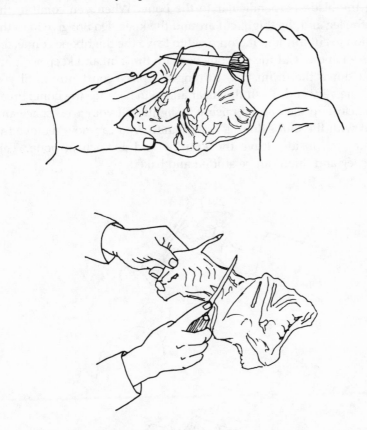

To make a chicken cutlet, pull and cut off the skin; cut off extra fat. (You have already removed the nerve.) Holding your knife parallel to your workspace, cut from the outside of the breast toward the center (where the meat is sealed) so that you can open the half chicken breast out like the pages of a book to a wide, flat piece (for an illustration, see pounding, page 12).

Turkey Breast. Boning a turkey breast is different from boning a chicken breast in that instead of removing the bones separately, we take out the breastbone and rib cage in one piece. Remove the wishbone first. Then start scraping the bones from the outside of the top of the rib cage, where the wing was attached, up to the breastbone. Repeat on the other side until you can pull out the whole frame.

Chicken Legs. Place the drumstick end toward you and find the end of the thigh bone. Cut around it, cutting the tendons away so that you can hold on to the top of the bone. Scrape the meat down toward the center, holding the blade perpendicular to the bone. When you come to the joint of the leg and the thigh, cut around the knee. Do not give in to the temptation to cut through it; you need to leave the thighbone connected to use as a handle. Cut the tendons beneath the joint and keep scraping the meat down the drumstick, turning the piece constantly until you are near the very end. Push the meat and skin back up the bone; break the bone close to the end by raising it slightly off your workspace and hitting it with the dull side of a heavy knife. You can now remove the bone from the inside; leave the knuckle and an inch of bone. This boneless leg and thigh can be stuffed and baked.

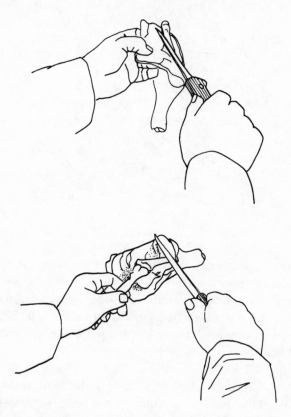

Turkey Legs. Turkey legs often present a problem as the drumsticks have a lot of hard tendons that make them impossible to slice. Bone them out as you would a chicken leg, then pull out the tendons using your apron or a towel for a grip or use tweezers.

Chicken Wings. Cut right through the first joint and wing tip; reserve the wing tips for stock. You can push the meat away from the knuckles to make drumettes that are ideal for cocktail parties and buffets. Cut through the joint between the two pieces of wing to separate them. Cut the skin at the smaller end of the larger wing piece; scrape down the meat toward the end of the bone so it looks like a little drumstick.

You can do the same thing with the smaller wing part by removing the small bone entirely, then scraping down the meat and skin from one end to the other. Cut off loose ends of cartilage to make the drumettes neater.

These little drumettes are easily cooked. Coated in bread crumbs, they can be baked or fried or they can be dipped in a beer batter and fried.

Turkey Wings. Turkey wings are no different from chicken wings; they're just bigger. You can make drumettes with them, as above, and roast them, or dip them in batter and bake them, or cook them in a casserole with a vegetable mirepoix.

Broiled Chicken Breasts

Boned chicken breasts cook very quickly under the broiler. Leave the skin on while cooking to prevent the meat from drying out. You want to cook the cut side a few minutes longer than the skin side.

2 *whole chicken breasts, boned,* *with skin on*	*Juice of half a lemon* *Rosemary*
1 *to 2 tablespoons oil*	*Salt, freshly ground pepper*

Wash the chicken breasts, cut them in half, and rub them with oil, lemon juice, rosemary, salt, and pepper. Let them marinate in the seasonings for at least 30 minutes before cooking.

Cook them in a preheated broiler for about 10 minutes, or until they are golden brown. Turn several times during the cooking and spoon some of the marinade onto them.

You can also flavor them with soy sauce or Worcestershire sauce.

SERVES 2 TO 4

Chicken Breasts with Tomatoes and Cream

If the breasts are very large, you will only need 3 whole breasts; cut each breast in half. You can, of course, remove the skin from the breasts if you prefer.

6 whole chicken breasts, boned
Salt, freshly ground pepper
Juice of 1 lemon
1 small onion, chopped
¼ pound (1 stick) butter or
  margarine
4 plum tomatoes, peeled, seeded,
  and cut into thin wedges or 1
  8-ounce can, drained

2 to 3 dried sage leaves
1 cup white wine
½ cup stock or water
1 teaspoon flour
1 cup heavy cream

Wash the chicken breasts and split them in half. Flatten them with a pounder or rolling pin; season with salt and pepper. Marinate them in the lemon juice for 10 to 15 minutes.

Prepare a little sauce by sautéing the chopped onion in 2 tablespoons of the butter until the onion is translucent. Add the tomatoes, salt, pepper, and the sage leaves. Cook for 15 minutes on a very low flame.

Heat the remaining 6 tablespoons of butter in a heavy skillet; when it is hot, cook the chicken breasts in the butter for 3 minutes on each side. Add the wine and cook until it is reduced by half.

Add the tomatoes. Cover the pan and simmer the chicken in the sauce on low heat for 15 to 20 minutes. Add a bit of stock or water if necessary to keep it moist.

Remove the breasts from the pan and keep them warm on a platter.

Stir the flour into the cream. Remove the pan from the fire and stir the cream into the tomato sauce. Return it to the stove and cook it on a low flame for at least 5 minutes. Pour the sauce over the chicken breasts and serve.

SERVES 6

Chicken Breasts with Capers

The ham and cheese slices should be slightly smaller than the butter-flied breast halves so that they will not hang out of the chicken rolls.

4 whole chicken breasts, boned	¼ pound (1 stick) butter
Salt, freshly ground pepper	¼ cup cognac
8 thin slices of ham	¼ cup dry sherry
8 thin slices of Gruyère or	½ cup chicken stock
fontina cheese	2 tablespoons capers, drained
16 dried sage leaves	1 cup light cream
Flour	A pinch of nutmeg

Wash the breasts, dry them, and split them in half. Butterfly each half and pound it lightly with a pounder or rolling pin. Remove the skin if you wish. Season with salt and pepper. Lay a slice each of ham and of cheese and 2 sage leaves on each piece of chicken. Trim off any overhanging ham or cheese. Roll the pieces up and tie them with white twine.

Dip the breasts in flour. Heat 4 tablespoons of the butter in a skillet; when it is hot, cook the breasts in the butter until they are golden brown, about 8 to 10 minutes.

Remove the chicken from the pan and discard all the butter. Return the pan to the fire and add the cognac. Flame it and reduce it by half. Add the sherry and reduce by half.

Add the stock, capers, the remaining 4 tablespoons of butter, and the cream. Stir the sauce well and cook for 2 or 3 minutes. Add the nutmeg.

Return the chicken breasts to the pan and taste for seasoning. Cook the breasts in the sauce for 5 minutes.

SERVES 4

Stuffed Chicken Legs

I got the idea for this recipe a few years ago when I was showing students at the school how to bone out chicken legs. I like this spicy stuffing, but any other of the stuffings suggested throughout the book would be good also.

8 whole chicken legs, drumsticks and thighs connected	2 tablespoons grated Parmesan cheese
1 pound or 1 10-ounce package fresh spinach; do not use frozen	1 tablespoon pignoli nuts
	¼ teaspoon nutmeg
	1 egg, beaten
½ pound hot Italian sausages	Salt, freshly ground pepper
	2 to 3 tablespoons butter

Wash the legs and bone them according to directions on page 44.

Wash the spinach and steam it briefly in its own water. Drain well, squeeze out any extra moisture, and chop coarsely.

Remove the skin from the sausages and place them in a bowl. Add the Parmesan, pignoli nuts, spinach, nutmeg, and the egg. Season with salt and pepper. Mix well.

Lay the stuffing in the center of the boned-out legs and tie them closed with twine (or sew them if you prefer).

Place the legs in a roasting pan skin side up. Season them with salt and pepper and dot with butter. Bake in a preheated 350° oven for 1 hour.

SERVES 6 TO 8

Variation: Stuffed Turkey Legs

Boned turkey legs can be stuffed, tied, and roasted in the oven on a bed of vegetables for mirepoix gravy (page 26) for about 1 hour and 15 minutes. Or braise them in a flameproof casserole on top of the stove. Use any stuffing that appeals to you, but remember to pull out the tendons.

Turkey Breasts

Europeans have been able to buy turkey breasts for a number of years, but this is a relatively new development in the United States.

Whole turkey breasts are sold with the rib cage, breastbone, and wishbone still in. The backbone will have been removed. You can roast a 7- to 8-pound breast just as you would a whole turkey, basting it with the juices and cooking it for about 2 hours. If you remove the bones (page 43) you can stuff the breast and sew it together before roasting. Or you can cook it like a whole boned turkey with the stuffing under the breast (page 57).

Turkey Braciole

The ham and cheese should be slightly smaller than the pounded turkey cutlets—about 3 by 6 inches in size. You can also use any stuffing that suits your fancy for these turkey rolls.

8 or 12 very thin slices of uncooked turkey breast
Salt, freshly ground pepper
6 thin slices of cooked ham
12 thin slices of fontina or Gruyère cheese
1 cup sliced button mushrooms, cleaned in acidulated water, page 8

1 cup sliced shiitake mushrooms
5 tablespoons butter
2 tablespoons oil
2 tablespoons flour
½ cup brandy or cognac
½ cup dry sherry
1 cup turkey or chicken stock
2 tablespoons capers, drained
½ cup cream

Spread the turkey slices on your work table and pound them with a pounder or rolling pin just as you would veal cutlets so that they are ⅛ inch thick (page 12). Season them lightly with salt and pepper.

Put half a slice of ham and a slice of cheese on each slice and roll them up lengthwise. Fasten with toothpicks.

Sauté the mushrooms in 3 tablespoons of the butter on high heat until they are just golden, less than 4 minutes. Remove them from the pan and set aside.

Heat the remaining 2 tablespoons of butter and the oil in a large skillet. Roll the turkey rolls in flour and brown them on all sides in the hot oil and butter. Remove the turkey rolls from the skillet and keep them warm.

Pour out the fat from the skillet and add the cognac. Reduce it by half, add the sherry, and reduce it by half. Add the stock and the capers and simmer on low heat for 3 minutes.

Add the cream, stir, and return the turkey rolls to the sauce. Add the mushrooms and cook together for about 5 minutes.

Serve with a risotto or rice pilaf.

SERVES 6

Breast of Turkey Verbena

When I had these turkey cutlets in Rome at Dante's Taberna dei Gracchi, I liked them so much I asked for the recipe. If you want to cut the slices off the breast yourself, see directions pages 11–12. Turkey cutlets can be an inexpensive substitute for veal cutlets.

8 or 12 very thin slices of
   uncooked turkey breast
Salt, white pepper
Flour
1 egg, beaten with 2 tablespoons
   milk or water

1 cup dried bread crumbs
2 tablespoons olive oil
4 tablespoons unsalted butter
16 asparagus tips, blanched
4 tablespoons grated Parmesan
   cheese

Spread the turkey slices on your work table and pound them with a pounder or rolling pin just as you would veal cutlets so that they are ⅛ inch thick (page 12). Season them lightly with salt and pepper and dip them in flour, then in the egg wash, then in bread crumbs.

Heat the oil and 2 tablespoons of the butter in a skillet. When they are hot, add the cutlets and cook until they are a golden brown, about 2 to 3 minutes on each side. Remove the cutlets to a paper towel and pat off any excess fat.

Place the cutlets in a baking dish and put 2 asparagus spears on each one. Sprinkle the Parmesan cheese over them and dot with the 2 remaining tablespoons of butter.

Finish them in a preheated 350° oven for 5 minutes.

SERVES 4

TO BONE OUT POULTRY

A boneless chicken or turkey filled with a succulent stuffing is a stunning dish for a party or holiday buffet. It is easy to slice and can be served hot or cold.

There are three ways to bone out a bird: The first method is to split the chicken down the back so that it lies flat; you will see the entire chicken laid out before you. The second method is to cut the skin straight down the back, then cut and scrape the meat away from the backbone and all the other bones (except the wingbones, which remain on the bird). The bones of the carcass are removed in one piece. The result is exactly the same. You stuff the bird, then roll and tie it. These two methods are particularly useful if you want the chicken or turkey for a galantine in the shape of a roll, like a salami.

The third method, glove-boning, is the art of removing the bones without cutting the skin. It is a little harder to learn, but once you get the hang of it, very satisfactory. This method gives you a boneless bird that still looks like a bird.

FIRST METHOD: SPLITTING THE BIRD DOWN THE BACK

Lay the chicken on your workspace breast side down with the tail away from you; split the chicken right down the back slightly off center of the backbone (page 31). Cut and scrape the meat away from the bones on both sides of the chicken as close to the bones as possible.

When you come to the thighbones connected to the body of the bird at the hip sockets on each side of the chicken, dislocate the bones from the sockets and cut the connecting nerves. Leave the legs and thighs in place. Continue cutting and scraping the meat from the rest of the frame.

Leave the wings and wingbones in place on the chicken by sliding the ball out from the shoulder wing socket.

Remove the breastbone as directed on pages 31–32, then the wishbone (page 42). Remove the rib cage exactly as you would remove the bones from a breast (pages 42–43), first on one side, then on the other.

The only bones left in the chicken are those in the wing (which will remain) and the leg bones and thighbones. Separate the hipbone from the thighbone by following with your knife around the bone in the socket. Bone out the thigh and drumstick bones on each side; remember not to cut the bone at the knee joint so that you keep the thighbone as your handle to hold on to while you work (page 44). Leave in the knuckles at the end of the drumsticks by cracking the bone (page 44).

SECOND METHOD: CUTTING THE SKIN DOWN THE BACK

Lay the chicken on your workspace breast side down with the tail away from you. Cut the skin the length of the backbone from the tail to the neck just at the center of the bone. Cut and scrape the meat away from the bones on both sides of the chicken as close to the bones as possible.

Dislocate the thighbones from the hip sockets and cut the connecting nerves. Leave the legs and thighs in place; continue cutting and scraping the meat from the rest of the frame.

Leave the wings and wingbones in place on the chicken by sliding the ball out from the shoulder wing socket.

The wishbone is right next to the wings; remove it as directed on page 42. Once the wishbone is out, continue scraping up the rib cage until you come to the breastbone. Remove it as directed on page 43.

All the bones except the leg and thighbones are now free of meat and can be removed.

Separate the hipbone from the thighbone by following with your knife around the bone in the socket. Bone out the thigh and leg bones leaving the knuckle of the drumstick in place (page 44).

This is the only way to bone out a turkey. The first method will not work because turkey bones are too hard; it is not possible to glove-bone a turkey.

THIRD METHOD: GLOVE-BONING

The backbone, ribs, and shoulder bones are removed in one piece; the wishbone and leg bones are removed separately; the wing bones are left in place. The skin remains attached to the meat in the shape of the bird. You will need a boning knife and a table knife that does not have a sharp blade. Allow yourself extra time when you first try this; you will probably be better at it the second time.

Lay the chicken on its back. Take the skin from the neck and gently pull it up over the start of the breast, being careful not to tear the skin. Feel with your fingers for the inverted V of the wishbone (it is attached to the wing on the bottom). Remove the wishbone by going under it with the point of the boning knife and opening it down to where it is attached to the wing.

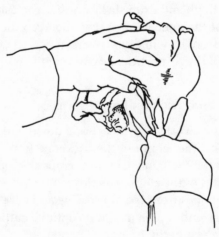

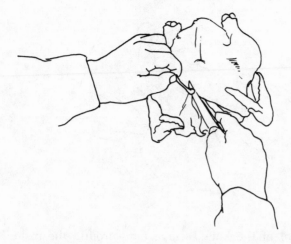

Lay the chicken on its side. Pull the skin off the shoulder and wing just to the point where you can see and feel the socket joint of the wing. Cut through to separate the wing from the carcass and scrape the flesh from the skeleton just below the wing toward the neck, leaving the wing attached to the skin. Repeat for the other wing.

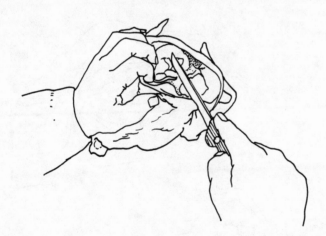

Cut the connecting tissue or flesh at the top part of the breast near the neck to reveal the collarbones; continue scraping and cutting flesh from the skeleton down the sides and back of the chicken, continuously turning the chicken while you work so that the skin and the flesh come down evenly all around until you come to the breastbone.

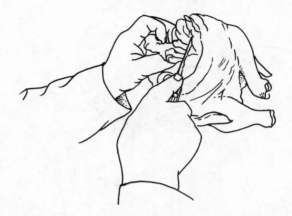

With the point of the knife, scrape hard around the inside of the curvature of its hook. This will cut the membrane separating the breast meat from the bone. Insert the table knife between the membrane and the breastbone and push the knife all the way down the breastbone. This will separate the meat in one piece from the breastbone. From this point on, do not touch the breast side, but continue scraping down the skeleton on the sides and the back with the table knife.

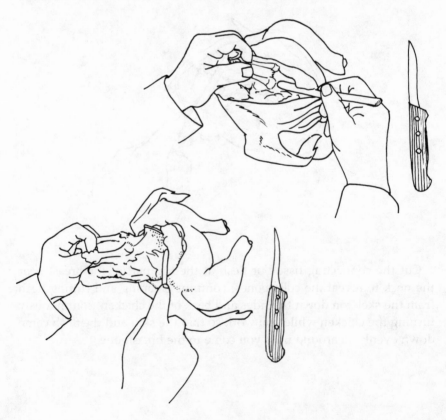

When you reach the thighbone area, hold the drumstick and thigh in the knee area with your fingers and use your thumb to push the thighbone out of the hip socket. Repeat with the other thigh.

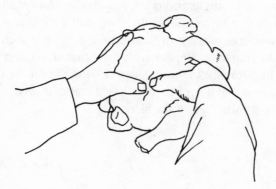

Continue scraping with the table knife down the back and sides of the skeleton until you reach the white cartilage at the end of the backbone just above the tailbone. You may have to cut a few of the connecting tissues around the femur bone that are attached to the hipbone; use the boning knife. Cut through the cartilage with the boning knife and pull out the entire bone structure except the thigh/drumstick bones and the wing bones.

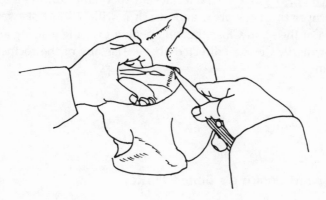

Turn the chicken so that the legs are facing you. Through the tail opening, take hold of one of the thighbones. With the boning knife, cut around the end of the thighbone, scrape down the thighbone, cut around the knee joint (being careful not to separate the thigh and drumstick bones), and then down toward the end of the drumstick bone, stopping approximately 1 inch above the knuckle (page 44). Hold the drumstick bone at an angle and crack it with the non-cutting edge of a heavy knife so that you do not cut the skin; pull the bones out from the inside of the chicken, leaving the knuckle and about 1 inch of bone at the end of the drumstick. Repeat with the other thigh and drumstick. (If you crack the drumstick bone while it is lying flat on the table, it will shatter; by holding it at a slight angle, it will crack cleanly.)

Leave the wings attached to the skin.

Stuffing and Cooking a Boned Chicken

After you have boned a chicken by one of the first two methods, place the stuffing in the center of the bird and fold the skin over it; do not overstuff or it will split while cooking. Sew up the back with a needle and thread. Rub the chicken with a little oil or butter if desired, season with salt and pepper, and roast it on a rack in a preheated 350° oven for 1 hour and 45 minutes, turning delicately once or twice. See recipes for stuffed chicken, etc., below.

After you have glove-boned a chicken, spoon the stuffing into it, pull the skin over the neck area, and attach it with a short skewer to the back area of the skin. Close the tail opening by tying a string around it or by sewing it. Cook as directed above. Use any of the recipes below for stuffing.

Stuffing and Cooking a Boned Turkey

You can bone and stuff a small turkey, up to 15 pounds. A turkey over 15 pounds is too big; it will cook out to a formless blob, and the stuffing will split the skin. Bone the turkey according to the second method, described on pages 51–52. Remember to pull out the tendons from the legs and be sure to include the oysters. I do not recommend the glove-boning process for a turkey.

Boned Turkey with All-Purpose Meat and Sausage Stuffing

One of the advantages of cooking a boned turkey is the considerably shortened cooking time. If your turkey is up to 8 pounds, the size of a large roaster or capon, stuff it in the same manner as you would a boned chicken.

If it is between 8 and 12 pounds, it needs a slightly different treatment. The stuffing is cooked under the turkey, which is draped over it like a tent. You can, of course, use this stuffing for a whole turkey, bone in. See below for cooking time.

Seasoning for a stuffing should be adjusted according to the ingredients you are using. Sausage meat is usually highly seasoned, so you may not want to add more salt and pepper. Other ground meats, like veal and pork, need to be seasoned. This all-purpose stuffing is suitable for a whole turkey, a breast, boneless turkey legs, or turkey braciole.

1 turkey, about 12 pounds, boned (pages 50–56)	1 onion, chopped
	½ cup white wine
4 tablespoons olive oil or butter	1 cup bread, about 4 slices, soaked in milk and squeezed
½ teaspoon rosemary	
Salt, freshly ground pepper	¼ teaspoon nutmeg
Turkey liver and heart, chopped	2 eggs, lightly beaten
1 pound sausage meat	3 tablespoons grated Parmesan cheese
1 pound veal, ground	
1 garlic clove, crushed	¼ teaspoon chopped lemon zest

Lay the boned turkey flat on your workspace and insert two long skewers, one on either side, so that they go through the leg meat and the wings like the handles of a stretcher. This will hold the turkey in shape. Coat the turkey with a little olive oil or butter, the rosemary, salt, and pepper.

Sauté the turkey liver and heart, sausage, veal, garlic, and onion in the remaining butter or oil until soft and thoroughly mixed. Add all the other ingredients and mix well.

Place the flattened turkey on a rack under a preheated broiler, cut side up, for 15 minutes. Remove the rack and spoon the stuffing into the center of the pan so that the turkey will cover it. Place the turkey, skin side up, over the stuffing, covering it entirely. Rub the skin side with oil or butter and season it with salt and pepper. Cook at 350° for 1 hour and 45 minutes.

SERVES 12

Variation: A Whole Turkey, Bone In

To cook a whole, fresh turkey without stuffing in a preheated 350° oven, first remove the breastbone and then truss. Roast according to the following chart.

8 to 9 pounds	2 to 2 hours and 45 minutes
12 pounds	3 to 3 hours and 30 minutes
18 to 20 pounds	4 hours and 30 minutes to 5 hours

To cook a turkey stuffed with a bread, oyster, celery, or cooked meat stuffing, allow 18 to 20 minutes to the pound. If the stuffing includes any uncooked meat like sausage, veal, etc., the turkey should cook an hour longer at 325° to insure that the stuffing cooks through.

To carve a whole turkey, remove the wishbone before cooking, page 42. Place the cooked turkey on the board with the legs toward you. Cut off one wing. Start slicing the breast from the front to the back until you have sliced down to the breastbone on one side. Cut off one drumstick and thigh and separate them; slice the thigh meat. Turn the turkey around and repeat on the other side.

Variation: Fruit and Nut Stuffing

This fragrant stuffing also goes beautifully in a glove-boned chicken.

¼ cup raisins
¼ cup pitted prunes, chopped
   coarse
¼ cup dried currants
¼ cup dried apricots, chopped
   coarse
¼ cup, or less, orange juice
¼ cup cognac
2 medium onions, chopped
2 tablespoons butter

White part of 2 leeks, chopped
2 celery stalks, chopped
2 tart apples, cored and cubed
¼ pound pecans, chopped coarse
¼ pound walnuts, chopped
   coarse
2 eggs, lightly beaten
¼ teaspoon nutmeg
¼ teaspoon ground mace
Salt and pepper if desired

Soak the dried fruit in the orange juice and cognac for at least 2 hours or overnight.

Sauté the onions in the butter for about 5 minutes; add the leeks and celery and cook another 5 minutes. Add the apples and cook for 3 minutes.

Mix all the ingredients together in a large bowl.

YIELD: STUFFING FOR A 7- TO 9-POUND BIRD

Chicken Parisienne with Meat Stuffing

This boned, stuffed chicken served with a mushroom velouté sauce is a lovely dish to offer guests.

1 chicken, about 6 pounds, boned
   (pages 50–56)
Salt, freshly ground pepper
¼ pound (1 stick) butter
2 tablespoons chopped shallots
1 cup finely chopped ham
½ pound veal, ground
¼ cup bread crumbs
1 tablespoon mixed herbs:
   parsley, thyme, basil,
   rosemary

1 egg, lightly beaten
2 tablespoons flour
1¼ cups chicken stock
¼ pound mushrooms, sliced and
   cleaned in acidulated water
   (page 8)
1 egg yolk
1 teaspoon lemon juice
1 cup light cream

Season the inside of the chicken with salt and pepper.

Melt 4 tablespoons of the butter in a small saucepan and cook the shallots in it until they are soft. Let cool a bit. Mix the ham, veal, bread crumbs, and herbs together in a bowl. Add the shallots and the beaten egg and mix well.

Stuff the chicken, sew it up, and sprinkle the outside of the bird with salt and pepper. Roast it on a rack in a preheated 400° oven for 1 hour and 30 minutes.

Make the velouté sauce: Melt 2 tablespoons of the butter in a saucepan. Add the flour and stir until lightly brown. Add the stock, bring it to a boil, lower the heat, and simmer for 3 or 4 minutes.

Sauté the mushrooms in the remaining 2 tablespoons of butter on high heat for about 5 minutes.

Add the mushrooms to the sauce, remove the pan from the fire, and beat in the egg yolk and the lemon juice. When they are thoroughly incorporated, add the cream and heat the sauce through. Taste for seasoning.

Cut the chicken into portions and cover with the velouté sauce. Serve immediately.

SERVES 6

Variations: Ground Meat Stuffings

¾ pound veal, ground
¾ pound pork, ground
3 tablespoons grated Parmesan
   cheese
½ teaspoon grated lemon zest

1 cup croutons, fried in butter
2 eggs, lightly beaten
¼ cup coarsely chopped walnuts
1 ounce cognac
Salt and pepper

Or use 2 ounces of sliced cooked ham and 1 tablespoon of pistachio nuts instead of the Parmesan cheese. Omit the croutons, walnuts, and cognac. Use only 1 egg and a hard roll soaked in milk, squeezed dry, and torn into pieces. Season with a pinch of nutmeg, a pinch of sage, salt, and pepper.

You can also place a blanched, peeled carrot in the center of any of the stuffings so that when you slice the bird, there will be a carrot slice in each serving.

YIELD: STUFFING FOR A 7- TO-9-POUND BIRD

Stuffed Capon alla Spoletina

1 capon or other roaster, 6 to 8
   pounds, boned (pages 50–56)
Salt, freshly ground pepper
4 eggs
¾ pound veal, ground
¾ pound pork, ground

¼ pound prosciutto, chopped
¼ pound cooked ham, chopped
¼ pound mortadella, chopped
¼ cup dry Marsala or any dry
   sherry
Olive oil or butter

Remove the fillet of the capon breast, the long extra piece that will separate from the rest of the breast when you bone the capon. Cut the fillet into strips. Season the capon with salt and pepper.

Separate the eggs and hard-cook the yolks in boiling, salted water for 8 minutes. Drain and cut the yolks into quarters.

Place the veal, pork, prosciutto, ham, and mortadella in a bowl. Add the egg whites and Marsala and mix the ingredients together well.

Spread some of the stuffing on the capon. Arrange the fillet strips and the egg yolks on the stuffing; add the remainder of the stuffing.

Pull the sides of the capon together and sew the skin closed with a large needle. You may want to tie strings in a few places across the body to help the capon keep its shape while it is cooking. Rub the capon with olive oil or butter.

Roast the capon on a rack in a preheated 375° oven for 1 hour and 45 minutes, basting it and turning it gently several times. Start with the breast side up; after about 30 minutes, turn it over so the fat ducts from inside the chicken skin melt down into the stuffing and onto the breast meat. Turn it again once.

To make sure the chicken is done, insert a skewer into the meat of the chicken; if the juices run clear, not pink, it is ready.

SERVES 8

Chicken Gallantina with Meat and Pistachio Nut Stuffing

This is a great dish for a cold buffet, but it needs two days for the preparation. The first day, bone the chicken, make the stock and the stuffing, stuff the chicken, and poach it. The day of the party, prepare the gelatin and decorate the chicken.

1 large roaster or capon, 8 to 9 pounds, boned (pages 50–56), the bones and all extra parts reserved for the stock

1 to 2 pounds chicken necks, backs, etc.

Chicken stock

1 fresh scalded calf's foot or a veal shin (or a package of unflavored gelatin)

2 ounces cooked ham, cut into strips

2 ounces cooked tongue, cut into strips

2 ounces unsalted pork fatback, cut into strips

1 small boneless, skinless chicken breast, cut into strips

1/3 cup dry sherry

3/4 pound veal, ground

3/4 pound pork, ground

1 teaspoon salt

1/2 teaspoon pepper

A pinch of nutmeg

2 egg yolks

2 ounces shelled pistachio nuts

2 egg whites

1/2 pound lean beef, ground

1 cup finely chopped carrots, onions, and celery

1 bouquet garni

Make a strong stock with the reserved bones and all extra parts from the bird, such as neck, wing tips, etc., plus a few pounds of chicken necks, backs, etc., and the calf's foot or veal shin. They will contribute the necessary gelatin to make the aspic. If you cannot get either ingredient, add unflavored gelatin to the clarification (see below). The stock should simmer for about 4 hours.

Marinate the strips of ham, tongue, fatback, and chicken breast in the sherry for 30 minutes. Mix the ground veal and pork together and season with salt, pepper, and nutmeg. Add the egg yolks, mix well, and moisten the forcemeat with some of the sherry.

Lay the roaster on your workspace skin side down and season with salt and pepper. Spread some of the stuffing over the chicken and lay the meat strips lengthwise over the stuffing to make a pattern. Sprinkle the nuts around. Push some of the stuffing into the leg cavities. Continue until the stuffing is all used. Sew the bird together.

Wrap the chicken in cheesecloth or any clean linen towel and tie it securely. After the stock has cooked for about 4 hours, add the chicken to it and poach the chicken in simmering stock for 1 hour and 30 minutes.

Remove the chicken from the stock and let it cool. Remove the towel and rinse it in cold water. Rewrap the chicken in the towel and place it in the refrigerator, weighted by a plate.

Strain the stock, cool it, and refrigerate overnight.

Skim off all the fat on top of the stock. Put 2 cups of the stock into a pot off the heat and stir in the egg whites (and crushed shells if you wish), ground beef, finely chopped vegetables, and the bouquet garni. (It is important that all the ingredients are cold.) When all is thoroughly mixed, add the remaining stock, put the pot on very low heat, and let it simmer slowly without stirring. The stock will begin to clarify, and you will see a thick foam come to the top, which will solidify as the impurities rise. Carefully move this crust to the sides of the pot and you will see the clear broth in the center. Carefully ladle out the clear stock into a clean pot. The clarification will probably take 30 minutes.

If you were not able to obtain calves feet or a shin of veal, soften the package of gelatin and add it to the clear broth and cook about 5 minutes. Test whether the broth has enough gelatin to set by putting a spoonful of it in the refrigerator for 5 minutes; if it hardens in that time, it is done.

Partially carve the chicken into 6 or 7 thin slices. Leave part of the chicken unsliced so your guests can see the presentation of the stuffed bird. Brush a coating of gelatin onto the platter and refrigerate for a few minutes. Arrange the slices next to the chicken on the platter, cover with gelatin, and refrigerate until the gelatin sets. Repeat several times until the slices and the chicken are well coated.

SERVES 8 TO 10

PORK

I<small>N THE DAYS BEFORE REFRIGERATION</small>, all pork slaughtering had to be done in the cold months. Pork spoils very quickly, so it was immediately preserved in salt. The packing industry in the United States began when the northeastern colonies shipped barreled pork to the West Indies in the 1650s.

Winter Meat

When I was a little boy in Italy, every fall my father and some of his friends and helpers slaughtered hogs. They processed them into hams, loins, shoulders, bacon, and fatback, rendered the lard, and made some of the hams into prosciutti.

I couldn't believe that so many different sausages, smoked and dried meats, and pickled meats could be made from one pig. The methods we used were primitive, but to me the products seemed fantastic. Our first taste of the pig was the blood sausages. They looked like long bolognas hanging on a pole immersed in a tall pot filled with aromatic boiling water. I don't know exactly how long they cooked, but I know it wasn't too long, because we were all waiting to taste them as soon as they cooled.

Then the men cut and trimmed the meat, squared off the bacon, and trimmed the hams and shoulders. All the trimmings were set aside for sausages, including the intestines, which were given to certain women who knew how to clean and scrape them.

Next the women cooked pieces of skin, ears, and parts of the head to make head cheese. At the same time the men prepared the meat that was to be cured with salt, sugar, and a very small amount of saltpeter, which was sometimes applied dry and sometimes in a pickling brine.

It took a good part of the winter to cure all the meat (two days per pound were needed for shoulders and hams), but we were always finished the day before Lent, Mardi Gras, when we had a feast. My mother made polenta—cooked corn meal from the year's new corn— and spread it over a special board that she used for bread and pasta making. She covered the polenta with a rich sauce made with all the pieces of pork, neck bones, spareribs, and some of the newly made sausages. Then she covered all of that with a lot of fragrant Parmesan cheese. We sat at the table and ate directly from the board, and as we ate, we made designs on what was left on the board. There was a lot of singing, and a lot of wine was drunk.

In the early years of this country, pork was more popular than beef, and Cincinnati was the pork capital of America. Salted pork was shipped all over the United States and to Europe; many of the famous Westphalian hams came from Cincinnati hogs.

Natural fat or lard from hogs was an important ingredient for cooking. It was packed into stone crocks to last out the year and as a preservative for sausages. If a hog didn't have a 2-inch-thick lard, the farmer was very disappointed.

Today we no longer need to rely on pork lard for our cooking needs, and we have found that our diets are healthier without that kind of fat. So hog growers are breeding pigs that are leaner and meatier than in the past. The coming of refrigeration and freezers also changed the processing methods for pork; we can safely buy fresh pork from our meat markets at any time of the year.

Pork is sold fresh or cured. It is the most processed of all meats; many parts of the pig rarely appear fresh in the supermarket, but are sold as cold cuts, sausages, etc. When meat is cured, it is preserved by salting; smoking is a further process that adds flavor. If the meat is given sufficient heat during the smoking process, it is then ready to eat.

Unlike other meats, pork does not lose its flavor after long cooking; I like pork cooked to an internal temperature of 170°, although some prefer it done to 180° or 185°.

Tips on Buying, Storing, and Freezing Pork

When you buy pork at the supermarket, look for firm, white fat with fresh, red bones under the fat. Beware if the fat is yellowish green and the bones gray.

Pork will keep three or four days if it is fresh when purchased. When you get home from the store, open the package and place the meat on a dish covered with a small sheet of waxed paper. Cover the meat with another sheet of waxed paper and put it in the coldest part of your refrigerator. The meat needs to breathe to prevent the juices from causing a bacterial growth.

Buying meat on sale for storage in your freezer is a good way to help your budget, but only if it fits into your space and menu needs. First, check the meat to see how much waste there is in fat and bones; you are not saving money if you have to throw out a good portion of what you buy. Second, think about the space available in your freezer and if you have time to cut and package the meat into small, usable portions.

Wrap the meat in freezer paper (shiny side in), then in aluminum foil. Label it clearly with the contents and date. If you are freezing several packages at once, do not pile them on top of each other in the freezer; spread them out singly until they are solidly frozen. Freezing should take place as quickly as possible; a slow freeze allows the cells to expand and rupture, so that when you thaw out the meat, it will lose half its juices. Ideal freezing temperature is −30°; the normal home freezer rarely gets below 5° to 0°.

Do not unwrap frozen meat or poultry that you buy at the supermarket for storage in your own freezer. The packages have been vacuum-packed for efficient freezing. Wrap aluminum foil over the package, label, and freeze.

It is better not to refreeze meat that has partially or completely defrosted. There is nothing dangerous about refrozen meat, but the loss of juices will leave the meat dry and tasteless.

To defrost meat, loosen package wrappings and leave it in the refrigerator for about 24 hours. Never leave meat out on the kitchen counter. When meat thaws at room temperature, all the juices run out.

To prepare pork up to 12 hours before using, rub a little peanut oil on any cuts not covered by their own fat. Place on a platter rubbed with a little oil, cover with plastic wrap, and keep in the refrigerator.

The Structure of Pork

Pork, lamb, veal, and beef are nearly identical structurally. They each have the same number of bones with the same shapes in the same places, except that pigs have fourteen ribs while lamb, veal, and beef each have thirteen. (Humans have twelve.) Some pigs have been "stretched" so that they have achieved fifteen ribs. (When counting ribs, start from the front of the animal.) The other differences between the four meat animals lie in size, in how the meat is cut by wholesalers, and in the names given to the cuts. The initial butchering of pork into large primary cuts is different from that of lamb, veal, and beef.

A whole side of pork—that is, half the pig from the jowl to the tail—weighs about 90 pounds. The three main cuts of pork are the shoulder, the ham, and the loin. A loin of pork is the body of the pig from the neck to the aitchbone of the leg after the hams, shoulders, bellie, and fatback have been removed. All fourteen or fifteen ribs are included in the loin (unless it is cut so that the first rib is left in the shoulder). This means the shoulder is cut at the very first rib after the joint of the arm

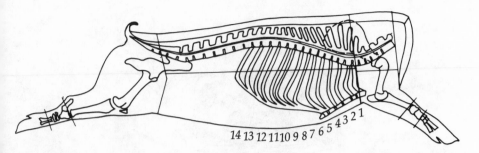

14 13 12 11 10 9 8 7 6 5 4 3 2 1

with the shoulder blade; most of the blade meat remains in the Boston butt of the shoulder.

Lamb, however, is cut so that the first four ribs are in the shoulder, eight are in the rib section, and one rib is in the loin. The blade meat is in the arm and forearm. A lamb loin is cut off at the beginning of the hip, whereas a pork loin is cut 5 inches below that point into the leg. (Veal is the same as lamb, but the ribs are sometimes divided so that three are in the shoulder, eight in the rib section, and two in the loin.) A side of beef is cut in half between the twelfth and thirteenth ribs.

Not only does a pork loin mean something entirely different from a loin of lamb, veal, or beef, there is also a good deal of built-in confusion in pork terminology itself. A ham is a whole back leg of a pig, but a picnic ham (formerly called a Calis or California ham) comes from the shoulder. The Boston butt is the other half of the shoulder; it is the muscle with the shoulder blade, the continuation of the loin toward the neck. It should not be confused with the butt end of the ham (that is, the leg), the round end that is not the shank end.

The Shoulder

The shoulders of the pig contain two important cuts, the Boston butt and the picnic ham. The Boston butt weighs 4 to 6 pounds and may be cooked whole or cut into steaks, slices (cutlets), or cubes. The muscles in the Boston butt are separated by membranes and fatty tissue, which makes the meat juicy and flavorful. The meat has some of the same uses as that from the ham, but if you like your pork lean, you will prefer meat from the ham. Boston butt is the best meat for sausages.

A porkette (sometimes called a pork tenderloin) is the 1½- to 3-pound boneless fillet of the Boston butt from which the blade bone and blade meat have been removed. (If the porkette weighs more than 3 pounds, it is probably heavy with fat.)

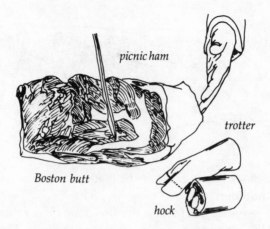

picnic ham

trotter

Boston butt

hock

You do not need special techniques to cut out the blade bone from the Boston butt. You will see a natural separation of membranes between the shoulder and the neck meat. Separate these two pieces so the blade bone and blade meat are no longer attached to the Boston butt. Blade meat is good only for sausages or cubed for stews. A smoked porkette or a smoked Boston butt can be baked and glazed just like a ham.

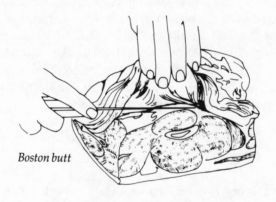

Boston butt

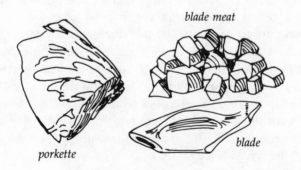

blade meat

porkette

blade

Boston Butt in a Casserole with Braised Fennel

Fennel bulbs, leaves, and seeds have long been appreciated by Italians, so much so that the fennel bulb is sometimes referred to as Florence fennel. Its slightly sweet, aniseed flavor complements the pork here.

1 boneless Boston butt, 4 to 4½ pounds	2 medium onions, sliced
1 teaspoon dried rosemary	2 celery stalks, chopped coarse
1 teaspoon dried sage leaves	2 carrots, peeled and chopped coarse
Salt, freshly ground pepper	1 cup red wine
4 to 5 tablespoons oil and/or butter, plus 1 tablespoon butter	1 cup meat stock or water
	1 tablespoon tomato paste
1 garlic clove, peeled and crushed	2 fennel bulbs
	¼ cup cream (optional)

Sprinkle the pork with the rosemary, sage, salt, and pepper and tie it in several places with white string (page 16.)

Heat 4 to 5 tablespoons of oil or butter (or oil and butter mixed) in a flameproof casserole; add the crushed garlic. As soon as the garlic begins to sizzle, add the onions and cook them for about 3 minutes. Add the celery and carrots and cook for another 3 minutes.

Add the pork to the casserole and brown it on all sides. Add the wine and cook until it is reduced by half; add the stock (or water) and the tomato paste. Stir well, lower the heat to simmer, cover the casserole, and cook for 1 hour and 30 minutes.

Cut the fennel bulbs into about 6 slices each and add them to the casserole. Put the cover back on the casserole and continue cooking for another hour.

Add the extra tablespoon of butter (and cream if desired) to the fennel slices and serve with pork.

SERVES 4 TO 6

Sweet and Sour Pork Cutlets

These cutlets can also be cut (pages 11–12) from the tenderloin or from any solid boneless piece. Beef bouillon cubes are very salty, so you may not need to add salt to the cutlets. Taste the sauce just before serving; if the tomatoes have absorbed the salt, season to taste.

1 large apple
4 plum tomatoes, peeled, seeded, and squeezed or 1 8-ounce can, drained
1 beef bouillon cube
4 tablespoons white wine
4 tablespoons wine vinegar

2 tablespoons Dijon mustard
8 thin pork cutlets, ¼ inch, cut from the boneless Boston butt
Flour
3 tablespoons peanut oil
Freshly ground pepper

Peel and core the apple and cut it into cubes. Put the apple pieces and the tomatoes through a food mill into a small saucepan. Shred or smash a bouillon cube and add it along with the white wine and vinegar. Stir the mixture together and cook slowly for 30 minutes.

Spread mustard over the cutlets, then flour them lightly. Sauté the cutlets in the hot oil, season them with pepper, and cook until they are golden brown on each side. Remove them to a baking dish, cover them with sauce, and bake them in a preheated 375° oven for 10 minutes.

SERVES 4

Pork Braciole

These boneless slices can also be cut (pages 11–12) from a fresh ham. Serve a pasta or polenta with the pork rolls so that you can mop up every drop of the delicious sauce.

8 thin pork cutlets, about ¼ inch, cut from the boneless Boston butt
Salt, freshly ground pepper
3 tablespoons grated pecorino romano cheese
2 tablespoons chopped parsley
1 garlic clove, chopped

¼ pound cooked ham, minced
½ cup bread crumbs
1 egg, lightly beaten
Flour
¼ cup cooking oil
1 16-ounce can peeled plum tomatoes, with juice

Place the cutlets on your workspace and flatten them slightly with a pounder or rolling pin (page 12). Season lightly with salt and pepper.

Mix the cheese, parsley, garlic, ham, bread crumbs, and egg in a bowl. Put a tablespoon or more of the mixture on each slice of meat. Tuck in the ends of the slices and roll them up. Tie each roll with two pieces of white string. Lightly flour the rolls.

Heat the oil in a large frying pan and brown the rolls in the hot oil, turning them several times to ensure uniform browning. Remove the rolls from the pan as soon as they are browned, and drain all the fat from the pan.

Return the meat to the pan and add the tomatoes. Bring the liquid almost to a boil, then lower the heat, cover the pan, and cook very slowly for 1 hour and 30 minutes. Salt and pepper if necessary.

SERVES 4

Pork Portuguese Style with Clams and Mussels

I fell in love with Lisbon on my first trip to Europe after the Second World War. The fountains, the pushcarts full of flowers, the sparkling streets, all enchanted me, as did the evening fish auction in Cascais, a fishing village within walking distance of Estoril. Spectators watched from the gallery of the market building in the plaza while women vendors bid for the freshly caught fish. Then I went down to one of the many little restaurants around the plaza and had pork, Portuguese style.

If you like leaner meat, cut the pork cubes from the loin end.

3 pounds pork, cut into 1½ -inch cubes	¼ cup oil
1 cup dry white wine	2 onions, chopped
¼ cup wine vinegar	Freshly ground pepper
3 garlic cloves, crushed	Hot red pepper flakes
2 bay leaves	1 dozen cherrystone clams, well washed
2 to 3 parsley sprigs	1 dozen mussels, well washed

Place the pork cubes in a porcelain or ceramic crock. Add the wine, vinegar, 2 of the garlic cloves, bay leaves, and parsley. Cover the crock with plastic wrap and refrigerate for 24 hours.

Remove the meat from the marinade and pat dry with paper towels. Reserve the marinade; remove and discard the bay leaves and garlic.

Heat the oil in a large skillet with the remaining crushed clove of garlic. As soon as the garlic begins to brown, add some of the meat and brown on all sides. (If you add the meat all at one time, it will steam, not brown.) Continue until all the meat is browned, removing the cubes from the pan as soon as they are browned.

Pour off half of the fat in the pan and add the onions to the pan. Cook the onions for 3 to 4 minutes; return the meat to the pan and cook for another 5 minutes.

Add the marinade to the pan, bring it to a boil, lower the heat, partially cover the pan, and simmer for 30 minutes.

Season the pork with pepper and hot pepper to taste. It is wiser not to add salt here; clams and mussels are salty, so taste for salt just before serving.

Add the clams and mussels and simmer, covered, for another 15 minutes. The clams and mussels should be completely opened and the pork tender.

SERVES 6

Fresh Shoulder of Pork with Sauerkraut

The picnic ham, the other half of the shoulder, is the least expensive cut of the pig. A whole picnic ham is about 6 to 7 pounds, half of which is meat; you can also use a 3- to 4-pound Boston butt for this recipe.

Go lightly with the salt here because sauerkraut is very salty. I like to serve this with a mixed-vegetable dish of red peppers, roasted and peeled, Brussels sprouts, and fennel.

A fresh picnic ham, 6 to 7
  pounds
Salt, freshly ground pepper
1 garlic clove, peeled and minced
6 juniper berries, crushed
1 cup beef stock or water
½ pound bacon, cubed

2 pounds sauerkraut
1 teaspoon caraway seeds
1 carrot, peeled and cut into
  large pieces
1 small onion, with 2 cloves
  stuck into it

Tie the ham in several places with white twine to help it keep its shape. Rub it with salt, pepper, garlic, and juniper berries. Place the meat in a deep roasting pan (with a cover), large enough to accommodate the meat and sauerkraut. Pour in the beef stock or water.

Place the pork in a preheated 350° oven and cook for 1 hour, turning it at intervals and adding liquid if needed.

While the pork is roasting, cook the bacon in a sauté pan until browned. Add the sauerkraut, caraway seeds, carrot, and onion and cook for 30 minutes. Add stock or water if it gets too dry.

Add the sauerkraut, bacon, and vegetables to the roasting pan, spooning the mixture around the pork. Cover the pan and cook for another 1 hour and 15 minutes, stirring the sauerkraut and turning the roast several times.

SERVES 6

Roasted Red Peppers, Fennel, and Brussels Sprouts

This is a colorful dish that is made a little more lively with the addition of a few drops of Pernod just before serving.

4 red peppers	3 tablespoons butter
2 small bulbs of fennel	1 garlic clove, peeled and crushed
Salt	A few drops of Pernod
1 pint Brussels sprouts	Freshly ground pepper

Roast the red peppers by charring them under the broiler. When they are cool enough to handle, peel them and discard the seeds. Cut into strips.

Cook the fennel bulbs in boiling salted water for about 20 minutes or until you can pierce them with a fork. Drain them and cut into strips.

Trim the Brussels sprouts and cook them in boiling salted water for about 15 minutes. Drain; if they are larger, cut in half.

Heat the butter in a pan and cook the garlic in the butter for a few minutes. Discard the garlic. Add the fennel and Brussels sprouts and cook for about 5 minutes. Add the red peppers, let them heat through, and flavor with the Pernod, salt, and pepper.

SERVES 6

The Loin

The two loins make up the body of the pig after the hams, shoulders, bellie, and fatback have been removed. Lightweight loins of pork from younger pigs weigh between 12 and 14 pounds; heavy loins, between 17 and 22 pounds. When a whole or half loin of pork is on special at the supermarket, it is probably a good buy. There is very little waste, because 70 percent of the loin is meat. It is not hard to divide the loin into usable cuts, and if you learn how to do it, you will save money.

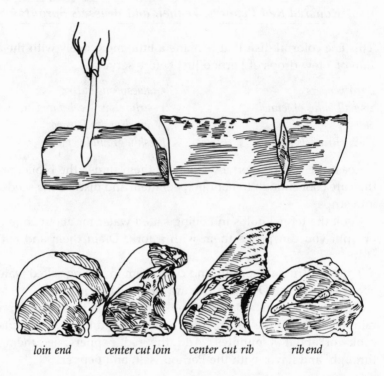

loin end   center cut loin   center cut rib   rib end

If you cut four ribs from the shoulder end of the loin, you will get a rib-end roast. Cut away the 2 to 3 inches of blade bone and its meat. Roast it in the pan with the loin for nibbling. If you take off 4 or 5 inches from the loin end, you will have a loin-end roast, sometimes called a rump roast. You can usually find a sale on these two end roast pieces. If either of the end roasts is about 3 to 4 pounds (from a lightweight loin), the roast will be tender. A 6-pound end roast from a heavy loin probably has too much fat.

To bone out the loin-end roast you need to remove the hipbone (the extension of the aitchbone, which together with the hipbone makes up the pelvic bone). The hipbone is a flat piece of bone kept together with the tailbone by cartilage and membranes.

Place the pork fat side down on your workspace. Separate the tenderloin that is under the finger bone and cut it away from the chine bone, but leave it attached to the upper part of the chop. You will have exposed the tailbone. Cut the membrane joining the tailbone to the hipbone and remove it. Cut around the end of the hipbone and remove it.

After the end roasts are cut off, you have left the center loin, one part rib section and one part loin section. Whole, it is a whole center loin,

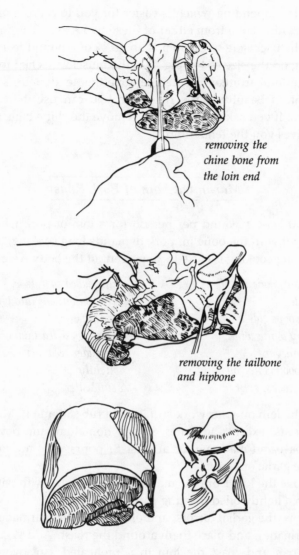

*removing the
chine bone from
the loin end*

*removing the tailbone
and hipbone*

but it can be cut into two or more center cut roasts or into ten rib and
ten loin chops. To bone out a center cut loin, place it fat side down on
your workspace. Starting from the chine bone, pull the tenderloin away
from it and from the little finger bones under it, but do not cut the
tenderloin off. With a saw, cut off the chine bone and feather bones
attached to it (pages 13–14). The eight ribs attached to the other end
can be removed in one piece to be used as baby-back ribs, page 86.
Remove the five finger bones under the fillet. Season the loin, tie it and
roast it as in Arista, Loin-End Roast of Pork, Tuscan Style, pages 76–77.

If you buy a whole loin or half a loin for roasting, ask for the rib side or loin side, depending which is easier for you to carve. Bone out and cut off the chine bone from either of these two roasts. The small fillet of meat on the back side of the loin is about ¾ of a pound to 1¼ pounds, depending on the size of the pig. It is the muscle attached to the inside part of the lumbar area. You can remove this tenderloin, stuff it, and cook it into a beautiful little roast. Or you can use it for cutlets or medallions. If you ask the butcher to remove the chine bone for you, be sure he gives you the tenderloin.

Marinated Loin of Pork Roast

Allow at least 1 pound per person for a loin of pork when you are cooking it with the bone in; pork demands long cooking, and shrinkage during cooking is close to 40 percent of the body weight.

1 *pork loin, bone in, about 5 pounds*	2 *cups cubed carrots*
2 *tablespoons salt*	1 *large onion, cut into large dice*
1 *cup dry white wine*	1 *bay leaf*
½ *cup vinegar*	½ *teaspoon dried thyme*
6 *tablespoons olive oil*	5 *coriander seeds, crushed*
4 *garlic cloves, split*	*slightly*
	½ *cup water*

Lay the loin on your work surface and rub salt into it. Mix the other ingredients, except the water, in any non-aluminum bowl; add the pork roast and marinate for at least 24 hours. It is not necessary to peel the garlic or carrots.

Remove the loin from the marinade and pat dry with paper towels. Place in a lightly oiled roasting pan, fat side up.

Remove the garlic, carrots, and onion from the marinade (reserving the marinade), and place them around the roast. Add ½ cup of water to the pan and roast the loin in a preheated 350° oven. Roast 30 minutes a pound or until the internal temperature on a meat thermometer reaches 170° to 185°, depending on your preference. Turn the roast at least twice during the cooking time, adding marinade juice as needed to keep the meat and vegetables moist.

When the pork is done, remove the pork to a platter. Scoop off any extra fat from the juices in the pan and put the juices and cooking vegetables through a food mill. If the resulting gravy is too thin, thicken it with 1 teaspoon of cornstarch mixed with a few drops of cold water, and cook a few minutes until you reach the desired consistency.

SERVES 5

Arista, Loin-End Roast of Pork, Tuscan Style

Ask the butcher for a 4-pound boneless roast from the loin side, or bone the meat yourself (pages 73–76). In either case cook the bones under the roast for added flavor. If you are unable to buy a boned roast and don't wish to go to the trouble of boning it yourself, use a center-cut loin piece with the bone in.

I started to cook with juniper berries only about six years ago. It seems to me that, like sage, they have a particular affinity for pork. You should crush them before using them to bring out their flavor. When I make this roast for my classes, I serve Pasta with Broccoli (see below).

1 boneless loin-end roast, about 4
    pounds, or 1 center-cut loin,
    bone in, about 6 pounds
8 garlic cloves
2 tablespoons dried rosemary
    leaves
12 juniper berries, crushed
1½ teaspoons salt

1 teaspoon freshly ground pepper
12 peppercorns, crushed
1 tablespoon olive oil
1 cup dry white wine
2 cups coarsely chopped onions,
    carrots, and celery for gravy, if
    desired (page 27)

Place the boneless roast cut side up on your workspace. Peel the garlic cloves and cut them into slices lengthwise. Mix them in a bowl with the rosemary, juniper berries, salt, and pepper. Rub the garlic mixture into the meat, then scatter peppercorns all over it. Roll the pork and tie it with white string.

If your roast has the bone in, saw the chine bones and feather bones so that they are still barely attached to the fat on the back of the loin (pages 13–14). Or ask the butcher to do this. Rub some of the garlic mixture and the peppercorns between the meat and these bones and fold them back together for the roasting. The bones will help keep the meat moist.

Turn the roast fat side up and make small incisions with the point of a knife; insert some of the garlic slivers and mixture into these incisions.

Oil a roasting pan lightly and place the roast in it fat side up. Roast the meat in a preheated 350° oven for 1 hour, turning the roast occasionally to ensure even browning.

After the first hour of cooking, pour in the white wine and continue cooking for another 40 minutes. Allow about 25 minutes a pound total cooking time.

When the roast is done, remove it from the pan and keep warm. Ladle off any fat remaining in the pan and serve the juices with the roast. Make gravy, if desired, from the vegetables in the pan. Or add to the pan juices a roux of equal parts flour and butter cooked together briefly; cook until it thickens.

SERVES 4 TO 6

Pasta with Broccoli

This easy pasta is a perfect accompaniment to roasted or broiled meat and chicken. It is also a great standby if you have unexpected guests arrive at your doorstep on a Sunday night. Serve a big bowl of the pasta with a loaf of Focaccia (page 5), and a green salad.

*1 bunch of broccoli, about 2
    pounds
Salt
2 to 3 tablespoons olive oil
4 garlic cloves, peeled, crushed,
    and finely chopped*

*½ teaspoon hot red pepper flakes
Freshly ground pepper
1 pound fusilli pasta
4 tablespoons grated pecorino
    romano cheese*

Clean a bunch of broccoli and cut it into florets. With a paring knife, clean the stems and cut them into little batons. Cook the broccoli in a large pot of boiling, salted water for 10 minutes or a little longer. You want the broccoli soft, not al dente. Start timing after you have added the broccoli and the water has come to the boil again.

Meanwhile, heat enough olive oil to cover the bottom of a large saucepan and cook the garlic in the oil until it just begins to color. Add a ladle of water from the broccoli pot to the pan to stop the browning process and season with red pepper flakes, salt, and pepper.

When the broccoli is cooked, lift it out of the boiling water with a sieve. Do not drain the broccoli; you will cook the pasta in the broccoli water. Add the broccoli to the garlic in the pan, toss gently, and continue cooking while you cook the pasta.

Bring the broccoli water to a full boil and add the pasta. Cook until al dente. Drain the pasta but save some of the water; return the pasta to the pot and gently stir in the broccoli. Moisten with some of the broccoli water. Turn the pasta and sauce into a large bowl and sprinkle with grated cheese and freshly ground pepper. Serve immediately.

SERVES 4

Variation: Butterflies of the South

This fanciful name for a simple pasta with broccoli refers to the shape of the farfallini (bow tie) pasta, which resembles little butterflies. This recipe and the one above also can be served cold as a salad.

Add 2 thinly sliced medium onions to the garlic just when it begins to color. Cook for 5 minutes. Add ¼ pound of ham, cut into thin strips, 2 tablespoons of capers, and 12 halved, pimiento-stuffed green olives, sliced in half. Stir well and cook for 3 minutes. Moisten with a ladle of broccoli water, and season with salt and pepper. Add the cooked broccoli and a few pieces of fresh tomato for color. Continue to simmer while you cook a pound of farfallini in the broccoli water. Mix and serve as above.

Stuffed Boneless Loin of Pork

If you are going to bone the pork yourself, buy a 4-pound rib-end roast or center-cut roast. Saw off the chine bones (see pages 13–14), or have the butcher do it. With a sharp boning knife, cut straight down between the meat and the ribs. You will have 3 pounds of meat, and baby-back ribs that you can serve as an hors d'oeuvre or save for barbecued ribs. Any stuffing will do nicely here. This one is very simple.

1 boneless loin roast, about 3 pounds	1 teaspoon dried sage leaves
Salt, freshly ground pepper	1 garlic clove, cut into thin slivers
1 pound fresh spinach	2 tablespoons pignoli nuts

Butterfly the loin so that it lies flat. Season it with salt and pepper.

Clean and wash the spinach well and blanch it quickly in boiling water. Shock with cold water to stop the cooking. Squeeze out the water, pat dry, and chop coarsely.

Sprinkle the sage and garlic slivers onto the pork. Mix the pignoli nuts with the chopped spinach and spread it on the meat. Roll the pork and tie it in several places with white string.

Place the pork fat side up in an open roasting pan and cook in a preheated 350° oven for 2 hours, about 30 minutes per pound.

SERVES 4

Stuffed Fillet of Pork

Here is a way to stuff and roast the fillet from the back side of the loin lumbar area. There is no reason to waste mushroom caps on the stuffing when stems will do. If you want to serve mushroom caps with the roasted fillets, buy ¾ of a pound of mushrooms, remove the stems, wash the caps briefly in acidulated water (page 8), pat them dry, slice them, and sauté in butter.

2 pork tenderloins, about ¾
    pound each
Salt, freshly ground pepper
1 onion, chopped fine
2 celery stalks, chopped fine
6 tablespoons butter or oil
½ pound veal, ground
¼ cup sherry
¼ pound fresh mushroom stems,
    chopped
2 tablespoons grated Parmesan
    cheese

1 egg, lightly beaten
1 tablespoon chopped parsley
½ cup stale bread, soaked in milk
    and squeezed
A pinch of marjoram
A pinch of dried sage
2 cups coarsely chopped onions,
    carrots, and celery for gravy, if
    desired (page 27)

Butterfly the tenderloins so that they lie flat, and flatten them a little more with a pounder or rolling pin. Lightly season them with salt and pepper and set aside.

Make the stuffing: Sauté the onion and celery in 4 tablespoons of the hot butter until the onion is translucent. Add the veal and cook for 5 minutes; add the sherry and cook another few minutes, until the sherry reduces by half. Add the mushrooms and cook another 5 minutes.

Pour the stuffing mixture into a bowl and let it cool a few minutes. Add the grated cheese, egg, parsley, bread, marjoram, sage, salt, and pepper and mix well.

Spread the stuffing on one half of each tenderloin and fold the other half over it. Tie with white twine; be careful not to tie too tightly, or the stuffing will pop out.

Oil a roasting pan that is not much larger than the 2 tenderloins. Season the surface of the meat with salt and pepper and dot with the remaining 2 tablespoons of butter; cover the meat with foil. Cook the fillets in a preheated 350° oven for 45 minutes. Remove the foil and continue cooking until the meat comes to a golden color, probably another 15 minutes.

Make a gravy if desired, or serve with the pan juices.

SERVES 4

Pork Noisettes with Cream Sauce and Prunes

Noisettes are small pieces of meat, ¾ inch to 1 inch thick; they are cooked differently from medallions, which are thin slices, like cutlets. If the butcher does not have tenderloin, ask him for eye of the rib or loin chops.

20 dried prunes
½ cup dry white wine
3 pork tenderloins, 2¼ to 3
*   pounds in all, cut into*
*   noisettes*
12 juniper berries, crushed
Salt, freshly ground pepper
2 tablespoons peanut oil

Flour
6 tablespoons butter or butter
*   and oil*
½ cup chicken stock
¼ cup heavy cream
1 tablespoon currant jelly
½ teaspoon lemon juice

Soak the prunes in the wine at room temperature for 4 hours.

Season the noisettes with juniper berries, salt, and pepper and rub with peanut oil. Let them set for 1 hour.

A few minutes before you start to cook the pork, cook the prunes and wine in any non-aluminum saucepan for 10 minutes. Drain and reserve the wine.

Dry the noisettes and dip them lightly in flour. Heat butter (or butter and oil) in a heavy frying pan and cook the noisettes in the butter for about 3 minutes on each side. Transfer the meat to a plate.

Pour out most of the fat from the pan, leaving just enough to cover the bottom, and add the wine in which the prunes were cooked. Bring the wine to a boil and cook on high heat until the wine has almost evaporated. Pour in the chicken stock, bring to a boil again, return the noisettes to the pan, and simmer gently on low heat for 30 to 40 minutes, until the noisettes are tender when pierced with a fork. Transfer the noisettes to a heated deep dish, cover, and keep warm.

Thoroughly skim all the fat from the juices in the pan, add the cream, and bring it to a boil, stirring and deglazing the pan. Cook briskly until the sauce thickens, then add the prunes, the currant jelly, and lemon juice. Cook and stir until the jelly is completely dissolved and the prunes are heated through.

Taste the sauce and correct the seasonings if necessary. Lift out the prunes with a slotted spoon and arrange them around the noisettes. Spoon the sauce over the noisettes and the prunes. Serve immediately.

SERVES 6

Crown Roast

A crown roast of pork, or lamb, is two center-cut rib sections of eight ribs each (ribs 7 or 8 through 14 or 15) tied together into the shape of a crown and roasted. A well-turned crown roast is beautiful to behold; it makes a spectacular, colorful presentation that enriches your dining table.

You have three choices when you want to serve a crown roast. If you have a good butcher, you can ask him to prepare the crown roast for you, and all you have to do is cook it. This is the most expensive method. Or you can ask the butcher for two center-cut rib sections of 8 ribs each (with the chine bone and feather bones removed) and tie them together yourself; see illustration and directions for Crown Roast of Lamb (pages 113–114). Here you will pay the price of center-cut pork chops.

The third possibility is to buy the rib sections of two pork half loins when they are on sale at the supermarket. The half-loin price will be about a dollar a pound cheaper than the center-cut pork chops. Be sure to ask the butcher to saw off the chine bone and remove the feather bones, or do it yourself (pages 13–14). Counting from the center of each loin (the small end) toward the shoulder (the large end), cut off one section of 8 ribs. The 4 to 5 inches you have left on each of the two shoulder ends can be frozen to serve as rib-end roasts, or cut into cubes for sweet and sour pork.

Crown Roast of Pork

As you will see in this recipe, I do not believe in cooking the stuffing inside the roast, as this makes the fat melt into the stuffing, and prevents the roast from becoming crispy. Also, by roasting the crown without the stuffing, you can cook it upside down and not have to worry about covering the bones to protect them from burning. Add baby peas or mashed potatoes with carrots in the center of the roast after it is cooked; you want a colorful center to offset the roast.

1 crown roast of pork, about 7 pounds
Juice of 1 lemon
1 to 2 garlic cloves, smashed and diced
½ teaspoon grated fresh ginger
½ teaspoon dried rosemary
½ teaspoon dried sage

12 juniper berries, crushed
Salt, freshly ground pepper

2 cups cooked green peas or 2 cups mashed potatoes and ½ cup cooked carrots
16 cherry tomatoes or olives (optional)

Place the roast on your workspace with the bones up. In a small bowl mix the lemon juice, garlic, ginger, rosemary, sage, juniper berries, salt, and pepper. Rub this seasoning into the fat on the inside of the crown.

Turn the roast upside down—that is, invert the crown—and place it in a roasting pan. Cook in a preheated 350° oven for 2 hours to 2 hours and 15 minutes, allowing 18 minutes a pound.

When the roast is done, turn it right side up, fill the cavity with the peas or the potatoes and carrots, and cover the rib ends with frilled paper chop holders or with cherry tomatoes or olives.

SERVES 8 TO 10

Pork Chops

A whole loin has 4 to 5 end chops and 8 to 10 center-cut chops, which may come together as a "combination package" at the supermarket. When center-cut chops are sold smoked, they are wonderful for dishes like Choucroute Garni (meat with sauerkraut, fermented white cabbage). Smoked chops are usually ready to eat and need only sufficient cooking to flavor the recipe you are preparing.

Pork Chops Piemontese

You need two pans for this recipe, one for the pork chops and one for the sauce.

6 pork chops, 1 inch thick each	3 tablespoons flour
Salt, freshly ground pepper	4½ cups stock
1 large onion, chopped fine	1 garlic clove, crushed
1 large carrot, peeled and diced small	2 tomatoes, peeled, seeded, and quartered
7 tablespoons butter or 5 tablespoons butter and 2 tablespoons oil	1 shallot, chopped
	1 tablespoon tomato paste
	1 bouquet garni

Season the pork chops with salt and pepper.

Cook the onion and carrot in 3 tablespoons of the butter (or 2 tablespoons of butter and 1 of oil) until they are lightly browned. Add the flour and cook until it is brown.

Add the stock, garlic, tomatoes, shallot, tomato paste, bouquet garni, salt, and pepper. Simmer the sauce slowly for 1 hour.

Meanwhile, brown the chops in the remaining butter or butter and oil; lower the heat and cook slowly for 30 minutes.

Pour the sauce over the chops and serve.

SERVES 6

TO CUT POCKETS IN PORK CHOPS

If the pocket is cut from the loin side, cut the slit to create it from the outer, fatty side of the chop; if from the rib side, then the pocket should be cut from the inside, the bone side.

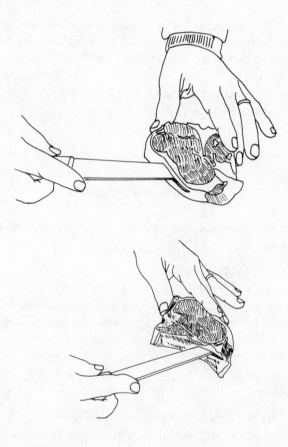

Stuffed Pork Chops San Danielli

The Danielli Company makes excellent prosciutto, and, as you can see, prosciutto flavors the stuffing for these chops so I have named this recipe for the company. Loin chops are best from the center cut, loin side or rib side.

4 center-cut pork chops, 1½ inches thick
1 garlic clove, peeled and crushed
2 tablespoons butter
½ pound mushrooms, chopped fine
½ cup cooked rice
2 tablespoons grated pecorino romano cheese

1 tablespoon chopped parsley
2 ounces prosciutto, chopped fine
1 egg, lightly beaten
Salt, freshly ground pepper
4 apples, peeled, cored, and cut into quarters

Cut a pocket in each chop. Sauté the garlic in hot butter. When it is nearly brown, remove it, and cook the mushrooms in the butter until nearly dry.

Turn the mushrooms into a bowl and add the cooked rice, cheese, parsley, prosciutto, and lightly beaten egg. Stir thoroughly and season to taste with salt and pepper.

Place a spoonful of stuffing in each pork chop pocket. Lay the chops flat in a lightly oiled roasting pan. Surround the chops with the apples and cover with foil.

Cook in a preheated 350° oven for 1 hour and 30 minutes; remove foil and cook another few minutes until the chops brown.

SERVES 4

Stuffed Pork Chops Santa Margharita

Santa Margharita is a very good saint, and these are very good pork chops. So here are pork chops Santa Margharita.

6 center-cut pork chops, 1½ inches thick
½ cup finely chopped onions
½ cup finely chopped celery
1 ounce prosciutto, chopped fine
2 tablespoons butter
2 slices of bread

2 tablespoons oil
¼ cup beef stock
A pinch of sage
Salt, freshly ground pepper
1 egg, lightly beaten
Fine bread crumbs

Cut a pocket in each chop. Sauté the onions, celery, and prosciutto in the butter for 5 minutes.

Make croutons by cutting the bread into small cubes and frying them in the oil. Pat dry with a paper towel and put them in a bowl.

Add the beef stock to the onions, celery, and prosciutto; season with sage, salt, and pepper. Stir the mixture together and pour it over the croutons.

Divide the stuffing among the pork chop pockets. Dip the chops in the beaten egg, press them in bread crumbs with the palm of your hand, and place them in a lightly oiled baking pan.

Cover the chops with foil and bake in a preheated 350° oven for 1 hour and 30 minutes.

SERVES 6

Variation

Season the inside of the pockets with salt and pepper. Fill each pocket with a slice of prosciutto, mortadella, or other ham, a slice of fontina cheese, and a sprinkling of nutmeg. Flatten the chops with a pounder or mallet and dip them in the beaten egg, making sure the inside of the pocket is wet with the egg. Press them in bread crumbs and fry in 3 tablespoons of hot oil for about 20 minutes.

Spareribs

So-called spareribs are another source of confusion. Regular spareribs are from the front of the rib cage and are held together by the sternum bone, so they are difficult to cut and to eat. Barbecue ribs are the same cut, but without the sternum. Baby-back ribs are cut from the rib side of the loin, are about 2 inches wide, and have more meat on them than either of the other two. Country ribs are really not ribs at all. They are the meaty section of the rib end of the loin split in half and then cut into chop-like strips.

All these ribs are delicious, especially when finished with a sauce under the grill or on the barbecue. The lighter-weight ribs cut from smaller hogs may be more tender than bigger ones. Allow at least three ribs per person; two racks will feed six people.

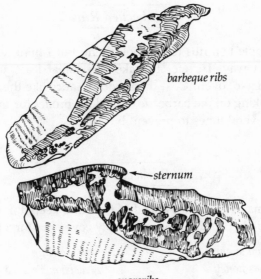

barbeque ribs

sternum

spareribs

baby back ribs   loin

country ribs

Barbecued Ribs

Many people boil ribs to precook them, but I think you lose a lot of flavor that way. I prefer to bake ribs for at least 30 minutes in a preheated 350° oven. Coat them with a sauce like the one below and finish cooking on the barbecue or under a broiler for 10 to 15 minutes, turning several times to prevent burning.

Barbecue Sauce

You can make this sauce ahead of time and keep it in the refrigerator until needed. This amount will amply cover ribs for 8 people.

⅓ cup brown sugar

4 tablespoons honey

2 garlic cloves, peeled and smashed

2 tablespoons Worcestershire sauce

1 teaspoon freshly grated ginger

¼ cup vinegar

½ cup water

½ cup ketchup

½ teaspoon Tabasco

½ teaspoon mustard seeds

½ teaspoon celery seed

½ teaspoon salt

½ teaspoon pepper

1 teaspoon cornstarch diluted in 1 tablespoon water

Place all the ingredients in a saucepan on low heat. Stir constantly until it comes to a gentle bubble. Continue cooking on low heat until the sauce coats a spoon, about 2 to 3 minutes.

Remove from heat and pass through a strainer. Cool and store in a jar until needed.

YIELD: 1½ CUPS

Spareribs and Mashed Potatoes

Here is an easy and unusual way to cook spareribs. It is a wonderful cold-weather dish.

2 racks barbecue ribs

Salt, freshly ground pepper

2 to 3 cups mashed potatoes

Place one strip of the ribs on a rack in a roasting pan. Season them with salt and pepper and spread the mashed potatoes over them. Season the second strip of ribs and place them over the potatoes.

Fasten the strips together with skewers or some white twine to make them easier to turn.

Bake the ribs in a preheated 350° oven for 1 hour and 30 minutes, turning several times. After 1 hour of cooking, separate the racks and remove the upper one to another pan, turning the inner sides up to give the potatoes a chance to brown.

SERVES 6

The Ham

The hams are the back legs of the pig. In other meat animals like lamb, veal, and chicken, a leg is called a leg; in a pig, the hind leg is called a ham. You can buy a whole ham, half a ham (butt or shank end), ham steaks (taken from the center), or a portion of a ham. If you need only a small amount, a portion is useful. Be careful, however; if you buy a large piece marked "portion" that looks like half a ham, the best slices have been removed from the center.

Hams are sold fresh, or cured, that is, salted to preserve the meat. (See the section on pork preserving, pages 250–254.) After a ham is cured, it can be treated in a number of different ways, but it must always be cooked before eating. Boiled ham, sold at delicatessens for cold meat platters or sandwiches, means just what it says: It is ready-to-eat ham that has been boiled after curing and formed into rectangular or pear shapes or put together into Pullman hams. It does not have the intense smoky flavor of hams that have been smoked after curing, such as Westphalian hams, or those that have been air-dried, like prosciutto and Smithfield hams.

Ninety-five percent of cured hams come to the market ready to eat and are so labeled. The remaining 5 percent are "farm hams" or "country hams," which have been smoked but not cooked, and the famous Virginia Smithfield hams, which are sold either cooked or uncooked. (Uncooked Smithfield hams are considerably less expensive than the ready-to-eat variety.) Usually a ham is labeled "ready to eat" or "must be cooked." If it is not labeled, be sure to ask.

There are several steps needed to cook a ham. The first step is to soak it in water to remove the salt. Smithfield hams are especially salty and need a 24-hour soaking; farm hams only need a 3- to 4-hour bath. Then the ham must be scrubbed and placed in a large pot covered with cold water. Bring the water to a boil and simmer for 3 to 4 hours. A smoked Boston butt or smoked loin of pork needs about 30 minutes in boiling water. The final step is to bake it in the oven to warm it before serving.

When cured and smoked hams are labeled "water added," the processor has injected just enough water into the meat to restore weight lost in cooking and smoking.

Glazed Ham

A large glazed ham is a popular and reliable standby for a buffet table. It requires very little effort on your part, looks stunning, and tastes wonderful.

You can also glaze a smoked Boston butt or a smoked loin of pork. Follow the recipe below, baking the Boston butt for 30 minutes, the first 20 minutes in a 350° oven, the last 10 minutes at 400°. Baste frequently with pan juices.

I have always decorated a ham with pineapple and maraschino cherries but now that maraschino cherries are out of favor because of red dye, we have to find an alternative. Stuffed olives are one possibility, or soak cherries in grappa (a strong Italian brandy) and arrange them on the ham with the pineapple slices.

1 cured, ready-to-eat-ham, 12 to
*   14 pounds*
Whole cloves
2 cups port (approximately)
2 tablespoons dry mustard
3 tablespoons brown sugar

4 whole slices of canned
*   pineapple and the juice from*
*   the can*
1 cup ginger ale
Raisins (optional)

Remove any skin remaining on the ham, and score the fat by making long vertical and horizontal cuts. Bake the ham in a 300° oven for 30 minutes.

Place a clove in each corner of the scored fat and return the ham to the oven for another hour and 30 minutes. During this time baste the ham with some of the port.

In a small bowl mix the mustard and brown sugar; add a few tablespoons of port to make a paste. At the end of the 2 hours, remove the ham from the oven and raise the oven heat to 425°. Spread the sugar/mustard paste over the whole fat side of the ham. Arrange the pineapple slices on the ham and pour the ginger ale, pineapple juice, and ½ cup of the port into the bottom of the pan.

Return the ham to the oven. After 10 minutes, baste the ham with the liquid in the bottom of the pan and bake for 10 more minutes.

If you wish a raisin sauce, soak the raisins in port and add them to the roasting pan with the ginger ale, pineapple juice, etc.

To carve a ham, place the ham with the glazed (fat) side up. Start slicing at a 15° to 20° angle from the round half, which is the large end. The first few slices will be practically the whole width of the ham, top and bottom. Where the aitchbone ends and the femur bone starts, continue slicing half slices down to the bone until you come to the shank. Turn the ham over to the other side. Start right after the bone and slice the first slice like a V. Continue cutting half slices. At the end you should have a clean bone ready for soup.

SERVES 20 TO 25

TO SEAM OUT A FRESH HAM

If the definition of eternity is half a ham and two people, a fresh, uncooked ham is an economy ticket. If you are good with your hands and a knife, you can separate out the muscles of the ham to get a number of small roasts, cutlets, rolladen, and cubes. Pork pieces cut from the ham are solid meat, leaner than those from the Boston butt.

Place the ham on your workspace with the round side (butt end) nearest you, the shank end away from you. Remove the skin and fat from the outer part of the ham. The first step is to remove the bone you can see as you look at the ham, the aitchbone, which is part of the pelvic bone. With a sharp boning knife, start cutting around this bone. Follow the bone with your knife until you come to a socket with the ball of the femur (leg) bone attached to it by a strong tendon. Cut this tendon and wiggle the aitchbone a bit. Continue to cut around the aitchbone as close to the bone as possible until you can remove it.

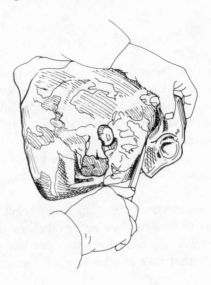

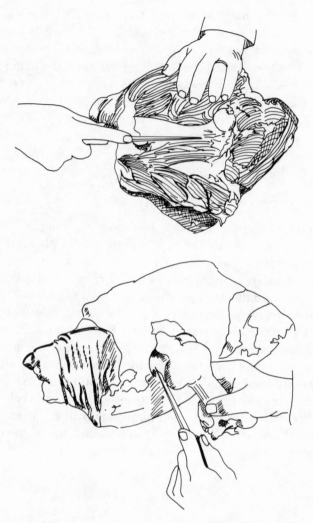

Now you remove the femur bone: Starting where the ball joint of the femur is exposed, make a cut along the femur bone and continue straight along the bone until you hit the kneecap. Cut around the knee-cap and cut through the joint (called the stifle joint) so that you can remove the femur bone.

The last bone is the shank bone. It can be boned out for stew meat, ground pork, or sausage; cooked whole for flavoring; or sawed into two small hocks.

The remaining four pieces of meat (three large muscles and one small one) are connected to one another by membranes that look like fatty tissues. With the shank side away from you, you will see the top sirloin, that is, the muscle that was attached to the femur bone (where the

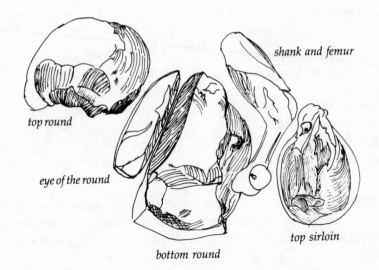

shank and femur

top round

eye of the round

top sirloin

bottom round

kneecap was). Separate it from the natural silver seam right underneath it and you will have a piece of meat the shape of a small football. This is the top sirloin, which makes an ideal small ham roast of about 2 pounds.

Then separate the top round—the round flat cushion that was on the other side of the femur bone and attached to the aitchbone—from the fatty tissue connecting it to the bottom round, a rectangular piece of meat. The top round and the bottom round are both about 4 pounds. The eye of the round is about 1½ to 2 pounds and is attached to the bottom round.

All these pieces—the top sirloin, top round, bottom round, and eye of the round—can be used as small boneless roasts. Or if you want a roast with the bone still in, do not bone out the femur, but separate the top sirloin from the top round and you will have a nice little roast.

Roast Fresh Ham (Leg of Pork)

A fresh ham is usually very large, rarely under 12 pounds. You will probably want to buy half a leg of 6 to 7 pounds, either a butt end or a shank end. If you buy the butt-end half, you can either make two roasts of 3 to 4 pounds each or you can make one roast and use the other half for cutlets, etc.

You may find fresh ham in the supermarket under its new name, leg of pork. You can also use a boneless ham for this recipe and its two variations; leaving the bone in the ham adds flavor but makes the ham harder to carve.

1 butt end or shank end half of a
   fresh ham, bone in, about 6
   pounds
12 juniper berries, crushed
2 garlic cloves, peeled and cut
   into slivers
1 teaspoon dried rosemary
3 to 4 dried sage leaves

¼ teaspoon paprika
Salt, freshly ground pepper
1 cup water or beef stock
2 cups coarsely chopped onions,
   carrots, and celery for gravy, if
   desired (pages 26–27)
1 cup dry red wine

If the meat has any fat or rind, leave it on. In a small bowl mix the juniper berries, garlic, rosemary, sage, paprika, salt, and pepper. Rub the mixture all over the pork and refrigerate for a few hours or overnight.

Place the meat (and optional vegetables) in a roasting pan or casserole, pour in the water or stock and cook in a preheated 350° oven for 1 hour. Add red wine and cook for another hour and 30 minutes, basting and turning occasionally. Make gravy with the vegetables if desired, or serve with the pan juices.

SERVES 8 OR MORE

Variation: Fresh Ham Baked in Milk

Marinate the ham as above. Flour it lightly and brown it in hot lard or oil until brown on all sides. Pour off all but 2 tablespoons of fat and sauté 1 chopped onion in the fat with the ham until the onion is translucent. Transfer the pork and onion to a deep roasting pan or casserole and pour 1 quart of warmed milk over all. Sprinkle with freshly grated nutmeg. Loosely cover the ham with foil and bake for 2 hours and 30 minutes.

Variation: Seasoned Fresh Ham

Add 1 finely chopped onion, the juice of 1 lemon, and ¼ cup of olive oil to the seasoning mixture. Marinate as above. Brown the ham in lard or oil, drain off the fat, and add the vegetables for gravy. Cook the ham with 1 cup of red wine and 1 cup of beef stock for 2 hours and 15 minutes.

Pork Cutlets

The top sirloin, top round, bottom round, and eye of the round can be sliced at an angle from the round side to get beautiful boneless, fatless slices (cutlets) suitable for boneless recipes.

Pork cutlets look like veal cutlets and may be cut (pages 11–12) and cooked in the same manner. Some people prefer them to veal because the cost is so much less (about one-third) and because pork cutlets contain a lot of vitamin B-1. The leanest pork cutlets are those cut from a fresh ham. Cutlets from the loin are tender because the tendons in the small of the back are very thin. They are really medallions of pork, but they may also be cooked in the same manner as veal cutlets. Pork cutlets from the Boston butt have the most fat and are, therefore, the most flavorful. The following three recipes can be made with pork slices cut from the ham, loin, or shoulder.

Pork cutlets cook very quickly. You can dip them in seasoned flour, egg, then bread crumbs and fry them. Served with lemon wedges, they are cutlets Milanese, with a fried egg on top, they become a Schnitzel. Or try one of these easy recipes.

Piquant Pork Cutlets

8 thin pork cutlets cut from a
   fresh ham, ¼ inch thick each
2 tablespoons flour
Salt, freshly ground pepper
1 egg, lightly beaten
6 tablespoons oil
2 tablespoons butter
1 onion, chopped

1 tablespoon capers, drained
2 anchovies, chopped
1 tablespoon chopped parsley
1 tablespoon vinegar
½ teaspoon potato starch
½ cup veal stock (or ½ bouillon
   cube dissolved in ½ cup
   boiling water)

Pound the cutlets with a pounder or rolling pin. Dip them in seasoned flour (salt and pepper mixed with the flour), then in the beaten egg.

Heat the oil in a frying pan. When it is hot, cook the cutlets a few at a time until they reach a nice golden color on each side, about 3 minutes per side. As they finish, remove them to a serving dish and keep them warm while you prepare the sauce.

Heat the butter in a small saucepan. When it is hot, add the onion and cook until it begins to color a bit. Add the capers and anchovies and cook for 2 to 3 minutes, then add the parsley, vinegar, and the potato starch dissolved in a bit of the cold stock. Add the rest of the stock, bring everything to a boil, lower the heat, and simmer for a few minutes. Taste the sauce and correct seasonings if necessary.

When the sauce has reduced to the proper consistency, pour over the cutlets and serve immediately.

SERVES 4

Pork Saltimbocca

Roman menus specialize in Veal Saltimbocca, little veal birds that jump into your mouth. Here is a variation using pork that is equally delicious and much easier on your budget.

16 very thin slices of fresh ham,
  1/8 inch thick if possible, about
  3 by 6 inches
Salt, freshly ground pepper
8 slices of prosciutto, chopped
12 black olives, chopped
1 garlic clove, chopped fine
8 dried sage leaves, crumbled
1 tablespoon chopped parsley
1 tablespoon chopped basil

2 tablespoons grated pecorino
  romano cheese
1 egg, lightly beaten with 1
  tablespoon water
6 tablespoons butter
2 ounces calvados
4 Granny Smith apples, peeled,
  cored, and sliced
1/4 teaspoon nutmeg

Flatten the cutlets with a pounder or rolling pin. Season them lightly with salt and pepper.

Mix together the prosciutto, olives, garlic, sage, parsley, basil, and cheese. Spread a tablespoon of this mixture on 8 slices of the meat. Cover with the remaining 8 cutlets. Wet the edges of the cutlets with egg wash and pound them lightly to help each pair of cutlets stick together.

Heat the butter in a skillet and brown the cutlets quickly on each side. Add the calvados and cook until it reduces by half. Add the apples, nutmeg, and a bit of water if necessary. Cook slowly until the apples are cooked to a puree, about 1 hour. Taste for seasoning.

SERVES 8

Other Parts of the Pig

A pig is a multipurpose animal; you can eat everything but the squeal. Fresh bellie is an important ingredient for sausages or as a flavoring for cured vegetables. Salted, it is called salt pork, used for cooking and seasoning. Salted and smoked, it is bacon. Bacon ends are not as neat-looking as center-sliced bacon, but they are inexpensive and useful in recipes calling for diced bacon, like Fresh Shoulder of Pork with Sauerkraut (page 72).

Canadian bacon is the boneless center-cut loin of pork that has been cured in the same fashion as bacon. It is flat in shape and ready to eat. Canadian-style bacon made in the United States is in the shape of a cylinder.

Back fat, fat from right under the skin, contains no lean at all and is sold fresh and salted as a fat for cooking, or sliced, to put around roasts or to line terrines. Caul fat, a lining from the abdomen that resembles lace, is used to wrap around roasts or around pork liver pieces for the barbecue and to line terrines.

The head is boiled and boned out to make head cheese, a type of sausage. My father's recipe for head cheese is on pages 249–250. The cheeks of a pig's head, the jowls, are cured like bacon and are used, especially in the South, to flavor greens. They are usually only found in special pork stores.

Hocks are the 3-inch pieces between the foot and the picnic ham on the front legs. They are used as flavoring. It is better to use cured and smoked meat with a fresh vegetable and fresh meat with a cured vegetable. Smoked hocks are good with split peas or fresh cabbage, fresh hocks with sauerkraut.

Crispy pork skin from a roast pig is a delicacy; the skin is also used in sausage recipes like Coteghini Milanese (page 245) and in some recipes for braciole.

The toes and feet of the front legs of a pig are called trotters. They are tasty pickled or boiled; see pages 226–227 for recipes.

Roast Suckling Pig

A roast suckling pig is an unusual, festive presentation that will serve 12 to 15 people at a party. Don't waste an inch of the crispy skin and the rich, juicy meat. You cannot carve a pig into slices; you must cut the meat off in chunks. A pair of poultry shears may be useful.

Suckling pig is not an Italian specialty; it belongs more to Spain, which is where I first tasted it. In Italy roast pig, porchetta, is an adult pig of about 125 pounds that is roasted on a spit in a baker's oven and often sold at fairs, where the tantalizing smell of the golden brown skin attracts the farmers and their families.

Suckling pigs are from 1 to 3 months old. Be careful to measure your oven first before you buy the pig. A 12- to 18-pound pig is the largest you can fit into a 24-inch oven. The Adolph Kusy Company, 861 Washington Street, New York, NY 10014, (212) 242-4755, is a good source for suckling pigs. You do not need to stuff the pig, but if you want to, I have given you a good stuffing at the bottom of this recipe. Your pig will be more flavorful if you rub the seasonings into the meat a few hours or the night before cooking.

1 suckling pig, 12 to 15 pounds	*2 tablespoons fennel seeds*
Salt, freshly ground pepper	*A small bunch of rosemary sprigs*
1 lemon	*A dozen fresh sage leaves* or
5 to 6 garlic cloves, peeled and	*dried leaf sage*
chopped	*24 juniper berries, crushed*
1 bunch of wild fennel or *the*	*About ½ cup olive oil* or *other oil*
leaves from a few fennel bulbs	

Wash and dry the pig. Pry the jaws open and insert a round stone about the size of a golf ball between the teeth. This allows you to put an apple in the pig's mouth at serving time.

Season the inside meat of the pig with salt and pepper. Cut the lemon in half and squeeze the juice onto the meat. Rub the garlic, fennel, rosemary, sage, and juniper berries onto the meat also. Let the pig marinate in these herbs and spices in the refrigerator for a few hours or overnight.

Fold the hind legs (the hams) underneath the belly of the pig so that they are practically under the head. Tie them in place. Place the pig in a large roasting pan. Brush oil all over the skin.

Cook the pig in a preheated 350° oven for 3 hours to 3 hours and 30 minutes, basting several times with olive oil and drippings. Cooking time is approximately 15 minutes per pound.

SERVES 12 TO 15

Stuffing for Suckling Pig

Salt, freshly ground pepper
Juice of 1 lemon
2 tablespoons fennel seeds
2 tablespoons rosemary leaves
2 tablespoons sage leaves
24 juniper berries, crushed
½ tablespoon peppercorns, gently
  crushed

2 pounds veal, ground
2 pounds pork, ground
2 cups stale Italian bread, soaked
  in milk and squeezed
2 eggs, lightly beaten
½ cup olive oil

Marinate the inside skin of the pig with salt, pepper, lemon juice, and one-half of the herbs and spices listed above—the fennel, rosemary, sage, juniper, and peppercorns. Let the pig rest for a few hours or overnight.

Mix the ground meats, bread, eggs, and the other half of the herbs and spices together. Season with salt and pepper and rub olive oil over the skin. Stuff the pig and sew up the incision. Continue to brush oil on the skin several times during the cooking. Cook as above.

LAMB

My FATHER WAS ONE OF FOUR BUTCHERS in Bevagna, our town of seven thousand people in the northern Italian province of Umbria. All year long each one tried to outdo the others preparing and displaying their merchandise. At Eastertime, the competition became intense. The butchers exhibited dressed baby lambs and kids (goats), abbacchi and capretti, which are traditional feast meats; everyone knew that the butcher who dressed them best was the top man for that year.

We did not have stoves as we have today; all the cooking was done either in a large fireplace or on small fireplaces that were waist-high. Lamb was so important at Easter that even the poorest family in town would sacrifice something to be able to buy a small piece of lamb. The lamb was usually cooked on a spit in the large fireplace. We took our traditional Easter cake, a high yeast bread called Pizza di Pasqua, made with cheese and eggs, to the baker's oven to be cooked. It was wonderful to walk home on Good Friday through the narrow side streets with the tantalizing smells of roasting lamb and fragrant cakes making you hungry at every step.

We do not eat a lot of lamb in the United States. (According to American Meat Institute figures for 1985, Americans eat 1.4 pounds of lamb annually, quite a difference from 62 pounds of pork and 78.9 pounds of beef.) The colonists brought cows and pigs with them, but not sheep; as settlers moved west, game was plentiful and it was easy and inexpensive to raise herds of cattle on the great open plains. There were some sheep brought up from Mexico before the 1860s, but the cattle ranchers thought sheep would pollute or use up all the grass; the range wars of the 1860s ensured that the cattlemen kept out the sheep.

In time it was found that sheep and cattle could exist on the same land, but for a number of reasons the fledgling sheep industry never grew to its full capacity. There was no experimentation to improve the stock by artificial insemination as there has been with such success in cattle. The price of wool fell as man-made fibers replaced wool and immigration laws kept out Basque and Mexican sheepherders who knew how to care for sheep. As land became increasingly expensive, it was far more cost-efficient to raise a thousand-pound steer than a ninety-pound sheep.

For all these reasons, and because of the popularity of beef and pork, lamb has never been popular here; in some parts of the United States, you cannot even buy lamb. It seems too bad that this tasty and nutritious meat has never enjoyed a good reputation. I have always thought of lamb as the purest meat and the most digestible, since sheep traditionally feed only on their mother's milk and on green grass, sometimes grass above the timberline. Europeans have always appreciated lamb, and you can usually find it in markets frequented by people from lands around the Mediterranean.

When I was in Paris in 1971, I had my first taste of pré-salé lamb, lamb from sheep that graze on the salt marshes near Mont-Saint-Michel in the northwest of France. It is exquisite, the naturally salted flesh an entirely new taste to me. Unfortunately, we have nothing like it in the United States.

Types of Lamb

There are three types of lamb: milk-fed lamb, spring lamb, and mutton. Baby milk-fed lamb, traditional for people of many cultures for the Easter holiday, is the most delicate. Baby hothouse lambs are milk-fed lambs under three months old and are almost always sold whole, halved, or quartered and roasted—often on a spit—for holiday feast days. (Baby lamb chops sold in restaurants are from three- to six-month-old lambs, not baby milk-fed lambs.)

Due to changes in lamb breeding in the last fifteen years, spring lamb (5- to 7-months old) is now available all year long, not just March through October as in the past. (Lamb sold between March and the end of October may still be legally stamped "genuine spring lamb.") The new lambs are leaner and about 20 pounds heavier than before, weighing 70 to 75 pounds when they come to market. Beware of older lambs 12 to 24 months; they are yearlings and fall into a sort of lamb limbo, too old for lamb and too young for mutton.

Mutton is a two-year-old castrated male lamb that has a strong taste particularly loved by the English. We do not raise true mutton in this country as they do in England, France, Italy, and Australia. Your best chance of tasting real mutton is at restaurants that import it.

You find a lot of New Zealand lamb in the supermarkets today. It arrives frozen, of course, but the quality is usually good. The lambs are raised the old-fashioned way, on mother's milk and grass (American lambs are now sometimes fed grain); 4- to 6-month old spring lambs are slaughtered by May 31st. The legs weigh 4½ to 5 pounds. Heavy pieces like 8- or 9-pound legs may be from older lambs. Marinate these in vinegar or lemon juice before cooking.

Tips on Buying, Storing, and Freezing Lamb

The best lamb has light red meat, not dark red like beef. The one-quarter to one-half inch of fat covering the outside of the meat should be firm and white, not oily or brittle. You should be able to see some red in the bones; if they are white and bleached out, the lamb is old.

Lamb will keep up to a week in the refrigerator. It can be prepared ahead of time for cooking and can be frozen in the same manner as pork (pages 65–66).

Structure of Lamb

Lamb is the smallest of the four-footed meat animals. You might get an idea of the difference between lamb and beef when you know that a leg of beef is about 42 inches in circumference and weighs about 80 pounds. A leg of lamb, on the other hand, weighs 6 to 9 pounds and is about 8 to 10 inches around, about one-tenth the size of a leg of beef.

You may remember from the pork chapter that although pork, lamb, veal, and beef are structurally identical, with the same number of bones with the same shapes in the same places, there is a difference in how they are divided into primary cuts. Lamb is cut so that the first four ribs are in the shoulder, eight are in the rib section, and one rib is in the loin. The blade meat of lamb is in the arm and forearm; the loin is cut off at the beginning of the hip, whereas a pork loin is cut 5 inches below that point into the leg. So a loin of lamb means something entirely different from a loin of pork, where the loin is the whole body of the pig from the neck to the aitchbone of the leg.

Lamb is a fatty animal, and, unlike pork, the fat is not edible. It is more like tallow. This contributes to the high price of lamb, because by the time the lamb is trimmed of its fat and other nonedible parts, the resulting meat is only about 40 percent of its weight. The fat is another reason the best time to buy lamb is from May to November, when the lamb has developed less solidified fat than when it is older.

The membranes separating the muscles on lamb and veal are clearer and easier to distinguish than those of pork, which resemble fatty tissue.

A lamb is divided into two parts, a foresaddle and a hindsaddle. The foresaddle, the front part of the lamb, has two parts, the chuck and the bracelet. The hindsaddle also has two, the loin and the legs.

The Chuck

Let's imagine that you have bought a whole chuck of lamb, the front section of the foresaddle. Ask the butcher to split it down the back so that you have two half chucks. Each half chuck has a piece of the neck, a shoulder with the shank attached, a rack of four ribs, and a brisket.

Like pork shoulder, lamb shoulder is juicy because it has fat running through it. It is an inexpensive cut, good for roasting. Saw off the lamb shank to which the brisket is attached just above the joint. (Or ask the butcher to do this if you are not handy with a saw.) Then, to square the roast, cut off a little piece of the neck, leaving about an inch of the neck on the chuck. You now have a square-cut shoulder of lamb, 6 to 7 pounds, bone in.

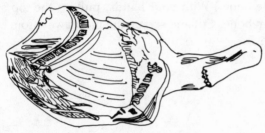

Because the shoulder is cut off between the fourth and fifth ribs, three-quarters of the shoulder-blade bone comes down into the shoulder where it is attached to the arm bone. These bones must be removed if you are to carve the roast successfully.

Place the shoulder on your workspace bone side up. The ribs, chine bone, and feather bones are on the surface and may be removed as a complete unit by following with your knife just under and around the sides of the ribs until they can be lifted off.

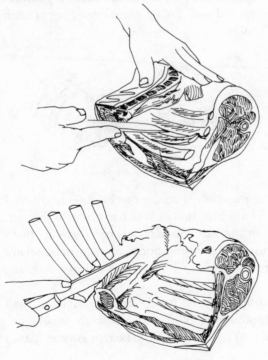

You will see the blade bone running in a straight line just below the eye of the chop. With the point of a boning knife, run along above the blade bone parallel to the arm bone. Open it up without cutting the skin and follow it into the square of the shoulder until you come to the joint of the blade bone and the arm bone. (It is easy to run your knife above the flat blade bone.) With your hands, pull up the top and expose the joint and arm bone. Cut and scrape the meat away from both bones and remove them.

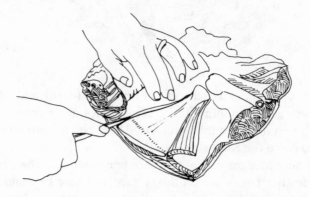

You now have a boneless pillow roast of about 4 pounds that is easy to slice; it can be stuffed and cooked like a boned leg of lamb or cut into cubes for shish kebab.

The chuck from the other shoulder can be cut into chops, but I do not advise doing it yourself at home. It is hard to saw the arm bone. Ask the butcher to run the half chuck on his band saw so that you get the standard U.S. cuts of four round bone chops (arm bone) and five or six long blade chops (blade bone), and the shank, brisket, and a piece of neck.

Or the half chuck may be totally boned, trimmed, and cubed for curried lamb, Irish stew, marinated for shish kebab, or ground for Moussaka (page 128) or Stuffed Grape Leaves Anwar (pages 126–127).

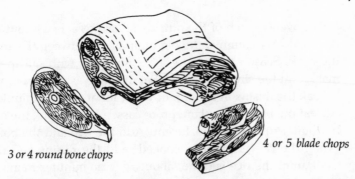

3 or 4 round bone chops

4 or 5 blade chops

Lamb shanks are not a fancy cut, but when prepared properly, they are delicious and help keep the budget in good trim. Shanks and the neck can be boned out for stew, curry, or ground meat. About the only use for the brisket, the thick part of the breast that has a thin coating of meat, is for ground meat or Scotch broth.

Shoulder of Lamb Greek Style

You stuff a boned shoulder just as you do a boned leg of lamb. Both are good; the difference is in appearance. The shoulder costs less, but the leg makes a better presentation and has finer-textured meat. I usually serve the shoulder for family meals. Use any other stuffing, such as recipes on pages 121–122; I like this Greek-type stuffing with lamb.

If you leave the shank bone in, you can tie the shoulder so that it is somewhat the shape of a cylinder. This makes it easier to carve than when the shoulder is boned out to make a flat pillow roast, but there is no room for stuffing; season with garlic, rosemary, thyme, salt, and pepper.

1 whole boneless shoulder of
    spring lamb, about 4 to 6
    pounds, the bones reserved
Salt, freshly ground pepper
A sprig of rosemary or 1
    teaspoon dried rosemary
1 small garlic clove, cut into
    slivers
½ cup raisins, soaked in water to
    equal 1 cup
4 tablespoons butter
1 onion, chopped fine

1 cup raw rice
2 cups boiling water
2 eggs
1 tablespoon chopped parsley
¼ cup pignoli nuts
Oil
2 cups coarsely chopped onions,
    carrots, and celery for gravy, if
    desired (pages 26–27)
A glass of dry white wine
1 cup beef stock

Remove as much of the outside fat as possible without uncovering the meat. Also remove the big lump of fat between the shoulder and the neck. Season the inside of the shoulder with salt, pepper, rosemary, and the slivers of garlic. Set the lamb aside.

Soak the raisins in the cup of water for at least 30 minutes.

Heat the butter in a flameproof casserole and cook the onion in the hot butter until it is translucent. Add the rice and the boiling water. When the rice is partially cooked, add the raisins and their water. Cook until the rice is done, about 17 to 20 minutes in all; let the rice cool.

Turn the rice into a mixing bowl and season with salt and pepper. Add the eggs, chopped parsley, and pignoli nuts and mix well. Stuff the cavity of the shoulder (where the blade bone was) with the mixture and sew the outer edges with a trussing needle and white thread.

Lightly oil a roasting pan. Lay the lamb bones in the pan and place the shoulder on them. Add the gravy vegetables and sprinkle the top of the lamb with salt, pepper, and rosemary.

Cook the roast at 400° for 1 hour and 30 minutes, basting with wine and stock several times during the cooking.

Remove the roast and keep it warm while you make gravy from the vegetables and juices from the pan.

SERVES 8

Braised Lamb Shanks

Lamb shanks should include about an inch of the arm chop and arm bone. Serve with rice pilaf or sautéed zucchini.

2 tablespoons oil	3 celery stalks, cut into 2-inch
4 tablespoons butter	pieces
2 garlic cloves, peeled and	Salt, freshly ground pepper
crushed	½ teaspoon thyme
4 lamb shanks	1 cup beef or veal stock
2 medium onions, chopped	1 16-ounce can peeled plum
2 carrots, peeled and cut into	tomatoes, juice included
2-inch pieces	

Heat the oil and butter in a large flameproof casserole; add the garlic. As soon as it begins to brown, add the lamb shanks. When the meat begins to brown, remove the garlic.

When the shanks are browned, remove all but 2 tablespoons of fat from the pan. Add the onions and cook for 5 minutes. Add the carrots and celery and season with salt, pepper, and thyme. Add the stock, bring it to a boil, and lower the heat to simmer. Add the tomatoes, cover the casserole, and cook on low heat or in a 350° oven for 1 hour and 30 minutes to 2 hours.

SERVES 4

Cubed Spring Lamb with Artichokes

¼ cup oil
2 garlic cloves, peeled and
   crushed
2 pounds boneless lamb shoulder,
   cut into 2-inch cubes
2 medium onions, chopped fine

1 cup dry white wine
Salt, freshly ground pepper
6 raw artichoke bottoms, trimmed
   and cut into quarters
2 egg yolks
Juice of 1 lemon

Heat the oil in a skillet large enough to hold the lamb; add the garlic. When the garlic begins to color, add the lamb cubes and brown them on all sides.

Remove the meat from the pan and drain off all the fat except about 2 tablespoons. Add the onions and cook until they are translucent; return the meat to the pan.

Cook for about 10 minutes. Add the wine and reduce it by half. Add salt and pepper to taste.

Lay the artichoke pieces in the bottom of a casserole. Pour the meat, onions, and juice over them. Cover the casserole and cook in a preheated 350° oven for another 35 minutes, or until the meat is done.

Just before serving, beat the egg yolks with the lemon juice. Remove the casserole from the oven and gently stir in the egg yolks and lemon. Serve immediately.

SERVES 4

French Lamb Stew

If you are in a hurry, you can cook all the vegetables with the lamb in this stew, but I think it is much more attractive to serve the stew surrounded by the onions, carrots, and turnips slightly glazed so they are shiny. In Italy we have small turnips like baby carrots, but white turnips cut into ovals are fine.

1 tablespoon flour	*1 cup veal stock*
3 pounds lamb from the shoulder	*1 teaspoon tomato paste*
and neck, cut into 2-inch cubes	*1 bouquet garni*
Salt, freshly ground pepper	*1¼ pounds white potatoes*
4 tablespoons butter	*24 small white onions*
2 tablespoons oil	*½ pound carrots*
1 garlic clove, peeled and crushed	*½ pound white turnips*
1 onion, chopped	*A pinch of sugar*
½ cup white wine	

Lightly flour the meat and season with salt and pepper. Heat the butter and oil in a large, heavy skillet and brown the lamb in the hot fat. When it is thoroughly browned, remove the meat from the pan and pour out all but 2 tablespoons of the fat.

Quickly brown and then discard the garlic. Sauté the chopped onion in the pan for about 3 minutes. Return the meat to the pan and cook the meat and onions together for a few minutes.

Add the wine, let it reduce, then add the veal stock, tomato paste, and bouquet garni. Turn the heat down to simmer. Partially cover the pan and cook on low heat for another hour and 30 minutes, making about 2 hours' total cooking time for the lamb.

Meanwhile, peel the potatoes and cut them into ovals. Add them to the stew for the last 30 minutes of cooking.

Peel the white onions, carrots, and turnips and cut the carrots and turnips into ovals about the size of your little finger. Place them all in a flameproof casserole with just enough water to cover and a pinch of salt and sugar. Cover them with a sheet of waxed paper cut to the same size as the casserole with a small hole for escaping steam. Cover the casserole as well and cook for 20 to 25 minutes or until the vegetables seem done when pierced with a fork. Place them around the serving platter as garnish.

SERVES 6 TO 8

The Bracelet

The bracelet is the second part of the foresaddle. It consists of eight ribs (the fifth to the twelfth) with the breast attached. When the breast is removed, it becomes a hotel rack with eight ribs on each side. The rack can be cooked whole, formed into a crown roast or Honor Guard roast, or cut into baby rib chops.

TO PREPARE A HOTEL RACK FOR COOKING

The chine bone and feather bones must be removed with a saw (pages 13–14). The chops must be frenched, that is, cleaned so that the rib ends are exposed. To do this, cut off 1 to 2 inches of meat and membrane from the rib end of the chop. You will be able to cover the rib ends with paper chop holders after cooking. Reserve the cut-off meat for ground-lamb recipes.

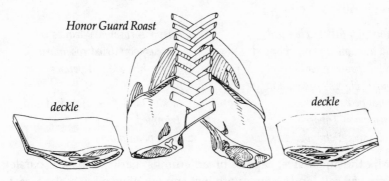

Honor Guard Roast

deckle   *deckle*

Next, you must decide what to do with the deckle, the thin line of meat between two layers of fat on top of the rack. When you order a hotel rack in a restaurant, the deckle will have been removed so that you eat only the eye of the chop; a rack from the store comes with the deckle on, and it is up to you if you wish to remove it or not. Some people like it. You can remove it from the last three ribs or from the whole rack, or you may want to keep the fat and just take off the end of the blade bone inside the deckle. Make a shallow incision with the point of a knife running the same direction as the chops between the seventh and eighth ribs. Remove the small piece of flat blade bone. At about the fifth rib, you will see the front part of the blade bone; cut around it closely and remove it. Lift off the deckle.

Rack of Lamb Chops with Cannes-Style Seasoning

A rack of lamb for two is dining high, as anyone knows who has ordered it in a good restaurant. I like to season the meat with this delicious mixture that I first tasted in France. I was traveling by train and realized after the train had left Nice that my wallet was gone. I reported the loss to the police in Cannes but did not expect any results. To my intense surprise and joy, the police returned the wallet with all the contents. I was so happy that I asked the young lady at the hotel which was the best retaurant in town, and she and I had dinner there. This is how they served rack of lamb.

This seasoning or any similar mixture may be used for other broiling cuts of lamb, like Denver Ribs (page 115) or barbecued leg of lamb.

A rack of lamb chops is a bit of a misnomer because it is structurally half the rack, that is, eight ribs of American lamb. New Zealand lamb has six ribs to the rack.

2 anchovy fillets, chopped	1 teaspoon rosemary leaves or
1 tablespoon capers, chopped	½ teaspoon dried rosemary
2 tablespoons bread crumbs	Salt, freshly ground pepper
2 garlic cloves, peeled and	Olive oil
chopped	1 rack of lamb ribs, frenched and
½ teaspoon Tabasco	trimmed
1 tablespoon chopped parsley	1 tablespoon honey

Mix the anchovies, capers, bread crumbs, garlic, Tabasco, parsley, rosemary, salt, and pepper with just enough olive oil to make a paste. Spread the seasoning over the meat side of the rack of lamb.

Cook the rack in a baking pan in a preheated 425° oven for 45 minutes.

Remove the pan from the oven and spread the honey over the lamb. Return the lamb to the broiler for a final 2 or 3 minutes of cooking. Serve on hot plates.

SERVES 2

Variation: Honor Guard Roast

Trim the surface fat from two racks, leaving only a thin coating, and french the ribs. Prop the two racks against each other so that the ribs interlock, with the fat facing outside. Score the fat in a crisscross pattern and season the meat with salt and pepper or with the above Cannes-Style Seasoning, and cook it for 45 minutes in a preheated 425° oven.

SERVES 5

Variation: Crown Roast

This is exactly the same as a crown roast of pork, except that since lamb is a more expensive meat, it is a more luxurious presentation. A crown roast of lamb is a good springtime party dish, while pork is more traditional in the winter holiday season. Invert the crown and cook for 1 hour in a preheated 425° oven, 15 minutes longer than the Honor Guard Roast because the meat is inside.

To serve, turn the crown right side up again and fill the cavity either with a meat stuffing that you have shaped to fit inside the crown and cooked in the pan beside the roast or with colorful vegetables such as baby carrots, peas, etc., surrounded by mashed potatoes.

TO PREPARE A CROWN ROAST

The chine and feather bones are often left on a crown roast. If this is done, however, you must make cuts in the chine between the ribs with a saw so that the racks can be bent into a crown.

Tie two frenched racks together to form a crown by bending the ribs backward with the meat on the inside. Place the two sections end to end. With a large needle threaded with white twine, pierce under the bottom side (the meaty part) of the last rib of one section and under the bottom side of the first rib of the second section. Tie the two ribs tightly together. Repeat this process farther up on the bare rib and tie together.

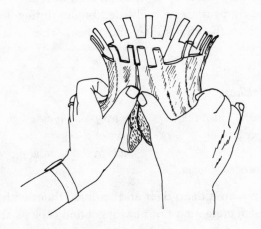

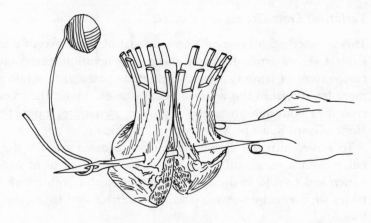

Take hold of the two ends of the rib section and turn them with the meat part inside so that the two ends meet to form a circle. Close the circle by tying the two sections together with your needle and thread once on the bottom part of the chops, then again on the bare rib side. It is important that your ties be strong and firm because you are bending the chops backward to create the crown shape.

SERVES 6 TO 8

Rib Lamb Chops

You can pan-fry rib lamb chops, broil them, or bread them for deep-frying. They are nice served with a mint sauce or any piquant sauce. For broiling, it is better to have them cut so that there are two ribs for each chop; this way the chop is thick enough to remain juicy. Cook one side of the chops under a preheated broiler until golden brown; salt that side, turn the chops over and repeat. The meat should be pink inside.

Marinated Rib Chops

8 rib chops, about 1½ inch thick
2 garlic cloves, peeled and
   chopped
A few sprigs of parsley, chopped

½ teaspoon thyme
Juice of 1 lemon
Salt, freshly ground pepper

Place the chops in a deep dish and sprinkle them with the above ingredients. Refrigerate for 1 hour or longer and cook as above.

SERVES 4

Breast

The other part of the bracelet, the breast, is very inexpensive. The breast is usually trimmed and cut into riblets, or it can be stuffed and roasted by opening a pocket between the ribs and the meat. Do not buy lamb breast from November through May because it will be much fattier and have less meat on it than when the lamb is younger.

Denver Ribs

Here is a cut from the breast that I call Denver Ribs in honor of the president of the Lamb Council, who is from Denver, Colorado. If the sternum bone is still attached to the base of the ribs, cut it off (see illustration of pork ribs on page 67). You do not need a saw for this; a knife will do, because you can cut just where the cartilage begins. Remove all the fat from the remaining 2- to 2½-inch-wide strip of ribs and cook the ribs like spareribs. Cut into individual riblets for finger eating.

Denver Ribs are good with Cannes-Style Seasoning (pages 111–112). Cook the ribs bone side up in a preheated 400° oven for 30 minutes, until the ribs have browned. Turn them over and spread the seasoning on the meat. Cook until crisp, about another 30 minutes. Trickle honey down the center of the ribs and finish them under the broiler for 3 to 4 minutes.

Or season them with Barbecue Sauce (page 88). Start them in a 400° oven as above, rib side up. Turn them over after the first 30 minutes and cook for another 15 minutes. Coat them with barbecue sauce and continue cooking, adding more sauce if necessary, for another 15 minutes. (If you put the barbecue sauce on too early, it will burn.)

SERVES 4 AS AN APPETIZER

Stuffed Breast of Lamb

This is an inexpensive cut of lamb that can be delicious when the lamb is young and not too fatty. Although there isn't much meat, what there is is very good. You can extend it with a meat stuffing like the one below or a pork chop or any meat scraps chopped up in a food processor and seasoned. (See seasoning for sausages, page 233.)

1 breast of lamb, about 1½
   pounds
1 small onion, chopped fine
1½ tablespoons butter or oil
½ pound sausage
1 egg, lightly beaten
½ cup bread, soaked in milk and
   squeezed

1 garlic clove, chopped fine
1 teaspoon chopped parsley
1 teaspoon chopped capers
2 tablespoons grated Parmesan
   cheese
Salt, freshly ground pepper
Oil

Remove most of the fat from the surface of the breast. With the point of a boning knife make a cut between the ribs and the meat where the small ribs are. Cut carefully all around so as to make a pocket without making any holes. Leave at least ½ inch of meat uncut on the edges.

Sauté the onion in the butter until translucent. Remove the sausage skin and cook the sausage meat with the onion for a few minutes. Turn the onion and sausage into a bowl and mix in the egg, bread, garlic, parsley, capers, Parmesan cheese, and ¼ teaspoon each salt and pepper.

Fill the pocket with the stuffing and close it with a skewer. Lightly season the outside of the breast with salt and pepper and sprinkle with a little oil.

Cook the breast in a preheated 350° oven for 1 hour and 30 minutes.

SERVES 4

The Loin

Now we move to the hindsaddle of lamb, the loin and the legs. When cooked together, this is called a baron of lamb. It weighs about 20 to 30 pounds, about 48 percent of the total weight of the animal. The baron can be cooked on a barbecue or a spit.

There are three or four things you can do with the loin. It can be cut into a roast of about 6 pounds, called a saddle of lamb. It can be cut into chops or boned out for noisettes or medallions. No matter how you cut it, it will be expensive, especially boned out.

Be careful when you order meat to make a saddle roast to specify that you want a loin of lamb, not a saddle of lamb. You might find yourself with the entire hindsaddle, loin and legs.

TO BONE OUT A SADDLE ROAST

Carefully cut the tenderloins free from the spinal bone, leaving them attached to the roast. Then remove the bone from between the loins, leaving the four pieces of meat joined together. To facilitate the removal of the bone after cooking, cut the 2-inch finger bones from the backbone with a saw.

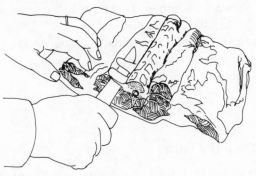

Saddle Roast

A saddle roast is all the loin of the lamb. If you remove the spinal bone, it is easier to carve, and you get attractive looking slices. When I cook the saddle, I replace the bone in the roast in order to give it shape and flavor.

1 boneless saddle roast, about 6 pounds, the spinal bone reserved

2 garlic cloves, peeled and cut into slivers

1 tablespoon rosemary

Salt, freshly ground pepper

2 cups coarsely chopped onions, carrots, and celery for gravy if desired (pages 26–27)

2 tablespoons oil or butter

½ cup white wine

¼ cup beef stock

Trim the loin by removing the kidneys, kidney fat, fell (the outer skin of the lamb that is like thin parchment), and most of the fat covering the meat. Bone out the roast; then cut off most of the flanks so that there are only 3 inches still attached. (Reserve the rest of the flank meat for ground lamb or meat for stuffing.)

Place the meat fat side down on your workspace and season the interior of the saddle with the garlic, rosemary, salt, and pepper. Replace the spinal bone and fold the fillets and the two pieces of flanks over them. The roast will have a somewhat flat shape. Tie it in several places with white string.

Soften the vegetables in the oil or butter in a roasting pan over low heat. Place the roast on them and cook on the upper rack of a preheated 450° oven for 1 hour. Turn the roast over, baste it with the fat in the pan, and cook for another 20 minutes. Turn again and cook 10 minutes more. It should now be nice and pink.

Remove the meat from the pan, add the wine, and reduce. Add the stock and cook a little longer. If you are using vegetables, pass them through a food mill with the pan juices.

To carve the meat, pull the spinal bone out and cut straight across. The slices will look like two chops side by side, commonly known as an English chop.

SERVES 8

Chops Cut from the Loin

A loin chop is over 1 inch thick, cut from a vertical split loin or a saddle of lamb. An English chop is over an inch thick, cut completely across the large end of the loin so that there are two chops connected to each other. A noisette is a boneless loin chop that has a small piece of lamb kidney inserted in the center and is wrapped in a slice of bacon.

All the above chops are especially suited for broiling. You can simply season them with salt and pepper, or marinate them for at least an hour before cooking in garlic, parsley, thyme, lemon juice, salt, and pepper, as suggested for broiled rib chops (page 114). Or you can cook them with the herb and bread crumb seasoning suggested for rack of lamb (pages 111–112).

A medallion of lamb is a slice of the eye of the loin, boneless and defatted. It is a delicate cut of meat suitable for sautéeing.

The Leg

The second part of the hindsaddle, the leg, is probably the cut of lamb you know best. A whole leg is 6 to 11 pounds, depending on the age of the lamb. Legs from new lambs bought in May or June will be 6 to 7 pounds. You can buy half a leg, shank end or butt end. The shank end of a lamb leg is the better end (just the opposite of the pork leg) because the butt end has less meat, is a little fattier, and is very hard to carve. You can easily recognize the shank end because the leg bone protrudes from it; in some markets the leg is sold with the leg bone bent under the leg. If the bone has not been cracked in this manner, do it yourself or ask the butcher to do it for you.

TO FRENCH A LEG OF LAMB

Scrape the membrane on the front of the shank above the knuckle vigorously with the blade perpendicular to the bone. With the scraped side up and the knuckle about an inch off the table edge, snap the joint apart. This process, called frenching the leg, makes the leg shorter and easier to fit into a roasting pan. It also allows you to put a frilled cap over the knuckle to present the roasted leg.

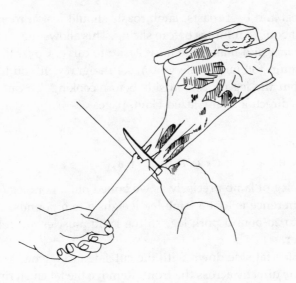

Roast Leg of Spring Lamb

1 leg of spring lamb, about 6 pounds
2 garlic cloves, peeled and cut into slivers
1 tablespoon rosemary
Salt, freshly ground pepper

2 tablespoons oil or butter
2 cups coarsely chopped onions, carrots, and celery for gravy, if desired (pages 26–27)
½ to 1 cup dry sherry or water

Remove the fell. (Some cooks like to leave it on to keep the juices securely inside; it is usually covered with grading ink, so I prefer to remove it.) Remove all the fat within the pelvic bone and whatever fat is on top of the round.

With a small knife make a few deep cuts near the bone, and in each cut place a sliver of garlic, some rosemary, salt, and pepper. Season the leg with salt and pepper and rub oil or butter on the surface of the leg.

Place the leg in a shallow roasting pan on a bed of chopped onions, carrots, and celery for gravy. Sprinkle with sherry or water. Cook in a preheated 350° oven 15 to 18 minutes per pound, basting several times with sherry or water. This is the right amount of time, a bit less than 2 hours' cooking, for delicate pink lamb. On an instant meat thermometer, 120° to 125° is rare, 130° to 135° medium. (If you are cooking half a leg, you will need to allow a few minutes more per pound.)

Like veal and beef roasts, lamb roasts should rest at room temperature for about 10 minutes before slicing. This allows the juice to come to the surface and makes the meat easier to carve. Cover the leg with an aluminum foil tent while you make the gravy. If you like a thick gravy, flour the leg on the outside before cooking. To carve a leg of lamb, see directions for Glazed Ham, pages 90–91.

SERVES 6 TO 8

TO BONE A LEG OF LAMB

You bone a leg of lamb precisely as we boned out a pork leg (pages 91–93). The difference is that a lamb leg weighs 7 to 9 pounds, contrasted with a 15- to 20-pound pork leg, so the lamb muscles are correspondingly smaller.

Place the leg fat side down with the cut side facing you. You will see the aitchbone directly across the front. Remove the fat clustering around the aitchbone. Very carefully separate the fillet from the hip end of the aitchbone where it is flat. If the tailbone is still attached at the hipbone, cut it off and remove it. With your boning knife, follow the aitchbone around to the ball and socket where the aitchbone meets the thighbone (femur), cutting and scraping the meat away from the aitchbone as close to the bone as possible as you go along. Cut the tendon and pull the bone away from the meat.

Starting from the ball and socket, cut the seam directly over the thighbone, cutting the meat just enough to follow the bone, until you come to the stifle joint, the knee part of the leg. Cut the meat away from the thighbone and remove it. There is meat only on one side of the shank bone, the only bone left. Cut away the meat and remove the shank bone.

Another method of boning out a lamb leg is called, appropriately enough, "tunneling" and is similar to boning out a chicken leg. Unlike the method above where the leg is completely open, by tunneling the leg, the major part of the leg will be intact, allowing you to stuff it and tie it into a roll for easy carving or to slice it into steaks.

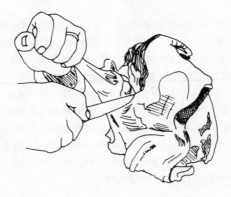

Follow the directions above for removing the aitchbone. Do not cut the seam above the thighbone. Instead, open up the seam on both sides of the shank bone and pull down the shank muscle. By pulling it down, you will reach the joint between the shank bone and the thighbone. The thighbone runs from the knee to the hip. Cut around the knee joint and scrape the meat away from the thighbone. When you have gone about 2 inches, stop and return to the ball that fits into the socket of the aitchbone. Scrape hard down the leg bone toward the center. Cut the tendon attached to the end of the bone. When you have almost reached the place where you had stopped working on the leg bone previously, twist the leg bone around a few times like turning a handle and it will come right out.

Once you have boned out the leg, you can roast it as a whole boneless roast of about 6 pounds (or less) or as small roasts like the 2-pound top round. Or you can butterfly it (lay it out flat) for barbecuing on the grill or for stuffing and roasting (see below).

Stuffed Boneless Leg

This is a very simple stuffing, more like a seasoning. For extra flavor, crack the bones taken from the leg and place them around the roast during cooking.

1 boneless leg of lamb, about 6
    pounds, the bones reserved and
    cracked
Salt, freshly ground pepper
1 onion, chopped fine
4 tablespoons butter
¼ teaspoon sage

2 tablespoons bread crumbs
1 tablespoon chopped parsley
Juice of half a lemon
2 cups coarsely chopped onions,
    carrots, and celery for gravy if
    desired (pages 26–27)
1 glass wine or water (optional)

Season the meat with salt and pepper. Cook the onion very briefly in 2 tablespoons of the butter on low heat, just to soften. Mix the onion with the sage, bread crumbs, parsley, salt, and pepper and place the stuffing mixture in the center of the cavity. Tuck in the small piece of shin meat and fold the rest of the lamb to form a nice roll. Tie it with white butcher twine; be careful not to tie it too tightly.

Rub the meat with the remaining butter, lemon juice, salt, and pepper. Place it in a lightly oiled roasting pan on a bed of chopped vegetables and sprinkle with wine or water. Cook 15 minutes per pound in a preheated 375° oven.

SERVES 10

Variation: Garlic and Pignoli Seasoning

2 garlic cloves, slivered
1 tablespoon pignoli nuts
12 juniper berries, crushed
½ teaspoon rosemary

¼ teaspoon sage
1 tablespoon chopped parsley
Salt, freshly ground pepper

This is a middle Eastern-style seasoning; mix all the ingredients together.

Variation: Sausage Stuffing

1 onion, chopped
½ pound Italian sausage meat
2 tablespoons butter
1 cup croutons, fried in oil

1 egg, lightly beaten
¼ teaspoon rosemary
Salt, freshly ground pepper

Soften the onion and sausage meat in butter over low heat. Mix with the other ingredients.

TO BUTTERFLY A LEG

In order to butterfly the leg, you need to separate the top round from the bottom round by cutting along the seam of membrane connecting these two pieces. (The top sirloin or sirloin tip is the other side of the meat from the round.) If the top sirloin is a bit thicker than the bottom, open that piece up, removing the little blob of fat in front where the fillet is. At the point where the bottom, top, and eye of the round come together, you will see a grayish gland the size of a quarter and about ¾ inch thick, encased in fat. Remove this gland as it can become bitter.

removing the gland

Butterflied Leg

When I make a butterflied leg for my classes, I usually serve Pasta Puttanesca (page 124) with it.

*1 boneless leg of lamb, 5 to 6
   pounds, butterflied*
2 teaspoons thyme
2 teaspoons rosemary
*2 garlic cloves, peeled and cut
   into slivers*

Juice of half a lemon
2 tablespoons olive oil
Salt, freshly ground pepper

At least 1 hour before cooking, season the leg with the thyme, rosemary, garlic, lemon juice, olive oil, salt, and pepper. Bake for 30 minutes in a preheated 375° oven, then finish under the broiler or on the grill for about 15 minutes, until it becomes crisp or until the inside temperature reaches 130° at the thickest part of the meat.

SERVES 10

Variation: Butterflied Leg with Cannes-Style Seasoning

Mix the ingredients for Cannes-Style Seasoning (pages 111–112) into a paste.

Brown the cut side of the leg first for about 15 minutes in a preheated broiler, then turn it over and brown the skin side.

Turn the meat so the cut side is again toward the heat and cover the top of the meat with the seasoning. Cook until done, about 15 minutes.

Pasta Puttanesca

I have wonderful memories of tasting Pasta Puttanesca for the first time on the island of Ischia during a trip to Italy in the 1960s. "Don" Ciacio, a fisherman and owner of a small restaurant on the water, insisted I try many of his specialties and was willing to share this recipe with me. You can usually find Gaeta or Calamata olives at a Greek delicatessen.

3 to 4 tablespoons olive oil
4 garlic cloves, peeled and
   chopped
1 onion, chopped fine
2 28-ounce cans peeled plum
   tomatoes with the juice
24 Gaeta or Calamata olives,
   pitted and chopped
2 tablespoons capers

6 anchovy fillets, chopped
1 teaspoon hot red pepper flakes
1 teaspoon oregano
2 tablespoons chopped parsley
2 pounds linguine or penne
Salt
½ cup grated pecorino romano
   cheese

In a large skillet heat enough oil to cover the bottom of the pan. Sauté the 4 garlic cloves and onion in the hot oil until the garlic just begins to brown. Add the canned tomatoes and their liquid. Crush the tomatoes with a fork. (Sometimes American canned tomatoes are hard; if so, put them through a food mill.)

Add the olives, capers, anchovies, red pepper flakes, oregano, and 1 tablespoon of the chopped parsley. Bring to a gentle boil, lower the heat, and simmer for about 30 to 40 minutes.

Cook the linguine or penne in a very large pot in boiling salted water until just al dente; drain and return to the pot.

Pour half the sauce onto the pasta and toss it with grated pecorino romano cheese and the remaining tablespoon of chopped parsley. Add more sauce to the pasta when serving.

It is wiser not to salt the sauce until you taste it at the end, because the anchovies and capers are already salty.

SERVES 8

Boned Leg of Lamb with Kidney Beans

This tasty dish is a variety of cassoulet; lamb and beans are flavored with salt pork and pork skins.

2 pounds white kidney beans,
    soaked in cold water overnight
1 pound fresh pork skins
1 boneless leg of spring lamb,
    about 6 pounds
2 garlic cloves
1 tablespoon rosemary, fresh if
    possible
Salt, freshly ground pepper
½ pound salt pork or pancetta or
    salted fatback, chopped into
    small cubes

2 tablespoons olive oil
2½ cups coarsely chopped
    onions, carrots, and celery
2 tablespoons tomato paste
1 cup dry red wine
1½ cups veal or beef stock
½ pound garlic sausages such as
    French saucisson, partly
    cooked and sliced
3 to 4 tablespoons bread crumbs

Drain the beans and place them in a saucepan with enough water to cover them by 2 inches; bring to a boil. Cook them on low heat while you prepare the other ingredients. Add more boiling water if necessary, but not too much; you don't want the beans too liquid.

Cover the pork skins with cold water in a saucepan and bring to a boil. Cook for 5 minutes; drain and shock under cold water. Let the skins rest in the water until 20 minutes before serving time; then cut them into 1- to 2-inch squares.

Season the lamb with 1 garlic clove cut into slivers, rosemary, salt, and pepper either by rubbing the seasonings over the surface or by inserting them into small cuts in the meat.

Heat the salt pork with 1 tablespoon of olive oil in a saucepan. Add the remaining garlic clove, peeled and chopped, and cook until the garlic just begins to color. Add 1 cup of the chopped onions, carrots, and celery, and cook until they are wilted. Add the tomato paste and simmer for about 5 minutes. Transfer the salt pork and vegetables to the bean pot and continue cooking the beans.

Heat the remaining tablespoon of olive oil in a roasting pan and cook the rest of the chopped onions, carrots, and celery for 3 or 4 minutes. Place the leg of lamb in the pan and brown it on all sides. Add the wine and reduce to one-third. Add stock, cover the pan, and cook in a preheated 350° oven for 2 hours. Add more stock if necessary.

Remove the lamb from the pan and cut it into slices. Put the vegetables and pan juices through a food mill. Discard the vegetables and remove as much fat as possible from the juices.

Line the bottom of the pan with the pork skins. Lay the sliced sausage on top of the skins, then add some of the beans, then some lamb slices. Repeat with beans and lamb, ending with a layer of beans.

Pour the pan juices over all and sprinkle with the bread crumbs. Finish in a 350° oven for about 10 minutes or until the bread crumbs have browned a bit.

SERVES 8 TO 10

Lamb Steaks

Lamb steaks should be cut ½ to 1 inch thick from the center of a tunneled leg. If you are cutting them yourself, chill the meat for about 20 minutes in the freezer before slicing. Marinate them as you would Butterflied Leg of Lamb (page 123) for an hour or two in thyme, chopped garlic, parsley, lemon juice, oil, salt and pepper. Cook under the broiler as you would a steak, until the meat is pink and rare.

You can also cut a boned leg into cubes for shish kebab, curry, or stews, but it is more economical to use the shoulder for stew meat.

Ground Lamb

Ground lamb from the shoulder combined with trimmings from other cuts can be made into lamb patties or into several succulent ethnic dishes.

Lamb patties, or lambburgers as they are sometimes called, are a good catchall for a number of parts of the lamb that cannot be used for broiling, roasting, or sautéing but, when trimmed of fat and membranes, are perfect for grinding. Season the meat after you grind it and shape it like a hamburger. You can wrap a slice of bacon around it if you wish, but it is not necessary. Oven-broiled or pan-broiled, these lamb patties are good and easily digested.

Stuffed Grape Leaves Anwar

I had an Egyptian customer who used to come into the store whenever he was home in New York from his business trips buying oil wells around the world. He told me he was a friend of Anwar Sadat's, and he always asked for ground lamb. So one day I got curious and asked him what he did with the lamb. He gave me this recipe. From then on, I always gave him an extra pound of lamb, and the next day his wife would bring a pan of stuffed grape leaves for me and my helpers.

As you can see, I have named this recipe for my customer's friend. You can prepare the grape leaves up to 24 hours ahead of time and reheat before serving, so they make a good party dish.

¼ cup Greek olive oil
2 garlic cloves, peeled and
   chopped fine
2 medium onions, chopped fine
1 28-ounce can imported peeled
   plum tomatoes, with the juice
A pinch of marjoram
A pinch of cumin
Salt, freshly ground pepper
4 tablespoons butter

1 cup raw rice
2 cups veal or chicken stock
3 pounds lamb, ground
2 tablespoons pignoli nuts
2 tablespoons raisins
1½ teaspoons crushed coriander
   seeds
2 tablespoons chopped parsley
1 jar of grape leaves

Heat the olive oil in a casserole and add the garlic. When the garlic begins to sizzle, remove it and add all but 2 tablespoons of the chopped onions. Sauté them for 5 minutes. Add the tomatoes and their juice, bring to a boil, lower the heat, and cook very slowly for 1 hour. Season with marjoram, cumin, salt, and pepper.

Sauté the remaining 2 tablespoons of chopped onions in a saucepan in 1 tablespoon of the butter. When the onion softens but before it browns, add the rice, and stir. Add the stock and cover the rice with a round of buttered waxed paper, cover the pot, and simmer on top of the stove or in a preheated 350° oven for about 18 minutes. Stir 2 to 3 tablespoons of butter into the hot rice and let the rice cool a bit.

Turn the rice into a large bowl; add the ground lamb, pignoli nuts, raisins, coriander, parsley, 1 teaspoon of pepper, and 1 tablespoon of salt. Mix well.

Wash the grape leaves under cold water and spread them on your work table. Place about 1 tablespoon of the meat mixture in the center of each leaf. Fold the leaves and pin them together with a toothpick.

In a deep baking pan place a layer of rolled grape leaves and cover them with sauce; add another layer and cover it. Continue until you have used them all.

Cover the pan with aluminum foil and cook for 1 hour and 30 minutes in a preheated 350° oven. If the sauce gets too dry, add water. Serve hot.

If you prefer to make this recipe in smaller quantities, unused grape leaves will keep in the refrigerator.

SERVES 18 TO 20 AS AN APPETIZER

Moussaka

This Greek dish is delicious when properly prepared. You will need a 9- by 13-inch baking pan 2 inches deep; the eggplant must be salted and refrigerated overnight. All but the last step can be prepared ahead of time.

2 medium eggplants, sliced
Salt
1 large onion, chopped
4 tablespoons oil
2½ pounds lamb, ground
½ pound pork, ground
1 35-ounce can peeled plum
    tomatoes, with the juice
Freshly ground pepper
Flour
Oil for deep-frying

1 quart milk
4 tablespoons butter
2 tablespoons flour
2 egg yolks
4 raw medium potatoes, sliced
    thin, to cover the bottom of the
    pan
4 medium zucchini, sliced thin,
    to cover two layers of the pan
2 tablespoons farina

Wash the eggplants and cut into ¼-inch slices. Place the slices in a colander and sprinkle with salt. Weight them with a dish and refrigerate overnight.

The next day sauté the onion in the 4 tablespoons of oil until it is translucent. Add the lamb and pork and cook for 5 minutes. Add the tomatoes and their juice, lower the heat to simmer, and cook slowly for about 1 hour. Season with salt and pepper if desired.

Rinse the eggplant slices under cold water and dry with paper towels. Lightly dip them in flour and deep-fry in hot oil until they turn brown. Drain on paper towels to remove any excess fat.

Prepare a béchamel sauce: Heat the milk in a saucepan almost to boiling. At the same time, in a separate pan, heat the butter and stir in the flour; do not let it brown. Ladle a little milk into the butter/flour mixture and stir; continue to add the milk, stirring vigorously on low heat until the sauce thickens. Remove it from the heat and let it cool a bit. Beat in the egg yolks, one at a time.

Butter the baking pan and layer potato slices on the bottom. Add a layer of eggplant, then zucchini, then the lamb mixture. Repeat with another layer each of eggplant, zucchini, and lamb. (If you wish, you can cover the pan and refrigerate it at this point until you are ready to cook the moussaka.)

Cover the top with béchamel sauce and sprinkle farina over all. Bake for 20 minutes in a 350° oven.

SERVES 8 TO 10

VEAL

W ITH VEAL WE MOVE to the larger animals. Every cut of veal (and even more so of beef) is bigger and has a lot more meat than do smaller cuts of pork and lamb. For example, on a breast of lamb the meat just covers the bones; on a breast of veal it is about an inch thick.

Types of Veal

Veal is a young calf from 1 to 26 weeks old. The smallest (and youngest) are bob calves, which may be only 1 week old and weigh about 50 pounds. Their meat is grayish white and lacks flavor.

On the other end of the scale is conventional veal, older calves up to 26 weeks, weighing close to 400 pounds. These calves drink mother's milk at birth but are weaned after twenty-four hours. They are then fed grass, hay, or other types of feed. Once the calves start eating solid food, they develop three stomachs like all ruminating animals and their meat darkens to a dark rose color and becomes less delicate. It can be very flavorful, although a bit chewy. Most of the veal sold in supermarkets is conventional veal.

The best-quality veal is "nature veal," that is, veal from calves born from Holstein-Fresian cows that drink only milk or milk replacements before they come to market at 16 or 17 weeks old. Only male calves, bulls, are raised for nature veal; female calves, heifers, are kept to replenish the herds.

The first week, nature calves drink their mothers' milk. Then they are weaned to a primary formula of milk replacers for eight weeks, then to a finishing formula for another eight or nine weeks, when they come to market at a live weight of 350 pounds. These milk replacer formulas are a Dutch invention first imported here in 1946. The meat of nature veal is a beautiful light pink color, the fat snow white. The flavor and texture are very delicate, and the meat is beautifully enhanced by sauces.

All European veal is nature veal (Europeans often enrich the Dutch formula with eggs), which is why so many travelers come back from Italy and France enchanted with the delicious veal dishes they have eaten. But all veal in this country is not nature veal, and you should be wary of veal that is advertised as coming from "naturally grown calves." These are not true vealers raised only on milk; their meat tastes like weak beef and is not delicate.

You will have to go to the best butcher shops or specialty supermarkets to find nature veal, and you will not be surprised to hear that nature veal is the most expensive type of veal. Plume de Veau is one trade name for nature veal; Provimi veal from Wisconsin is another.

Of course, even among these carefully raised animals some calves are better than others. In order to get the best veal for my customers, I used to play a little game with Mr. Berliner of Berliner & Marx, for many years the largest and best wholesale veal house in New York City. My store was very small, but it was known as one of the best in the city. The walk-in refrigerator at Berliner & Marx was large enough to hold about 2,500 calves. Every Friday I would come to buy one calf. I was probably Mr. Berliner's smallest customer, but he knew I wanted the best, so we had a wager. We would walk through the refrigerator with his top salesman and I would try to choose the best calf; if I lost, I would pay for breakfast. Needless to say, I lost more times than I won. Mr. Berliner, however, would wink at me and tell me I might have paid for breakfast, but I always walked out with the best calf in the house.

Different Styles of Cutting Meat: American vs. European

This is a good time to discuss the difference between American and European styles of cutting meat. European butchers separate each muscle at its seam into small roasts or slices for cutlets, etc. This type of butchering favors the customer who receives pieces or slices of solid meat without any connecting membranes. Most veal in good butcher shops is cut European style. The initial cost may seem high to you, but you are buying pure meat with no waste.

American-style cutting, on the other hand, is not so precise and cuts across whole muscles. In many supermarkets veal steaks are made by cutting whole slices from the leg with the band saw, so that in one slice you will have portions of the sirloin tip, the top round, the bottom round, and the eye of the round—all the muscles that make up the leg. To make this method of cutting possible, the meat is chilled. When you buy it, the slice may look like a solid piece of meat, but when it begins to soften, the muscles start separating.

Tips on Buying, Storing, and Freezing Veal

Nature veal is light pink, while conventional veal is reddish and bob veal grayish white. Veal is a moist meat and does not keep well. It will become slimy after two days in the refrigerator.

Veal can be frozen in the same manner as pork (pages 65–66). If veal cutlets, scaloppine, chops, and roasts are prepared ahead of time, they should be kept in the refrigerator, covered with a towel that has been soaked in ice water and wrung out.

Structure of Veal

Veal is divided into the foresaddle and the hindsaddle. The foresaddle has two shoulders, the neck with three ribs, the rack with eight ribs, and two breast pieces. The hindsaddle consists of the loin, including the last two ribs, and the two legs. As in lamb, the membranes separating the muscles are clear and easy to distinguish.

The cost of veal varies greatly, depending on the cut. The breast is the least expensive; next are the neck and shoulders from the chuck; then the rack and the leg; then the loin. A boned-out loin of veal is very pricey. In some of the following recipes I will show you how to treat the less costly cuts of veal.

Veal bones are excellent for stock because they are so gelatinous. If you use veal bones for aspic, you will never need gelatin. So if you bone out meat yourself, don't worry if you leave a little on the bone; it will add to the stock. If you ask the butcher to bone a piece of veal for you, be sure to ask him for the bones to put in your freezer until you are ready to make stock.

White Veal Stock

This recipe is for a white veal stock—that is, the bones have not been browned in the oven before boiling. For a brown veal stock, follow directions for Beef Stock (page 173).

2 *veal bones, cracked*	2 *carrots*
1 *veal shank, cut in two*	2 *celery stalks, with leaves*
(optional, but wonderful if you	1 *onion, split in half, with 3*
can get it)	*cloves inserted*
1 *calf's foot, scalded (also*	*A few peppercorns*
optional; superb for gelatin)	

Wash the bones and meat and place them in a stockpot or any tall pot. Cover with cold water 2 to 3 inches above the meat (about 8 quarts) and bring to a boil. Lower the heat and skim the froth off the top. Add the vegetables and peppercorns.

Cook gently for 3 hours. *Be very careful not to let the stock boil hard, because that will make it a milky white color and you will not achieve a clear stock.*

Strain the stock and cool it. Place it in the refrigerator overnight. Scrape off the fat that covers the top of the gelled stock. Stock will keep for 4 days in the refrigerator, or indefinitely in the freezer.

YIELD: ABOUT 4 QUARTS

The Shoulder and Neck

A shoulder of a nature veal weighs about 20 pounds. It has three bones (blade, arm, and shank), many small, narrow muscles, and a solid center muscle, called a shoulder clod. When the clod is boned out, it weighs anywhere from 4 to 9 pounds, depending on the size of the calf, and looks like the map of South America. It is a lovely piece of meat that can be stuffed and roasted. You can buy a clod or half a clod from a prime butcher, or buy a whole shoulder and bone it out yourself.

TO BONE OUT A VEAL SHOULDER

Place it on your workspace with the smooth side down; the shank bone should face away from you, the blade bone toward you. The blade bone is a flat bone that runs 6 to 7 inches to the center of the meat in the shape of an inverted V. Make an incision running along the top of the

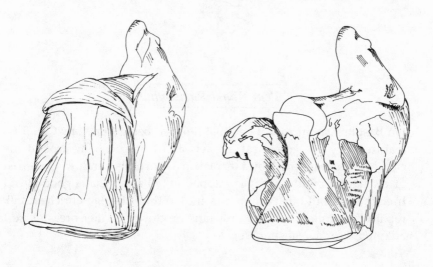

blade bone. You should be able to feel the blade bone with your fingers. Cut until you come to the joint of the shoulder blade and the arm. Cut around the joint so that you separate the blade bone from the joint; cut underneath and down the sides of the blade bone until you have separated most of the meat and membrane from the blade bone. Remove it.

Make an incision over the joint of the arm bone and follow the arm bone until you meet the joint of the arm and the elbow. Cut and scrape the meat away from the arm bone and remove the bone.

You now have two choices. If you have a saw, you can cut off the shank and cut it into three sections for Osso Buco (pages 161–162). Or you can continue cutting at the seam to separate the meat from the shank bone; shank meat is good for stew. In either case, once the shank meat is removed, you will have a whole shoulder clod, to be used as a roast or for cutlets, and a number of smaller muscles that can be separated and sliced, cubed, or ground.

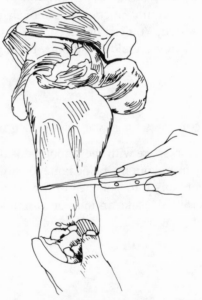

Veal Roast Parisienne

On Bastille Day in 1971, I had just finished being filmed by CBS for a feature story on Paris meat markets and I was walking around the city. My eye was struck by a display in a butcher's window of a breast of veal stuffed with sausage wrapped in fatback. What a good idea! I tried it here, but our veal breasts are too thin (the egg-enriched milk replacer formula used by Europeans produces meatier breasts), so I adapted it for a veal shoulder clod.

1 boneless veal shoulder clod,
   about 4 pounds
½ teaspoon rosemary
1 2-inch slice of lemon zest, cut
   into slivers
Salt, freshly ground pepper
¾ pound veal, ground
¾ pound pork, ground
1 egg
¼ teaspoon nutmeg

¼ teaspoon cinnamon
½ cup stale bread soaked in milk
   and squeezed
8 thin slices of fatback or
   unsalted bacon
2 cups coarsely chopped onions,
   carrots, and celery for gravy, if
   desired (pages 26–27)
Butter or oil
White wine

Butterfly the boned clod so that it is like an open book; use a pounder to spread it out as much as possible. Season it with the rosemary, lemon zest, salt, and pepper and set aside.

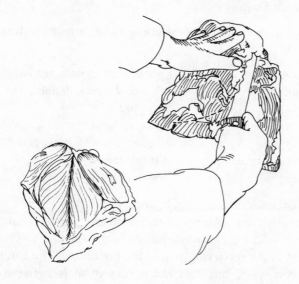

Mix the ground veal and pork, egg, nutmeg, cinnamon, and bread; add salt and pepper and mix well. Roll this mixture so that it is in the shape of a fat sausage.

Place 4 slices of fatback around the rolled mixture and put it in the center of the veal. Roll the veal so the stuffing is inside and place the other 4 slices of fatback along the outside of the roast. Tie it securely in several places.

Place in an open roasting pan on a rack or on a bed of chopped vegetables. Dot the top with butter or rub with oil. Cook for 2 hours to 2 hours and 30 minutes in a preheated 350° oven; baste with white wine every half hour. (If you are making an 8- to 9-pound roast, you will need nearly a bottle of wine.) For a small roast you should allow 20 to 25 minutes per pound, or until the internal temperature comes to 150° to 160° and, when pierced with a fork, the juices run white, not pink. Unlike veal chops, which are delicious a little rare, roast veal should be well cooked, especially if you are using a stuffing with raw pork. It seems strange, but the time for cooking increases as the roast gets smaller; an 8-pound roast should cook about 18 minutes a pound.

Keep the veal warm while you make gravy from the vegetables and pan juices. (Like lamb and beef, veal roasts should rest at room temperature for about 10 minutes before serving.)

SERVES 8 TO 10

Variation: Frittata Stuffing

A frittata—a thick, open Italian omelette—makes a nice stuffing for veal.

½ teaspoon dried rosemary leaves
Salt, freshly ground pepper
6 eggs
3 tablespoons grated pecorino
    romano cheese
1 tablespoon chopped parsley
¼ teaspoon nutmeg

1 pound fresh spinach, washed,
    blanched briefly, drained, and
    chopped
4 tablespoons butter
½ pound Gruyère cheese, sliced
½ pound mortadella or cooked
    ham, sliced (optional)

Season the veal with rosemary, salt, and pepper.

Beat the eggs with the pecorino romano cheese, parsley, nutmeg, salt, and pepper. Add the chopped spinach to the eggs.

Cook the eggs in a large frying pan in the hot butter. You can turn the frittata if you wish, but it is not necessary; it is better if the omelette is not overcooked.

Place half of the Gruyère (and mortadella) slices along the inside of the meat and place the frittata on them. Top with the remaining cheese (and mortadella) slices. Tie the roast and cook as above.

Slices, Cubes, and Ground Meat from Shoulder and Neck

After the clod has been removed from the boned-out shoulder, you can get nice slices from the other small muscles to use for veal rolls. The shoulder meat can also be cut into cubes for Veal Marengo à la Ubaldi (pages 139–140) or any other stew-type dish, or it can be ground for dishes like Crepes Fiorentina (pages 141–142).

The neck is an inexpensive cut of veal that can be cut into cubes for any kind of veal stew, or ground for ground-meat dishes. If you have good-quality nature veal, the neck can be boned out, butterflied, stuffed, and roasted. Remove the neck bone (it will come out in one piece) and the large tendon (backstrap); cook about 25 minutes per pound.

Veal Rolls à la Lombardy

Although you need good-quality veal for this recipe, there is no reason the slices must come from the leg; shoulder slices are fine (see pages 11–12 to slice). Serve with potato puree and buttered spinach.

6 thin slices of veal, about 3 by 5
   inches, about 2 pounds
2 slices of prosciutto, about ⅛
   inch thick, cut into thin strips
   of about ¼ inch
3 eggs
1 tablespoon chopped parsley
1 garlic clove, chopped fine
2 tablespoons grated Parmesan
   cheese
7 ounces heavy cream

½ teaspoon dried rosemary
A few sage leaves
Salt, freshly ground pepper
6 ounces sliced fontina cheese,
   cut into thin strips
6 tablespoons butter
1 onion, sliced thin
½ cup dry white wine
1 16-ounce can peeled plum
   tomatoes, drained

Flatten the veal with a pounder and cut off any uneven pieces. If you have a sufficient amount of trimmings to make ½ pound (or some tucked away in the freezer), grind the meat in a meat grinder together with any trimmings left after slicing the prosciutto into strips.

Hard-boil 2 of the eggs and cool them in cold water. Shell them and cut them into wedges.

Mix the ground veal with the remaining egg, parsley, garlic, grated cheese, and 3 tablespoons of the cream. Season with rosemary, sage, salt, and pepper.

Spread the veal slices on your work table and sprinkle with a bit of salt and pepper. Place 2 strips each of prosciutto and fontina, 1 tablespoon of the stuffing, and a wedge of hard-boiled egg on each slice of meat. Roll them up and tie them (page 16).

Heat the butter in a heavy skillet and cook the onion slices in the hot butter until soft. Add the veal rolls and brown them on all sides. Add the wine and let it reduce, then add the tomatoes. Season lightly with salt and pepper, partially cover the pan, and simmer for 1 hour.

Toward the end of the cooking time, add the remaining cream.

SERVES 6

Veal Catalane Sauté

I first tasted this dish at a restaurant in Cannes. The chef shared some of his recipes with me; in exchange, I shared my bottle of Scotch with him.

2 pounds veal shoulder, cut into 2-inch cubes	2 carrots, chopped coarse
½ pound thin pork sausages, cut into 2-inch pieces (luganica sausages are good, or any small breakfast sausage)	1 cup dry white wine or ½ cup wine, ½ cup stock
	2 fresh ripe tomatoes, peeled, seeded, and chopped
Flour	¾ cup veal stock or water
4 tablespoons oil	3½ ounces pitted green olives
6 tablespoons butter	20 small white onions
Salt, freshly ground pepper	2 tablespoons sugar
1 garlic clove, crushed	20 chestnuts, peeled

Dredge the veal cubes and sausage pieces in flour. Brown in 2 tablespoons of the oil and 2 tablespoons of the butter in a heavy pan. Remove the meat and set aside; discard the fat in the pan. Season the cubes lightly with salt and pepper as they cook if you wish, but remember olives are salty; it is safer to adjust the seasoning at the end.

Add 2 more tablespoons of butter to the pan and cook the garlic clove in the hot butter for a few minutes. Add the carrots and cook for another 5 minutes. Return the meat to the pan, cook the meat and carrots together for a few minutes, then add ½ cup of the white wine and let it reduce by half.

Add 1 tablespoon of flour, if desired, for a thick gravy; the tomatoes, and the stock. Turn the heat down to low, cover the pan, and simmer partially covered for about 1 hour and 30 minutes.

Blanch the olives in boiling water for 3 minutes. Drain them and add them to the meat.

Peel the white onions and brown them in 2 tablespoons of butter and 2 tablespoons of oil for 10 minutes, stirring continuously. Add 1 tablespoon of the sugar and the remaining ½ cup of wine, cover the pan, and cook on low heat until tender.

Cook the chestnuts in 1 tablespoon of sugar and wine or stock as you do the onions until they are tender and slightly glazed.

Add the onions and the chestnuts to the pan 5 minutes before serving the veal. Adjust the seasonings before serving.

Note: Peeling chestnuts is not difficult. When fresh chestnuts are available in the fall, slash them with a knife and either roast them lightly for 10 to 15 minutes or boil them for 5 to 10 minutes until you can remove the skins easily. Once peeled, they can be frozen until needed. Unsweetened, peeled chestnuts are available from France in jars.

SERVES 4 TO 5

Veal Marengo à la Ubaldi

When Napoleon's chef hastily improvised a chicken, crayfish, and egg dish for his hungry master after his victory at Marengo, June 14, 1800, he created the recipe that has come to be known as Chicken Marengo. As we cook Veal Marengo today, the meat is browned in oil and cooked slowly with tomatoes, garlic, parsley, white wine, and cognac. Evidently there was a General Ubaldi serving in the Napoleonic Wars, so in his honor, here is my version of the recipe in a quantity to serve a very small army. Serve over a bed of green noodles or on toasted slices of garlic bread.

6 pounds veal shoulder, cut into
   2-inch cubes
1 cup olive oil
10 ounces (2½ sticks) butter
3 tablespoons flour
Salt, freshly ground pepper
3 medium or large onions,
   chopped
½ cup chopped parsley
2 cups dry white wine

3 cups veal or chicken stock
1 6-pound, 9-ounce can peeled
   tomatoes, drained
6 garlic cloves, crushed
3 bay leaves
36 small white onions
2 cups pitted green olives
2 pounds button mushrooms,
   cleaned in acidulated water,
   (page 8)

Cut the meat into fairly large pieces to allow for shrinkage during cooking.

Heat ½ cup of the olive oil and 4 tablespoons of the butter in a large, heavy casserole. Brown the veal cubes in the hot oil in small batches so that not too many cook together. Sprinkle the flour on the veal while it is browning. You want the veal to brown, not steam and ooze water. Remove the meat from the pan. Season lightly with salt and pepper if desired, but as the olives are salty, it is better to adjust the seasoning at the end.

Pour out all the fat and add the remaining ½ cup of oil, plus ¼ pound of butter. Heat the oil and butter and cook the chopped onions in it for 5 minutes. Add the meat and half of the chopped parsley and cook another 3 or 4 minutes.

Add the wine to the casserole and let it reduce on high heat until it evaporates. Add the stock, tomatoes, garlic, and bay leaves and bring to a light boil. Lower the heat, partially cover the pan, and cook the stew slowly.

Meanwhile, peel the white onions and brown them in 4 tablespoons of butter; add them to the veal.

Blanch the olives briefly in boiling water, drain, and add to the veal.

Quickly brown the cleaned mushrooms in the remaining 4 tablespoons of butter for about 4 to 5 minutes. Add them to the veal.

Continue to simmer the stew until the veal is tender, about 2 hours to 2 hours and 30 minutes. Adjust for seasonings and sprinkle the remaining chopped parsley over the stew.

SERVES 18

City Chicken

A young fellow used to come into my store and ask for two pounds of "city chicken." What he wanted was cubed veal and pork. When I had a little extra time to talk to him one day, I found out what he did with it. So here is City Chicken, kebabs of veal and pork marinated and grilled with pieces of bread and bacon.

1 pound veal shoulder, cut into
   1-inch cubes
1 pound pork butt, cut into
   1-inch cubes
Juice of half a lemon
2 tablespoons olive oil
1 garlic clove, chopped very small
A pinch of thyme

A pinch of sage
Salt, freshly ground pepper
6 thick slices of dense bread, cut
   into cubes
4 thick slices country bacon, cut
   into small pieces
A dash of wine (optional)
Fresh sage leaves (optional)

Marinate the veal and pork cubes in the lemon juice, olive oil, garlic, thyme, sage, salt, and pepper for at least 1 hour.

Thread the meat onto skewers with the bread and bacon pieces, alternating the different pieces.

Put the skewers on a cookie sheet and brush with some of the marinade. Sprinkle with wine if desired. Fresh sage leaves interspersed between the meat would enhance the flavor.

Cook under the broiler for 30 minutes, turning once.

This recipe can be partially prepared ahead of time by marinating the meat in the morning of the day you are planning to serve it.

SERVES 4

Crepes Fiorentina

This recipe comes from the Ristorante degli Antellesi on the Piazza Santa Croce in Florence. Cook the veal, pork, and beef as whole pieces (not cut into cubes), then grind them together for the crepes stuffing.

¾ ounce dried porcini mushrooms	½ cup stock or bouillon
1 tablespoon butter	4 tablespoons grated Parmesan cheese
1 tablespoon oil	½ pound spinach, washed, blanched, drained, and chopped fine
1 garlic clove, chopped	
1 onion, chopped	
½ pound veal shoulder	1 egg
½ pound pork butt	A pinch of nutmeg
½ pound beef, top round	Salt, freshly ground pepper
½ cup dry red wine	8 large crepes, 8 to 9 inches
1 tablespoon tomato paste	1 cup heavy cream

Soak the mushrooms in warm water for at least 20 minutes.

Heat the butter and oil in a saucepan. Cook the garlic until it just begins to color; add the onion and cook for another 2 or 3 minutes.

Add the three pieces of meat and brown them on all sides. Add the wine and reduce by half.

Drain the mushrooms and squeeze them dry. Chop them coarse and add them to the meat with the tomato paste and stock. Lower the heat, cover the pot, and simmer until the meat is well done, about 30 minutes. Add more liquid if necessary to keep it moist. This part of the recipe can be done ahead of time.

Lift the meat pieces out of the sauce with a slotted spoon and grind in a meat grinder or a food processor.

Mix the ground meat with 2 tablespoons of the Parmesan cheese, the spinach, egg, nutmeg, salt, and pepper.

Spread the crepes on the table and place some stuffing on each one. Roll up the crepes and put them in a shallow baking dish.

Reheat the rest of the sauce from the meat pan and add the cream. When it just comes to a simmer, add 1 tablespoon of the Parmesan.

Spoon some of the sauce over the crepes to cover them and cook them in a preheated 350° oven for 5 minutes. Top with the rest of the sauce and the remaining tablespoon of Parmesan and run under the broiler to finish.

YIELD: 8 CREPES

The Breast

A whole breast of nature veal will weigh about 9 to 10 pounds with the bone in. Boned and stuffed, it will serve 12 to 14, but you can ask the butcher for half or a smaller part of a breast.

To stuff a breast of veal, you either make a pocket between the meat and the ribs or remove all the bones and butterfly the breast. It depends on how you like to carve it.

TO MAKE A POCKET IN THE BREAST OR BUTTERFLY FOR STUFFING

Remove the sternum bone by cutting across where the cartilage separates the breastbone and the ribs. With the point of a boning knife, make a slit right on the center of the membrane on the bone side of each rib, so that you barely cut the membrane. As the breast cooks, the skin will pull away from the bones. Just before serving, the ribs will come right out if you give each one a little twist.

If you would rather butterfly the breast and roll it up, remove the rib bones as well as the sternum bone. Slice it open from the side so the brisket can be spread out like the leaves of a book, in order to double the width of the breast. After you place the stuffing in the center, roll it lengthwise into a thin long roast, not a thick short one. Use no more than an inch of stuffing.

Or you can cut a breast into 13 individual riblets that can be broiled like rib lamb chops (page 114). A boned breast can also be poached like Chicken Gallantina (pages 61–62).

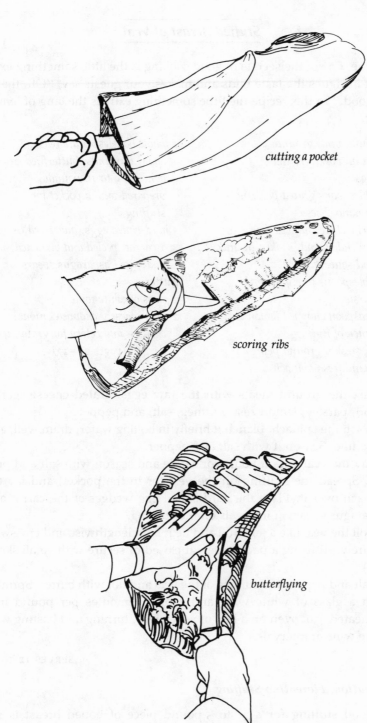

cutting a pocket

scoring ribs

butterflying

Stuffed Breast of Veal

To me, one of the secrets of good cooking is the little something extra that intrigues the taste buds and makes your guests say, "Oh, that is *so* good." In this recipe the little something extra is the tang of lemon zest.

1 pound veal, ground
1 pound pork, ground
2 eggs
3 tablespoons grated pecorino romano cheese
1 garlic clove, minced fine
1 cup stale bread, soaked in milk and squeezed
2 tablespoons finely chopped parsley
½ teaspoon chopped lemon zest
A pinch of nutmeg
Salt, freshly ground pepper
1 pound fresh spinach

1 whole boneless veal breast, about 6 pounds, butterflied or bone in, 9 to 10 pounds, prepared with a pocket for stuffing
3 hard-boiled eggs, quartered or 1 carrot, peeled and blanched, and 3 to 4 asparagus spears
Butter
1 glass of white wine
2 cups coarsely chopped onions, carrots, and celery for gravy, if desired (pages 26–27)

Mix the ground meats with the raw eggs, grated cheese, garlic, bread, parsley, lemon zest, nutmeg, salt, and pepper.

Wash the spinach, blanch it briefly in boiling water, drain well, and chop fine. Season it with salt and pepper.

Lay the veal out on your workspace and season with salt and pepper. Spread the stuffing on the veal (or in the pocket) and lay the spinach over it. Place the hard-boiled egg wedges *or* the carrot and asparagus spears at intervals on the stuffing.

Roll the veal like a jelly roll and tie it both lengthwise and crosswise securely. (If using a pocket, sew it closed or secure with small skewers.)

Salt and pepper the surface of the veal and dot with butter. Sprinkle with a glass of white wine and cook 18 minutes per pound in a preheated 350° oven on a bed of vegetables, turning and basting with more wine at intervals.

SERVES 12 TO 14

Variation: Fiorentino Stuffing

A good stuffing for a 4- to 5-pound piece of boned breast is 1½ pounds of spinach, prepared as above, 6 ounces of fresh ricotta cheese, 2 ounces of finely chopped prosciutto, 2 ounces of pignoli nuts, 4 tablespoons of grated Parmesan cheese, 2 lightly beaten eggs, 1 tablespoon of finely chopped parsley, a few gratings of fresh nutmeg, salt, and pepper.

Variation: Frittata Stuffing

The frittata stuffing on page 136 also works well with a 4- to 5-pound piece of boned veal breast.

Breast of Veal with Beer

Here is a good, homey recipe that would be nice served on a bed of polenta garnished with strips of steamed green cabbage.

4 pounds breast of veal, cut into 2-inch cubes, or 3 pounds boned breast	1 garlic clove, chopped
	2 tablespoons butter
	1 beef bouillon cube
Flour	½ teaspoon fennel seeds
6 tablespoons olive oil	1 bay leaf
1 large onion, chopped coarse	½ teaspoon honey
1 large carrot, peeled and cut into large pieces	1 12-ounce bottle of beer
	Salt, freshly ground pepper
2 celery stalks, cut into large pieces	

Lightly dust the veal cubes with flour.

In a large skillet heat 4 tablespoons of the olive oil. Cook the onion, carrot, celery, and garlic in the hot oil on moderate heat.

At the same time in another pan, heat the remaining 2 tablespoons of olive oil and the butter. Brown the veal cubes; as they become thoroughly browned, add them to the pan with the vegetables.

When all the meat has been added, stir the vegetables and meat together and cook another 5 minutes.

Crumble the bouillon cube over the skillet and add the fennel, bay leaf, and honey. Cook another 5 minutes.

Pour in half of the beer, cover the pan, reduce the heat, and simmer for about 2 hours, adding the rest of the beer a little at a time throughout the cooking.

Season with salt and pepper to taste.

SERVES 6

Rack of Veal

There are eight rib chops on a rack of veal, four of them well formed, the other four somewhat truncated where the shoulder has been cut away; these four look like neck chops. You can season and roast a whole rack or cut it into chops.

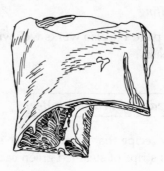

Loin

The loin, the front part of the hindsaddle, is a fancy piece of meat. Half a loin (that is, one side of the animal) will provide eight loin chops or a saddle roast, a roast valued for fine flavor and texture. When the queen of England visited the White House some years ago, I noticed that a saddle roast of veal was on the menu for the state dinner. When you want to serve something very elegant, try my recipe for saddle roast.

A note about seasoning: Although I season roasts and large pieces of meat in the beginning of the cooking, when I cook chops I prefer to taste for salt and pepper at the end. The trend now is to season cautiously, but I like a positive approach to seasoning; a bland style doesn't suit me.

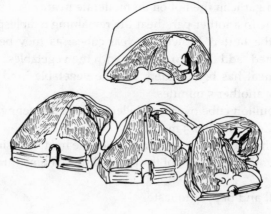

Saddle Roast of Veal

You need veal stock for this recipe, so if the butcher is boning the roast for you, ask him for the bones from the roast and a few extra. You can, of course, substitute another stuffing if you wish.

Half a veal loin, about 7 pounds
* untrimmed, 5 pounds boned*
¼ teaspoon grated lemon zest
A few leaves of fresh rosemary or
* ¼ teaspoon dried rosemary*
Salt, freshly ground pepper
½ pound veal, ground
½ pound pork, ground
1 egg, lightly beaten

½ cup stale bread, soaked in milk
* and squeezed*
1 garlic clove, chopped fine
A pinch of marjoram
A few gratings of fresh nutmeg
Olive oil
1 cup dry white wine
1 cup veal stock

Trim and bone the loin, but leave about 2 inches of the flank attached.

Lay the veal on your workspace and season it with lemon zest, some of the rosemary, salt, and pepper. Set aside.

Combine the ground veal and pork with the beaten egg, bread, garlic, marjoram, and nutmeg. When all is well mixed, spread the stuffing on the cut side of the veal and fold in the flank. Tie lightly with white twine.

Season the surface of the meat with a few more rosemary leaves, salt, and pepper and rub it with olive oil.

Cook the roast in a pan that is just a little larger than the meat in a preheated 350° oven for 2 hours, basting often with wine and stock.

SERVES 8

Veal Chops

Veal chops cook very quickly (about 10 to 15 minutes) and, unlike a roast, are good slightly rare. They adapt very nicely to sauces, as you will see in the following recipes. You can use rib chops or shoulder chops instead of loin chops, but remember that shoulder chops, the least expensive, do not make as attractive a presentation as loin chops.

Veal Chops in Marinara Sauce

A marinara sauce is a quick, tasty tomato sauce for meat, pasta, or fish. It will keep a week in the refrigerator or can be frozen. This is an easy, family-style recipe.

4 tablespoons olive oil
4 loin or rib chops, ½ inch thick
2 garlic cloves, peeled and
  crushed
1 35-ounce can peeled plum
  tomatoes, with juice

½ teaspoon oregano
A few hot red pepper flakes
  (optional)
2 tablespoons chopped flat-leaf
  parsley
Salt, freshly ground pepper

Heat 2 tablespoons of the oil in a large, heavy skillet and brown the chops on both sides. Remove the chops and throw out the fat in the pan.

Add the remaining 2 tablespoons of oil and lightly brown the garlic. Add the tomatoes and cook for a few minutes. Squash the tomatoes with a fork and add the oregano, red pepper flakes, parsley, salt, and pepper. Return the chops to the pan and simmer them slowly in the sauce for about 30 minutes.

SERVES 4

Veal Chops Parco dei Principi

When I stayed at the Parco dei Principi Hotel in Sorrento in 1985, my room had a balcony overlooking the beautiful bay. I had time to talk with the chef during our visit and came away with this recipe.

2 tablespoons olive oil
4 loin or rib chops, ½ inch thick
3 tablespoons butter
8 asparagus spears, blanched
4 tablespoons baby peas, blanched
4 large mushroom caps, cleaned
  in acidulated water (page 8)
  and sautéed

½ cup cognac or brandy,
  warmed
½ cup veal or chicken stock
½ teaspoon cornstarch (if needed)
Salt, freshly ground pepper

Heat the oil in a skillet large enough to hold the veal chops without overlapping. Brown both sides of the chops quickly in the hot oil on fairly high heat; lower the heat and cook for 10 minutes.

Remove the chops and pour out the oil; add 2 tablespoons of the butter and return the chops to the pan. Place 2 asparagus spears, 1 tablespoon of peas, and a sautéed mushroom cap on each chop.

Raise the heat, add the cognac, and flame carefully. Add the stock and simmer for 5 minutes.

Gently remove the chops and their vegetables to a warmed platter. Add the remaining tablespoon of butter to the pan and stir it with the pan juices. If the pan juices have dried out, stir in a little more stock. Or, if the sauce is too liquid, dissolve the cornstarch in a little water and add it to the pan. Add salt and pepper to taste and pour the sauce over the chops.

SERVES 4

Veal Chops Savoyard

Leo's Santa Croce is a friendly little restaurant in the Piazza Santa Croce in Florence. I found Leo's place when I was visiting Italy in 1984, and I went back again and again. Olive oil from his own farm near Perugia is stored in fifty-gallon stone jars, and all the prosciutti, cold cuts, and wine served in the restaurant also comes from his land. Leo is small in stature with a full head of white hair, but he is a man large in heart; he was kind enough to share a number of his recipes with me.

4 loin or rib chops, ½ inch thick	8 to 12 thin slices of black or
2 tablespoons olive oil	white truffles
4 tablespoons butter	4 tablespoons grated Parmesan
1 ounce cognac, warmed	cheese
12 asparagus tips, blanched	2 tablespoons tomato sauce
8 mushrooms, sliced and lightly	¼ cup light cream
sautéed	Salt, freshly ground pepper

Pound the chops lightly with a pounder or rolling pin. Sauté them on high heat in the hot oil and 2 tablespoons of the butter in a skillet large enough to accommodate them without any overlapping. When they are brown on both sides, lower the heat and cook for 10 minutes.

Pour off the fat and add the remaining 2 tablespoons of butter. Add the cognac to the pan and flame it. On each chop place 3 asparagus tips, 2 mushroom slices, and 2 to 3 truffle slices. Cook on low heat for 3 or 4 minutes.

Put a spoonful of grated cheese and a few dots of tomato sauce on each chop and pour the cream into the pan. Season to taste with salt and pepper.

Finish the chops in a very hot oven or under the broiler for just 3 minutes.

SERVES 4

Loin Veal Chops Busoni

Here is another of Leo's specialties.

4 loin or rib chops, ½ inch thick
2 tablespoons olive oil
5 tablespoons butter
¼ pound pancetta or bacon, cut
    into small squares
2 ounces sliced salami, cut into
    small pieces

12 pitted black olives
1 cup dry red wine
A dash of Worcestershire sauce
A dash of kirsch
¼ cup cream
Salt, freshly ground pepper
Chopped parsley

Pound the chops lightly with a pounder or rolling pin. Heat the oil and 2 tablespoons of the butter in a skillet large enough to accommodate the chops without any overlapping. Sauté the chops on high heat until they are brown on both sides. Throw out the fat in the pan and add another 2 tablespoons of butter. Lower the heat and add the pancetta, salami, and olives. Cook for about 10 minutes.

Add the wine and let it reduce to less than half; add Worcestershire sauce and kirsch. Cook for 3 or 4 minutes.

Remove the chops from the pan and keep warm. Add the remaining tablespoon of butter and the cream to the pan and simmer for about 1 minute. Adjust for seasonings.

Pour the sauce over the chops and sprinkle with chopped parsley.

SERVES 4

Loin Chops Fantesca

This recipe comes from the Grand Hotel de Bains at the Lido in Venice.

4 loin chops, ½ inch thick
Flour
Salt, freshly ground pepper
2 tablespoons olive oil
6 tablespoons butter
4 slices of cooked ham

4 slices of fontina cheese
½ cup dry white wine
½ cup heavy cream
1 green or red pepper, roasted,
    skinned, and cut into thin
    strips

Dip the chops in flour seasoned with salt and pepper. Heat the oil and 2 tablespoons of the butter in a large skillet. Sauté the chops until they are well browned on both sides. Lower the heat and cook for 5 minutes.

Discard the fat in the pan and add another 2 tablespoons of butter. Place a slice of ham and a slice of cheese on each chop, add the wine, cover the pan, and cook on low heat for a few minutes.

Add 2 more tablespoons of butter and the cream and stir well. Place slivers of pepper over each chop and cook gently for another 2 minutes before serving.

SERVES 4

Frenched Veal Chops with Eggplant and Fresh Tomato

4 rib chops, ½ inch thick, frenched (page 111)	1 garlic clove, chopped
1 medium eggplant	Freshly ground pepper
Salt	A few basil leaves
2 ripe, solid tomatoes	3 tablespoons butter
Flour	¼ teaspoon meat extract
½ cup olive oil	½ cup dry white wine

Pound the chops with a pounder or rolling pin to remove any tough membranes. Peel the eggplant and slice thick. Spread the slices on a rack and salt them.

Scald the tomatoes and peel them. Chop coarse, removing seeds.

Dry the eggplant pieces with paper towels and dredge them in flour. Heat the oil and fry the eggplant slices in it until they are golden brown. Remove and place on paper towels.

In the same skillet and the same oil put the garlic and the tomatoes. Season with salt and pepper and cook on low heat for 10 minutes. Add the basil leaves toward the end.

While the tomatoes are cooking, dredge the chops in flour, shake off any excess flour, and sauté them in hot butter, being careful not to let the butter burn. When the chops are well cooked on both sides, about 15 minutes, transfer them to a serving dish. Cover each chop with some eggplant, then with the cooked tomatoes.

Add the meat extract and wine to the pan and cook on high heat to let the wine reduce. Adjust the sauce for seasonings and pour over the chops.

SERVES 4

The Leg

Butchers who sell nature veal usually cut the leg European style by separating the individual muscles out from each other. So you will have the top sirloin, the top round, the bottom round, the eye of the round, the rump, the fillet head, and the little heel of the round.

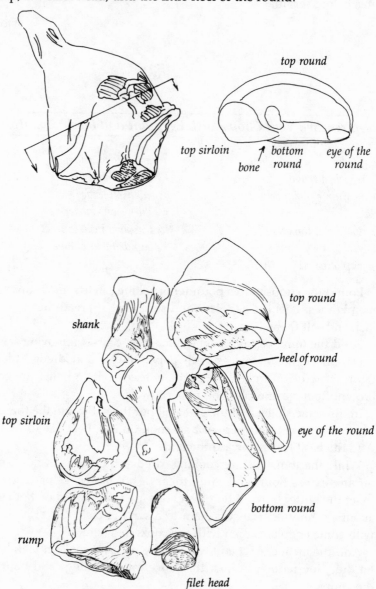

With the exception of the heel, all these cuts can be used for individual roasts or to cut into slices for cutlets and scaloppine. You can, of course, use any of the shoulder clod recipes for leg roasts.

The heel of the round is full of tendons, so its best use is boned out for veal stew.

Veal Roast alla Catherine de Medici

I got this recipe twenty years ago from the owner of a little pensione I stayed in near the railroad in Florence. It is for feast days, so I named it for the Florentine who became queen of France. Boneless top sirloin is a perfect cut for this recipe.

1 solid piece of boneless leg
    muscle, 5 to 6 pounds
A few sprigs of rosemary
Salt, freshly ground pepper
1 veal kidney
2 tablespoons olive oil
¼ cup brandy
4 tablespoons butter
1 garlic clove, crushed
1 onion, chopped fine
½ pound chopped mushrooms

2 tablespoons chopped parsley
¼ cup bread crumbs
1 egg yolk
A few strips of salt pork, if
    necessary
2 cups coarsely chopped onions,
    carrots, and celery for gravy
    (pages 26–27)
1 bay leaf
½ glass of dry white wine

Spread the veal on your work table and butterfly it: Hold the veal flat on the table with one hand and your knife horizontal to the table with the other. Cut the meat from the outside until you are about ½ inch from the outer edge. Open the meat out flat, pound it a bit, and season with rosemary, salt, and pepper.

Clean out the veal kidney: Remove all the fat and membrane from the center, wash it well, and pat dry. Cut the kidney into thin slices.

In a small frying pan, heat the olive oil and cook the kidney slices for a few minutes on fairly high heat. Add the brandy and flame it. Remove the kidneys and set them aside in a bowl.

Add 2 tablespoons of the butter to the pan. When the butter is hot, brown the garlic clove and discard. Add the chopped onion and cook for 2 or 3 minutes. Add the mushrooms, season lightly with salt and pepper, and cook another 5 minutes.

Add the mushrooms and onion to the kidney, along with the parsley, bread crumbs, and egg yolk. Mix well and taste for seasoning.

Place the kidney mixture in the center of the leg, roll up the leg, and tie it with white twine. If the veal is lean, tie a few strips of salt pork around the outside of the veal.

Place the veal in an open roasting pan with chopped vegetables for gravy and a bay leaf. Dot with butter and cook for 2 hours and 30 minutes in a preheated 350° oven. Baste with wine during the cooking.

Remove the roast, cover it with foil to keep it warm, and let it rest while you make gravy from the juices and vegetables in the pan.

SERVES 10 TO 12

Veal Orloff

Veal Orloff is a classic preparation that calls for some work on your part; you need to make three sauces, a duxelle (shallots and mushrooms cooked in butter), a soubise (pureed onions and rice), and finally a Mornay sauce (a white béchamel with cheese). It isn't hard, it just takes time, but you will be richly rewarded with a delicious and beautiful presentation.

1 solid piece of boneless leg muscle, 4 to 5 pounds
Salt, freshly ground pepper
¼ pound (1 stick) and 2 tablespoons butter
½ cup dry white wine
1¾ cups veal stock
3 tablespoons finely chopped shallots
½ pound mushrooms, cleaned in acidulated water (page 8) and chopped fine

Juice of half a lemon
1 small onion, chopped
¼ cup raw rice
4 tablespoons flour
1 quart milk
2 egg yolks
2 ounces grated Gruyère cheese
¼ cup heavy cream
A pinch of nutmeg

Season the veal with salt and pepper. Heat 2 tablespoons of the butter in a casserole large enough to hold the veal comfortably. Add the veal and gently brown it on all sides. Add the white wine; when the wine has reduced, add 1 cup of the veal stock. Reduce the heat, cover the casserole, and simmer it slowly for 1 hour and 30 minutes.

For the duxelle sauce, heat 2 tablespoons of the butter in a medium pan; add the chopped shallots and cook for 3 minutes on moderate heat. Add the mushrooms and season them lightly with salt and pepper. Add the lemon juice, cover the pan, and simmer on low heat for 30 minutes.

For the soubise sauce, heat 2 tablespoons of the butter in a medium saucepan and add the chopped onion. Cook until translucent; add the rice. In a separate pan, heat the remaining veal stock and add it to the rice. Cover the pan and cook the rice for 20 minutes. Stir 2 tablespoons of the butter and 2 tablespoons of the flour into the rice. Pass the rice through a food mill and add it to the duxelle sauce.

For the Mornay sauce, heat the remaining 2 tablespoons of butter in a saucepan and add the remaining 2 tablespoons of flour. Cook and stir these together until they are very smooth but not brown. Heat the milk just to the boiling point and add it a little at a time to the butter and flour, stirring constantly on low heat. When all the milk has been added, remove the sauce from the heat and let it cool a bit. Stir in the egg yolks one at a time. Stir in all but a few spoonfuls of the grated cheese. Stir in the cream and season the sauce with a pinch of nutmeg, salt, and pepper.

Slice the veal and cover each slice with the soubise sauce. Replace the slices to re-form the shape of the roast. Spoon the Mornay sauce over the roast and sprinkle the top with the leftover grated cheese.

Finish the roast in a preheated 350° oven for 20 minutes.

SERVES 8 TO 10

Leg of Veal in Aspic

Here is another elaborate preparation that is lovely for a summer buffet. It is somewhat the same procedure as that for Chicken Gallantina (pages 61–62), except that here the meat is roasted, not poached. There is no question that your own stock is the best base for the gelatin, but you can substitute powder or sheet gelatin dissolved in water if you wish. You can also make this recipe with a boned shoulder clod, or you can substitute any of the stuffings I have suggested earlier for this one. Make this the day before serving so it has time to set.

Although sirloin tip or top round is fine for this recipe, I recommend the bottom round because its flat shape makes it easy to butterfly and roll.

1 solid piece of boneless leg
    muscle, 4 to 5 pounds
Salt, freshly ground pepper
2 carrots, cut into large pieces
1 onion, sliced
Olive oil
¼ pound (1 stick) butter
1 bay leaf
1 tablespoon meat extract
½ cup water
½ glass of dry white wine
½ pound liver pâté, canned
A few drops of Worcestershire
    sauce
1 tablespoon cognac

1 quart white veal stock of
    sufficient strength to make
    gelatin (pages 132–133)
2 egg whites
½ pound lean beef, ground
1 cup finely chopped carrots,
    onion, and celery
1 small can of peas, drained
1 green or red pepper, roasted,
    skinned, and cut into thin
    strips
3 hard-boiled eggs, cut into thin
    slices
6 ounces prosciutto, sliced thin
Garnish: lettuce, tomato wedges,
    hard-boiled egg wedges

Lay the veal on your workspace. Butterfly it (page 153), season it with salt and pepper, and tie it into a roll. Put the carrots and onion in a roasting pan. Rub the veal with oil and place it on the vegetables; dot it with 4 tablespoons of the butter. Add the bay leaf and cook for about 2 hours in a preheated 350° oven. Baste at intervals with the meat extract that you have dissolved in water and wine. If the top begins getting crusty, cover the roast with foil. Let the roast cool.

Mix the liver pâté with the remaining 4 tablespoons of butter, Worcestershire sauce, and cognac.

Add some of the strained juices from the roasting pan to the veal stock if desired. The stock should be cool. Using the egg whites, ground beef, and chopped vegetables, clarify the stock, following the directions on page 62. Cool the clarified stock.

Pour stock into a loaf pan to a depth of ½ inch. The pan should be just large enough to hold the roast. Place the pan in the refrigerator until the gelatin hardens, about 30 minutes.

When the gelatin is firm, place the peas and pepper strips over it in a pattern of your choosing. Cover the vegetables with a light layer of gelatin and return to the refrigerator.

Untie the veal and slice it into thin slices, keeping them in the form of the roast. On one side of each slice spread a thin coating of pâté, then a slice of egg, then a slice of prosciutto. When each slice is covered and the slices are all back in the roast form, tie it lengthwise with a white string to hold it together.

Place the veal in the loaf pan and pour the rest of the gelatin around it so that it is nearly covered. Refrigerate at least 6 hours or overnight.

Just before serving, pour a bit of hot water on the base of the loaf pan and slide it out, upside down, onto a serving platter decorated with lettuce leaves. Garnish with fresh tomatoes and hard-boiled eggs or other garnish of your choice.

SERVES 10

Vitello Tonnato

Here is another festive summer dish that is not as much work as the Leg of Veal in Aspic. The sirloin tip is the best cut for this, although you can also use the shoulder clod.

1 solid piece of boneless leg muscle, 4 to 5 pounds	12 peppercorns, crushed
	A few sprigs of parsley
1 carrot, peeled and cut into large pieces	Salt, freshly ground pepper
	1 bottle of white wine
1 onion, cut in half, with 3 cloves stuck into each half	1 8-ounce can tuna, packed in oil
	1 cup mayonnaise (see Note)
1 celery stalk, including leaves, cut into large pieces	1 tablespoon capers
	4 anchovies, chopped
2 bay leaves	2 tablespoons white vinegar

Tie the veal lightly to hold it together. Place it in a stainless steel or enamel pot, cover it with the carrot, onion, celery, bay leaves, peppercorns, parsley, salt, and pepper. Pour in all but 1 cup of the white wine. Roll the veal around in the marinade. Cover the pot and refrigerate overnight.

The following day, put the pot on the stove and bring the liquid to a boil. Immediately lower the heat and simmer the veal, partially covered, for 1 hour and 30 minutes. If you think the veal needs more liquid, add water. Remove the pot from the heat and let the veal cool in the juices.

Put the tuna through a food mill and stir it into the mayonnaise with the capers and anchovies. Slowly add the vinegar and some of the reserved white wine, stirring constantly. You may not need the entire cup of wine.

Slice the cooled veal into thin slices and arrange on a serving platter. Cover the slices with the tuna mayonnaise and set the platter in the refrigerator until needed.

Note: To make mayonnaise, mix 1 egg yolk with 1 teaspoon of lemon juice, ½ teaspoon or less of dry mustard, salt, and pepper in the bowl of a food processor. With the machine running, dribble in ¾ cup of olive oil until you have a satisfactory emulsion. The mayonnaise will be better if it has been made a few hours ahead of time.

SERVES 8 TO 10

Veal Paillard

Quarter-inch slices of veal cut from the top round of the leg are wonderful grilled in the summer. Serve them on lettuce with lemon wedges, a mountain of matchstick fried potatoes, and Eggplant Parmigiana Neapolitan.

4 slices of top round, ¼ inch thick	½ teaspoon marjoram
Juice of 1 lemon	1 tablespoon chopped parsley
1 garlic clove, chopped fine	½ teaspoon rosemary
	Salt, freshly ground pepper

Place the veal slices in a large dish so they do not overlap and sprinkle them with the lemon juice, garlic, marjoram, parsley, rosemary, salt, and pepper. Marinate for at least 1 hour.

Place the veal slices between the two sides of a wire grill that you put over a charcoal fire. Cook for about 3 minutes on each side, basting with the marinade during the cooking. Be careful not to overcook; you want medium veal. (If your broiler is very hot, you can also grill the veal under the broiler.)

SERVES 4

Eggplant Parmigiana Neapolitan

Fried eggplant finished with a cheese and tomato sauce goes very nicely with broiled or roasted meat.

2 medium eggplants, unpeeled	4 ounces Gaeta or similar Greek olives, about ½ a jar
Salt	
2 tablespoons olive oil	1 tablespoon chopped parsley
1 garlic clove, peeled and chopped	Freshly ground pepper
2 medium onions, chopped fine	Flour
1 28-ounce can ground tomatoes, with juice	Oil for frying
2 tablespoons capers	½ cup grated Parmesan cheese
	½ pound mozzarella cheese, sliced

Wash the eggplants, cut off the ends, and cut into ½-inch slices. Sprinkle them with salt, place on a dish, and cover with another dish topped by a small weight. Let sit at least 30 minutes.

Heat the olive oil in the bottom of a saucepan, and gently brown the garlic. Remove the garlic, add the onions, and sauté until soft. Add the tomatoes, capers, olives, and parsley. Season with salt and pepper and simmer slowly for at least 30 minutes.

Drain the water that has come off the eggplant slices and pat them dry with paper towels. Dip them in flour, then fry them in hot vegetable oil until they turn a golden color, turning to ensure even browning. Set on paper towels to absorb any excess oil.

Put a bit of the tomato sauce in the bottom of a shallow baking dish. Add a layer of eggplant slices. Sprinkle the eggplant with a handful of grated Parmesan cheese, a few slices of mozzarella, and more sauce. Repeat until all the eggplant is used. Top with sauce and cheese.

Cook in a preheated 350° oven for 20 minutes. Let set at room temperature a few minutes before serving.

SERVES 6

Veal Pillows

I first had these cuscinetti at the Gracchi Restaurant, about five blocks from St. Peter's in Rome, where salamis and prosciutti hang from the ceiling and the fish is out of this world.

4 slices of veal cutlet, about 4 by 6 inches each	2 tablespoons oil
Flour	8 tablespoons chopped mushrooms
Salt, freshly ground pepper	4 tablespoons butter
4 thin slices of prosciutto	8 tablespoons green peas, blanched and drained
4 ounces mozzarella, cut into small cubes	3 tablespoons tomato paste

Dust the veal lightly with flour on one side only. Lay the cutlets on your work table with the floured side down. Season the cutlets on the clean side with salt and pepper. Lay a slice of prosciutto on each slice and a tablespoon of mozzarella on the prosciutto. Fold the cutlets over so that they each form a small pillow. Pound the edges of the cutlets so they will stick together.

Heat the oil in a large skillet. Brown the meat on fairly high heat for about 10 minutes, turning carefully to keep the cushion shapes.

(If the heat is too low, the juices will ooze out of the meat and be lost.)

While the veal is browning, quickly sauté the mushrooms in 2 tablespoons of the butter.

Add the mushrooms, peas, and tomato paste to the veal and cook on low heat for 5 minutes.

Taste the sauce for seasoning and adjust if necessary. Remove the veal, mushrooms, and peas to a serving dish and finish the sauce with the remaining 2 tablespoons of the butter.

SERVES 4

Veal Scaloppine

Slices for scaloppine are cut in the same manner as any cutlet (pages 11–12) from meat that has been chilled in the refrigerator for 20 minutes. They are usually cut from the eye or bottom round and are thinner and smaller than slices for cutlets. (If cut from the eye round, the slices will be round; if from the bottom round, they will be rectangular, about 3 by 5 inches.)

Cutlets from the center of the top round are used in recipes like Veal Parmigiana (deep-fried, covered with tomato sauce and grated Parmesan cheese, topped with fontina cheese, and finished in a hot oven), Veal Milanese (coated with bread crumbs and deep-fried), or Schnitzel Holstein (Milanese with a fried egg over it.)

Like cutlets, scaloppine cook very quickly. It is a good idea to remove any membranes or tendons and flatten the meat with a pounder before cooking.

Scaloppine Negresco

Here is another favorite of mine from my Florentine friend, Leo. Like all good cooks, Leo has a few extra touches he adds to recipes to make them his own. Here he enriches the sauce just before serving with a "point of tomato" and a bit of cream.

1½ pounds from the center of the leg, cut into thin slices
Flour
1 egg, lightly beaten
3 tablespoons butter plus 1 tablespoon oil or 4 tablespoons clarified butter
½ cup dry white wine

1 cup white veal stock
Scant teaspoon tomato paste
2 tablespoons chopped parsley
Scant ¼ teaspoon oregano
Salt, freshly ground pepper
4 tablespoons grated Parmesan cheese
1 tablespoon cream (optional)

Dredge the veal in flour, then in the beaten egg. Heat 1 tablespoon of the butter and the oil (or 2 tablespoons of clarified butter) in a frying pan and brown the veal for 2 minutes on each side. Cook only a few of the cutlets at a time; if the pan is crowded, the meat will ooze water and steam.

Remove the veal from the pan and discard the fat. Add the remaining 2 tablespoons of butter to the pan. When it is hot, add the wine and let it reduce. Add the stock, tomato paste, parsley, oregano, salt, and pepper. Cook for 2 or 3 minutes, then return the veal to the pan.

Spread the cheese over the veal and cook for 5 minutes more. Just before serving, stir in the cream. Place the veal on your serving platter and cover with the sauce.

SERVES 4

Variation: Scaloppine al Marsala

Return the veal to the pan after you discard the fat. Add ¼ cup of Marsala wine or sherry and let it reduce. Add ½ cup of white veal stock, salt, and pepper. Simmer for 8 minutes and finish the sauce with a little butter.

Variation: Scaloppine alla Crema

Dredge the veal slices in flour but not in beaten egg. Brown the veal as above. After you throw out the fat in the pan, add ½ cup of dry sherry, then ½ cup of white veal stock. Return the veal to the pan and let it simmer. In a separate pan lightly sauté ½ pound of sliced fresh mushrooms in 2 tablespoons of butter; sprinkle a little lemon juice on the mushrooms while they cook to keep them white. Add the mushrooms to the veal, season with salt and pepper, and cook another 8 minutes. Place the veal on a serving dish with the mushrooms over them; finish the sauce with 2 tablespoons of butter and ½ cup of heavy cream.

Osso Buco

Osso Buco, veal shins cooked slowly in a casserole with wine and vegetables, is a delectable dish that is not always easy to find. On a recent trip to Italy, I ordered it in a nice-looking trattoria in Rome near the Castel Sant'Angelo. To give the restaurant credit, the fettuccine was wonderful, but the Osso Buco was nothing more than a small piece of beef shank with a few fried mushrooms over it. Well, said the waiter when I complained, that is Osso Buco in this restaurant. Two weeks later I was in Milano on Ferragosto, the height of the August summer vacation, and every restaurant was closed for the holiday. I was walking around La Scala opera house trying to find a place to eat and decided to try a hotel dining room. There was Osso Buco on the menu, "alla Milanese"; I figured I couldn't get stuck twice, and I didn't. It was delicious.

For the best Osso Buco, buy hind shins; they are meatier and have more marrow than fore shins. (Shins are also known as shanks.) Many people prefer Osso Buco without tomatoes, so I have listed them as an optional ingredient. Risotto is the traditional accompaniment; serve a spoonful or two of the sauce over the rice.

2 leg shins, cut into 6 2½-inch
    pieces
Salt, freshly ground pepper
Flour
4 tablespoons butter
2 tablespoons olive oil
1 garlic clove, crushed
1 large onion, chopped
2 celery stalks, chopped

2 medium carrots, chopped
½ cup dry white wine
1 16-ounce can peeled plum
    tomatoes, drained (optional)
1 teaspoon marjoram
1 teaspoon grated lemon zest
1 teaspoon grated orange zest
1 to 2 tablespoons chopped
    parsley

Sprinkle the shin pieces with salt and pepper and dredge in flour.

In a casserole large enough to hold all the meat in one layer, heat the butter and oil. When hot, add the garlic clove until it is just brown; discard.

Add the veal pieces to the hot fat and brown them on all sides. Add the onion, celery, and carrots and cook for about 20 minutes.

Add the wine, let it reduce a bit, and add the tomatoes and marjoram. Simmer for about 1 hour and 30 minutes, or until the meat is tender. Do not overcook, or the veal will fall off the bones.

Remove the meat to a serving dish and keep warm. Put the sauce through a food mill. Add the lemon and orange zests and the parsley; enrich with a little butter if desired. Pour some of the sauce over the veal; serve the rest of it separately.

SERVES 4 TO 6

Risotto

Many short-grain rices go very quickly from the al dente stage to mush. Arborio, an Italian short-grain rice, is not so temperamental and, therefore, a bit more reliable.

2 cups raw short-grain rice
5 cups chicken broth
4 tablespoons butter
1 onion, chopped fine

¼ cup dry white wine
A pinch of saffron strands
* (optional, see Note)*
Salt, freshly ground pepper
4 tablespoons grated Parmesan
* cheese*

Rinse the rice. Heat the chicken broth and keep it simmering during the entire cooking time.

Heat 2 tablespoons of the butter in a heavy saucepan and sauté the onion in it until translucent but not brown. Stir in the rice. As soon as the rice begins to stick a little, add the white wine. When the wine bubbles up, add 2 ladles of the hot broth, stirring continually.

Continue stirring and adding broth until the rice is al dente; the entire cooking time with the broth is about 18 minutes. The last 5 minutes of cooking, dilute saffron threads in a little hot stock and add to the rice. Taste for seasoning and add salt and pepper if necessary.

Remove the pan from the heat and stir in the remaining 2 table-spoons of butter, cut into pieces, and the Parmesan cheese.

Note: I like the taste of saffron and the lovely yellow color it gives to the risotto. If you prefer not to use saffron, add 1 tablespoon of tomato paste dissolved in a little stock. Do not use saffron powder.

SERVES 6 TO 8

Variation: Risotto with Dried Mushrooms

Dried porcini, shiitake, or cèpes add a lovely woody flavor to a risotto. Soak the mushrooms in warm water for about 20 minutes. Drain them, reserving the water, and squeeze out the liquid. Strain the mushroom water and add about ½ cup to the stock. Chop or slice the mushrooms, discarding any hard stems, and add to the rice near the end of the cooking time.

BEEF

WHEN THE COLONISTS CAME to America, they brought with them Devon cattle from the southwest of England. As early as 1623, the "old red cow" supplied the settlers with milk, beef, ox teams, and leather. Today they are raised in the south and used solely as beef cattle.

Devon is only one of thirty-three registered breeds of beef cattle in the United States. Other well-known breeds are Black Angus, a cross of Scottish bulls and native Texas Longhorns, Hereford, and Santa Gertrudis. The Santa Gertrudis breed, widely distributed in the southern United States and exported to fifty-two different countries, is solely descended from a single bull calf who was a cross of three parts Brahman bull and five parts Texas Shorthorn.

Today it is not necessary to bring the bull to the cow. Semen from the bull is frozen and, when kept at −360°, will be potent for twelve years. Recently, American breeders have been experimenting with semen from so-called exotic breeds like the Charolais and Limousin of France, the Italian Chianina, and the Swiss Simmental. By crossing these very large animals with our native Holsteins and Herefords, they have been able to attain a larger percentage of meat per animal, 78 percent, compared to about 68 percent from Black Angus and Herefords.

How Meat Is Sold

I want to explain to you some of the facts of life of how meat gets to the consumer. When I started my butcher shop in 1936, I went every week to the wholesale meat houses to choose the meat I wanted for my customers. Beef carcasses hung in long rows in the cold rooms, and butchers would walk down the rows with the salesmen to select hindquarters or forequarters of beef based on their experience of what to look for to get good meat. Transactions were confirmed by a handshake. Back at the store, my assistant and I would cut these 200-pound pieces down into secondary cuts, then into smaller pieces to suit the needs of our customers.

Any cuts that were not used by our clientele, we sold back to the processors, and of course we always sold back the fat. In order to buy refrigerators, hooks, and blocks for my store, I borrowed $750 from my "fat man." Every month he deducted the fat and skins I sold back to him until I had the loan paid back. Butchers still sell back the fat, which is melted down to make tallow, soap, etc.

Although a small amount of meat is still selected and cut by a few prime butchers, 90 percent of the meat sold in the United States today is purchased at the supermarket. The meat manager of the supermarket does not personally select each carcass; instead, he fills out a requisition for the meat he thinks he will need. Meat is no longer slaughtered at the stockyards in Chicago, but at the feeding plants where an assembly line of workers cuts the beef into secondary cuts, packs them in Cry-O-Vac in boxes containing no more than seventy pounds each and labeled as to content and grade, and dispatches them to the supermarket. The use of Cry-O-Vac, an airtight container, means that meat will keep an extra two weeks under refrigeration. The down side of the system is that the supermarket meat manager has not chosen the meat, nor does he have a chance to examine what is in the box before it is delivered to him. Needless to say, once the meat is in his store, it is up to him to sell it, regardless of the quality.

In New York City there are still about five wholesale houses that sell carcasses for a few prime butcher shops and fancy hotels. To me, it is sad that most butchers have lost the pleasure of selecting the meat they will sell to their customers and the detailed knowledge of how to cut the meat in the precise way the Europeans do.

LABELING

As you know, meat in a supermarket is packaged, wrapped in plastic, and labeled before it is displayed in refrigerated cases. The label should tell you exactly what is in the package. For example, there are 127 different cuts of beef sanctioned by the United States Department of Agriculture. (This federally approved labeling is in response to some pretty cute ways of retailing meats some years ago, when nondescript pieces of meat were being sold as "his and her steaks" or "lollipop steaks.") Now when the label says "porterhouse steak," you should feel confident that that's what you are getting, not a piece of chuck steak.

DEFINITION OF BEEF

Beef is the muscle meat from a steer (a castrated male animal) 18 months old or older. Steers have finer meat than do cows or bulls. Heifers, young females who have not yet calved, may also be sold as beef.

Beef is the largest of the meat animals, ten times larger than lamb, three times larger than veal. Live cattle weigh between 1,110 and 1,300 pounds. They lose 40 percent of their weight when dressed, leaving about 600 pounds of bone, fat, and meat of which 35 to 40 percent is fat and bones.

GRADING

You may be surprised to know that meat grading is not compulsory; it is a voluntary service on the part of a wholesaler or slaughterhouse, which pays a fee to the United States Department of Agriculture, whose inspectors make the designation. What *is* compulsory is the USDA's stamp of approval, which certifies that an animal is healthy and good for human consumption. The cost of federal inspection is borne by the U.S. government. All meat animals must have this federal inspection, but lamb is the only other meat that is graded. (The lamb grades are prime, choice, and commercial, a grade rarely seen in the stores.)

There are seven different grades of beef; you probably have heard of only two or three. The top of the line is prime, light-colored meat with firm, white fat and fine-textured, even marbling throughout the meat. Less than 2 percent of the meat you can buy is prime meat. Supermarkets do not carry prime meat; it is used mainly by fancy hotels and restaurants and can be found in a few prime butcher shops. That is why, unless you have access to a prime butcher shop or prime steaks by mail order, you may have to go to a high-priced restaurant to get really good prime steaks.

The next grade is choice, a grade that accounts for 20 percent of all beef sold and is probably what you buy in your supermarket. The meat in this grade is also light-colored and the fat is firm and white, but there is a subtle difference. The marbling is not even, or there might be some little pockets of fat; the texture of the meat might be just a bit coarser.

There can be quite a difference between top choice and low choice, since about ten years ago the breeders and growers changed the grades, incorporating plain choice into top prime and the grade below choice, good, into choice. So choice is now a large grade that encompasses a wide range of quality. This is why you will see some meat advertised as "top choice." No one, however, ever labels meat "bottom choice," so it is clearly to your advantage when you are buying meat in a supermarket or from a new butcher to know what you are looking for.

Good grade (formerly commercial) is popular with people who do not like fatty meat. It is a plain meat with hardly any marbling and is apt to be tough, with little flavor.

Commercial, the next grade, may include some cows and young bulls. The last three grades—utility, cutters, and canners—are seldom seen in retail markets. They are used by processors of frankfurters, bologna, knockwurst, and other sausages that require a percentage of beef.

Aging

Aging beef for two to three weeks after the kill breaks down the tissues and makes the meat more flavorful and tender. Only whole pieces of meat still covered with the natural fat can be aged, not cut pieces like individual steaks. It is best to get a whole hindquarter, but a butcher can age loins or prime ribs; rounds and chucks are never aged. During the aging process the meat is kept in constant dry refrigeration at 34° to 36°. (If the temperature is lower, the meat will blacken.) It loses water and 1 percent of its weight each day, one reason aged meat is more expensive.

If you have an extra refrigerator that is not in daily use, you can age a whole rib or a shell of beef yourself. Do not open the door of the refrigerator until the aging process is finished.

Tips on Buying, Storing, and Freezing Beef

Beef should be a bright color, a dark pink, with delicate thin lines of fat (marbling) running through the meat. The fat should not be coarse or mottled, and there should not be pockets of fat. (See the description of grading above.)

Like lamb, beef will keep up to a week in the refrigerator. BUT ground meat should never be kept more than 24 hours before using. If you cannot use it within 24 hours of its purchase, freeze the meat in its supermarket package by wrapping it with a sheet of aluminum foil. If the outside of the ground meat is gray, return it to the store; it is too old. (Sometimes the interior of ground meat discolors and darkens. This may be due to lack of oxygen inside the package, or the meat may have absorbed water and become moist.)

Beef can be prepared ahead of time for cooking and can be frozen in the same manner as pork (pages 65–66).

Structure of Beef

Just as all the meat animals have the same bones in the same places, so beef is divided into sections in exactly the same way as are pork, lamb, and veal. The only difference is that since beef is so much larger, it can be broken down into many more individual pieces.

Each of the two sides of a steer is cut across between the twelfth and thirteenth ribs. The forequarter is that part of the animal from the twelfth rib to the neck; the hindquarter is from the thirteenth rib to the tail.

Forequarter

With the exception of the prime ribs, forequarter meat should be cooked with liquid—that is, braised, pot-roasted, or stewed. A few separate muscles of the chuck, like the top blade, under-blade, and eye, can be sliced and broiled, marinated and broiled or barbecued, or sliced thinly to be cooked for pepper steak, sukiyaki, etc. Any of these will be fine if the meat is good, but you will not get the same tenderness or taste as you will from a porterhouse steak or any other steak cut from the loin.

Forequarter meat is juicy and flavorful because the muscles are interspersed with fat and tissue. It takes well to braising and pot-roasting and does not get dry or tough with long cooking.

The major secondary cuts of a forequarter of beef are the chuck, brisket, prime ribs, and plate.

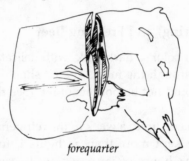

forequarter

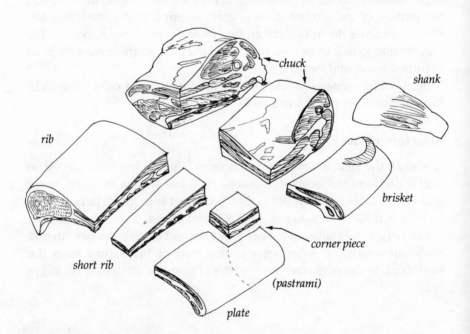

chuck

shank

rib

brisket

short rib

corner piece

(pastrami)

plate

The Chuck

The chuck is the largest of the forequarter cuts. It is separated from the rib and the plate by cutting straight across the forequarter between the fifth and sixth ribs. This is a cross-cut chuck and weighs about 100 pounds. When the brisket is removed, it becomes an arm chuck. When the foreshank (arm) is removed, it becomes a square-cut chuck, which is then cut into chuck, or blade, steaks. The foreshank is sinewy meat, good only for stews.

It is hard not to be confused by this terminology. And to complicate things further, different parts of the country, like Boston, New York, Philadelphia, and California, all have different ways of cutting meat. In some areas, parts of the chuck may still be called shoulder or shoulder clod, or a boneless arm pot roast may be called a cross rib. The center-cut chuck is sometimes known as a blade roast.

The neck—that is, the front part of the chuck—is used only for soup meat or, boned out, for stewing or for ground meat.

Flanken-style ribs, the continuation of the five ribs on the chuck from the chine bone that is right next to the shoulder, can be braised or marinated, then barbecued; usually they're cut into short ribs. Other cuts for short ribs are cross-cut ribs from the prime rib and the three ribs under the plate. Of these three, short ribs cut from the chuck are the leanest.

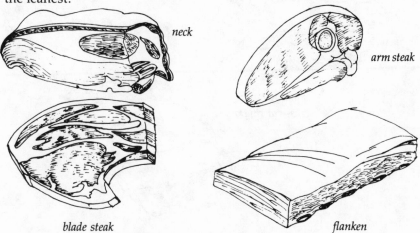

neck

arm steak

blade steak

flanken

There are four large muscles in the square-cut chuck, as well as many small ones. If these muscles are separated at the seam where the membrane holds the muscles together, the European style of cutting meat, solid pieces of meat (muscles) of different sizes result.

The largest of these four muscles, the eye of the chuck, the total center of the chuck, is sometimes sold as a chuck eye roast. Under-blade meat may be called under-blade steak or under-blade pot roast; it can be terrific marinated and barbecued. Top chuck, called top-blade meat, is a small, triangular muscle attached to the upper side of the shoulder blade. All these cuts make a fine pot roast, or any of them can be sliced for pepper steak, sukiyaki, etc. Oval boneless slices of top-blade meat used to be called chicken steaks; they are tender and can be sliced thin or 1 inch thick for pan-frying or broiling. The smallest of the big muscles, the mock tender, is on top of the blade bone opposite the top-blade steak and is recognizable because it is shaped like an ice cream cone. It can be used in the same ways as the other muscles.

If you are watching your budget carefully, look for center-cut chuck roast on sale, especially in the summer, when many people are buying steaks to cook on the barbecue. (Conversely, steaks are often put on special in the wintertime.) Ask the butcher to cut you a center-cut chuck steak about 4 to 5 inches thick. By running your knife along the membranes that hold the muscles together, you can separate it into top-of-the-blade meat, under-blade meat, an eye roast, and small pieces suitable for grinding. For minimal cost, you have possibilities of a wealth of recipes that will give you three or four nutritious meals for your family.

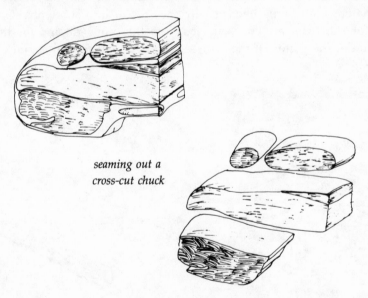

seaming out a
cross-cut chuck

The following recipes are suitable for meat cut from the chuck. There is, of course, no law that says you cannot make stew or pot roast with a piece of round from the hindquarter. But unless the round is on sale, you will pay more for the meat, and there is no reason for using the higher-priced cut.

Beef Stock

This is a brown stock; that is, the bones are browned in the oven before cooking in water.

1 pound beef, chuck or any inexpensive cut	2 carrots
1 beef shank, cut crosswise, or a piece of short ribs	2 celery stalks, with leaves
Beef bones	1 onion, cut in half, with 3 cloves inserted
	Peppercorns

Place the meat and bones in a roasting pan with the vegetables for about 45 minutes in a preheated 350° oven. Turn once or twice during the browning.

Place the meat, bones, vegetables, and peppercorns in a stockpot and cover with cold water. Bring to a boil, lower the heat, and skim off any froth that comes to the surface. Cook gently for 3 to 4 hours.

Strain the stock and cool it. Place it in the refrigerator overnight. Scrape off the fat covering the top of the gelled stock. The stock will keep in the refrigerator for 4 days or in the freezer indefinitely.

Pot Roast

This is an old-fashioned dish that is lovely in the winter and particularly helpful to your pocketbook when you buy the meat on sale. You can use any part of the chuck—the arm steak, the mock tender, the eye, or the under-blade meat suggested here.

1 boneless under-blade roast, 4 to 5 pounds	¼ pound salt pork, cut into cubes
Flour	1 cup dry red wine
Salt, freshly ground pepper	1 16-ounce can peeled plum tomatoes
6 tablespoons rendered suet fat (page 174) or 6 tablespoons oil	2 bay leaves
1 garlic clove, peeled and crushed	1 tablespoon chopped parsley
4 tablespoons butter	1 cup beef stock or water (if needed)
2 cups coarsely chopped onions, carrots, and celery for gravy (pages 26–27)	

Roll the meat in flour and season it with salt and pepper. Heat the suet fat in a large skillet; brown the garlic and meat in the hot fat.

Meanwhile, heat the butter in a casserole and begin to sauté the vegetables and salt pork in the butter. When the beef is well browned, add it to the casserole and let it cook with the vegetables for about 5 minutes.

Add the wine and reduce it to less than half. Add the tomatoes, bay leaves, parsley, salt, and pepper. Lower the heat to simmer, partially cover the pan, and cook for 2 hours, checking the amount of juices and turning the meat from time to time. If it gets dry, add beef stock or water.

Put the vegetables through a food mill with the juices in the pan for a slightly thickened gravy.

SERVES 6 TO 8

Suet Fat

Suet fat is the fat around the beef kidneys. It is strong, can tolerate high heat, and will render (melt down) almost 95 percent of its weight. It is a good browning fat and excellent for cooking french fries.

To render 1 to 2 pounds of suet fat, cut it into small cubes. Cook on very low heat in a saucepan with 1 to 2 cups of water. When it is practically all melted down and the cracklings—the little solid pieces left in the fat—begin to get brown, remove from the heat. Carefully strain into a bowl, being careful not to let the hot fat burn you. Cool to room temperature and refrigerate. The clear fat will rise to the surface and any water and impurities will sink to the bottom. Separate the fat from the water and store in the refrigerator until needed.

Carbonnade Flamande

3 tablespoons oil
2 shoulder steaks or cross rib
  steaks, 1 inch thick, about 2
  pounds each
Salt, freshly ground pepper
1½ pounds onions, sliced
4 garlic cloves, peeled and
  crushed

1 cup beef stock
3 cups beer
2 tablespoons brown sugar
1 large bouquet garni
1 tablespoon potato starch or
  cornstarch
1 tablespoon vinegar

Heat the oil in a large frying pan and brown the beef in the hot oil. With salt and pepper, season the meat on the side you have cooked first. When both sides are well browned, remove the beef. Add the onions and garlic to the pan and cook for about 10 minutes.

Spoon some of the onions and garlic into a flameproof casserole and place one of the steaks on top of the onions. Put more onions on the steak, then the other steak, and top with the remaining onions.

Deglaze the browning pan with the stock and pour it over the meat. Add the beer so it just about covers the meat. Stir in the brown sugar and the bouquet garni. Bring the liquid to a simmer, then cover the casserole and put it in a preheated 350° oven for 2 hours. Check the meat to see if it is tender; if not, cook a little longer.

When the meat is cooked, remove it and the onions to a deep serving dish and keep warm. Pour the juices into a saucepan and remove any fat. Mix the potato starch or cornstarch with the vinegar and stir it into the juice. Correct the seasoning and pour over the meat. Serve with egg noodles.

SERVES 6

Swiss Steak

For this recipe you can also use shoulder arm steak or any boneless cuts, such as top chuck, middle chuck, or chuck eye. Arm pot roast (cross rib steak) is also used today for London broil (page 195).

Serve Swiss Steak with any root vegetables—potatoes, turnips, or rutabaga—mashed or cut into sticks and sautéed in butter or with noodles.

2 tablespoons flour
1 slice of boneless arm pot roast,
    1½ inches thick, about 2
    pounds, or 1 piece of arm steak
    or chuck steak, about 4
    pounds, bone in
4 tablespoons rendered suet fat
    (page 174) or 4 tablespoons oil
4 tablespoons butter

2 onions, sliced
2 celery stalks, chopped
2 carrots, peeled and chopped
1 cup dry red wine
2 bay leaves
1 cup beef stock
2 teaspoons tomato paste
½ teaspoon paprika
Salt, freshly ground pepper

Sprinkle 1 tablespoon of flour over each side of the meat and massage it in.

Heat the suet fat in a heavy skillet that will hold the meat comfortably. Brown the meat on all sides in the hot fat. Remove the meat and discard the fat.

Heat the butter in the skillet and sauté the onions in the hot butter for 3 to 4 minutes. Add the celery and carrots and cook another 2 to 3 minutes.

Return the meat to the pan and let it cook with the vegetables for a few minutes. Add the wine and the bay leaves and cook to reduce the wine. Add the stock, tomato paste, paprika, salt, and pepper.

Cover the pan and put it in a preheated 350° oven for 2 hours.

SERVES 4 TO 6

Pepper Steak

I like to use ½-inch slices of meat for this dish, but you can also make it with thin slices of under-blade meat, arm pot roast, or chuck eye. You will need 8 thin slices of meat to feed 4 people.

4 slices of top blade meat, ½ inch
  thick, about 1½ to 2 pounds
Flour
6 tablespoons oil or 4 tablespoons
  oil and 2 tablespoons rendered
  suet fat (page 174)
1 onion, sliced
4 ripe plum tomatoes, peeled and
  seeded or 1 16-ounce can

1 tablespoon chopped parsley
A pinch of marjoram
Salt, freshly ground pepper
4 green and red peppers (2 of
  each, if possible), cut into
  strips

Dip the steaks in flour. Heat 2 tablespoons of the oil (or the suet fat) in a skillet and brown the steaks on both sides in the hot fat. Discard the fat.

Add 2 more tablespoons of the oil, add the onion, and cook it with the meat for 3 or 4 minutes. Add the tomatoes and the parsley and season lightly with marjoram, salt, and pepper. Turn the heat to simmer and cook slowly at least 30 minutes.

In a separate pan, heat the remaining 2 tablespoons of oil and quickly cook the pepper strips in it on high heat.

When the meat is done according to your taste, add the peppers to the meat, taste for seasonings, and serve.

SERVES 4

Beef Bourguignon My Way

Lean cubed meat from the chuck is excellent for any kind of stew. (You can, of course, also use meat cut from the round.) The French have a way with stews, as I think you will find if you try this classic preparation that I have adapted slightly. This lovely seasoned bourguignon is perfect for easy entertaining because it tastes better when you make it a day ahead of time. I suggest you follow the directions precisely the first time you make this recipe.

6 ounces bacon or salt pork, cut into strips by ¼ by ¼ inch, or cubed
¼ pound (1 stick) butter
6 tablespoons oil
3½ pounds lean beef, cut into 2-inch cubes
2 garlic cloves, peeled and crushed
2 onions, sliced
2 carrots, peeled and cut into pieces
1 fresh tomato, peeled, seeded, and quartered

1 16-ounce can plum tomatoes, drained
1 tablespoon flour
3 ounces cognac
¼ teaspoon rosemary
Salt, freshly ground pepper
2 cups good red Burgundy wine
3½ cups beef stock
20 small white onions
1 tablespoon sugar
1 pound mushrooms

If you are using bacon, remove the rind and cut it into strips or cubes. Blanch it (or the salt pork) in a quart of just boiling water for 10 minutes. Drain and dry.

Heat 2 tablespoons of the butter and 2 tablespoons of the oil in a large, heavy skillet. Brown the beef in the hot fat, a little at a time so you do not crowd the meat. Set the meat aside and discard the fat in the pan. Pour a little water into the skillet to deglaze it; save this liquid for later use.

Add another 2 tablespoons each of the oil and the butter to the pan and brown the garlic and the blanched bacon or salt pork in the hot fat for a bit. Add the onions, carrots, and the fresh tomato. Cook for about 5 minutes and add the canned tomatoes.

Add the beef to the pan and sprinkle the flour around. In a separate pan heat the cognac, then flame it. Pour it around the meat and season with rosemary, salt, and pepper. Add the wine, 3 cups of the stock, and the liquid from deglazing; partially cover the pan and lower the heat to simmer. Cook for about 2 hours.

Meanwhile, peel the white onions and brown them in 2 tablespoons each of the butter and the oil for 10 minutes, stirring continuously. Add the sugar and the remaining ½ cup of stock (or wine). Cover the pan and cook on low heat until tender.

In a separate pan sauté the mushrooms in the remaining 2 table-spoons of butter.

When the meat is tender to a fork, remove it from the pan with a slotted spoon. Pass the vegetables and juices through a food mill; remove all fat. Taste the juices for seasonings and thickness. If it is to your liking, return the meat and juices to the pan, add the onions and mushrooms, and cook for another 5 minutes.

Note: You may not want to bother with the extra step of passing the vegetables and juices through the food mill. You should, however, be sure to defat the juices.

SERVES 6

Ground Meat

The chuck is particularly good for ground meat for hamburgers, meat loaf, and other ground-meat recipes. A mixture of meat from the neck, the front part of the chuck, and the hanging tenderloin (also called the false or butcher's tenderloin, the thick muscular dorsal attachment of the diaphragm) is an excellent combination because it is so juicy. Leaner ground meat from the round works all right for rare hamburgerrs, but well-done hamburgers will get dried out unless you mix in some meat from the chuck.

By law, hamburger meat is chopped fresh or frozen beef from any part of the animal except the heart, esophagus, or cheek, containing no more than 30 percent fat, with no water, binders, or extenders. (Simi-larly, beef stew meat can be cut from any part of the cattle except the cheek, esophagus, or tongue.) Hamburgers can be pan-broiled (brush the skillet with a little butter or oil) or grilled under a very hot, pre-heated broiler. Here is a meat sauce that can be made with hamburger meat or with leftover hamburgers.

Bolognese Meat Sauce

2 tablespoons butter	½ cup red wine
1 garlic clove, peeled and crushed	1 6-ounce can tomato paste
2 ounces lean salt pork or bacon, chopped	1 cup beef stock or broth
1 large onion, chopped fine	1 bay leaf
1 pound beef, ground, or leftover hamburgers	Salt, freshly ground pepper
	2 tablespoons heavy cream

Heat the butter in a flameproof caserole and lightly brown the garlic in it. Remove the garlic and add the salt pork and onion. When the onion is translucent, add the meat and brown it.

Add the red wine and let it cook down for 2 minutes without stirring. Dissolve the tomato paste in some of the broth and add the paste and all the broth to the pan. Stir well, add the bay leaf, and taste for seasoning.

Simmer the sauce for about 30 minutes. Stir in the cream just before serving with 1½ pounds of pasta cooked according to manufacturer's directions.

SERVES 6

Meat Loaf

There is no reason meat loaf cannot be cooked to please the eye and taste buds as well as stretch the family budget. This layered-look meat loaf is a cut above the ordinary.

2 pounds beef, ground, cut from
    the neck or chuck
½ pound pork, ground, any
    inexpensive cut
½ pound veal, ground, any
    inexpensive cut
½ cup stale bread, soaked in
    milk, squeezed, and shredded
3 tablespoons grated Parmesan
    cheese
2 eggs, lightly beaten
¼ teaspoon nutmeg
Salt, freshly ground pepper
Oil

½ pound string beans, cleaned,
    blanched, and drained
1 carrot, peeled, blanched, and
    cut into long strips
6 pitted green olives, halved
1 pound fresh spinach, washed,
    blanched, drained, and
    chopped or 1 10-ounce package
    frozen spinach
1 tablespoon pignoli nuts
2 tablespoons butter
1 8-ounce can peeled plum
    tomatoes (optional)

Place the meats in a mixing bowl with the bread, cheese, eggs, nutmeg, salt, and pepper. Mix well with your hands. Do not taste for seasoning when you are working with raw pork.

Line the bottom of a 9- by 5- by 2¾-inch baking pan with a piece of waxed paper oiled on both sides. Place one-third of the meat mixture on the paper and flatten it out. Place the string beans over the meat and arrange carrot strips and olive halves on the beans.

Cover these vegetables with another third of the meat. Place the chopped spinach in the center of the meat so that it does not come to the edges of the pan and sprinkle with pignoli nuts.

Cover the spinach with the rest of the meat and squeeze the edges together. Dot the top with butter. Cook 1 hour and 15 minutes in a preheated 350° oven. If you wish, pour the can of tomatoes over the meat at the start of the cooking.

Unmold the meat loaf by turning it upside down onto a serving platter.

SERVES 8

Brisket

The brisket is the front part of the breast, which includes the sternum bone and part of the first five ribs. A whole boneless brisket weighs 12 to 13 pounds. Its most common use is as corned beef, that is, pickled meat. Before refrigeration, beef was pickled for preservation by immersion in kegs of brine (salted water). In those days salt contained saltpeter, a preservative, so that the meat kept well and when it was cut, it still had a nice rosy color. Like many butchers, I corned beef in my store in a stone crock; it was a good way to preserve meat I hadn't sold.

Today, meat is preserved by refrigeration, but beef is still often pickled because the taste is popular. The modern pickling process injects brine into the meat by machine, thereby lessening the curing period from several weeks to a few days. Nitrite has replaced saltpeter as the preserving agent.

Corned Beef Boiled Dinner

You can buy corned beef in packages or loose. If it is in a package with seasoned brine, you can use that liquid as the base for cooking.

1 piece corned beef, 6 pounds
1 onion, cut in half, with 2
   cloves stuck into the halves
5 to 6 carrots, peeled and cut into
   large pieces
1 to 2 celery stalks

A few peppercorns
1 bay leaf
1 head of cabbage, cut into
   wedges
6 to 8 medium potatoes, peeled

Place the meat in a large pot with water to cover. Bring the water to a boil and skim off the scum that rises to the surface. Add the onion, 1 carrot, celery, peppercorns, and bay leaf. Simmer for 1 hour and 30 minutes.

Add the cabbage, potatoes, and remaining carrots and cook another 30 minutes. Do not add salt.

Serve the corned beef on a large platter, attractively surrounded by the cooked vegetables.

SERVES 6

Braised Beef with Wine

Fresh brisket is a perfect cut for this dish, as are arm steaks, any of the cuts of the middle chuck, and flanken. Serve with rice, or mashed potatoes and turnips, or noodles.

3 pounds beef, cut into 2-inch cubes
1 large onion, sliced
2 carrots, cut into pieces
2 celery stalks, sliced
1 bay leaf
6 peppercorns, crushed
1 tablespoon chopped parsley

Enough dry red wine to cover the meat, about 2 to 3 cups
Flour
Salt, freshly ground pepper
4 tablespoons rendered suet fat (page 174)
¼ cup oil
2 teaspoons tomato paste

Place the meat in a bowl or enamel pot with the onion, carrots, celery, bay leaf, peppercorns, and parsley. Pour the wine over all and cover the bowl with plastic wrap. Refrigerate overnight.

Remove the meat from the marinade and dry it. Season a few tablespoons of flour with salt and pepper and roll the meat in the flour. Brown the cubes in small batches in the hot suet fat. Put the meat aside.

Discard the fat in the skillet and add the oil. Strain the vegetables (save the wine) and cook them in the hot fat for 5 minutes. Add the meat and cook another 5 minutes. Add the wine, bring to a boil, and lower the heat to simmer. Mix in the tomato paste, partially cover the pan, and cook for 2 hours.

SERVES 4 TO 6

Prime Rib

A prime rib roast is the most flavorful, and most expensive, roast of beef. Always buy the roast from the small end of the rib, that is, the twelfth rib up toward the seventh rib. The very best are the first three ribs of the short end, the twelfth to the tenth. A trimmed two-rib roast will weigh approximately 5 to 7 pounds and serve 4 people. For 6 or 7 people you need a three-rib roast of 6 to 8 pounds.

You can, of course, have the roast boned and rolled in order to make the carving easier, but my preference is always for a standing rib.

To cook a standing rib roast, place it in an open roasting pan, fat side up. Sprinkle salt and pepper over the fat. Fill the bottom of the pan with 2 cups of chopped vegetables (see page 25), a crumbled bay leaf, and a glass of water.

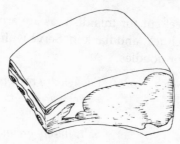

Cook the roast in preheated 350° oven for 15 minutes per pound for rare meat, 18 minutes for medium. A meat thermometer should read 125° for rare, 140° for medium. A boneless rolled rib roast will need a few minutes' more cooking per pound; place on a rack in the roasting pan.

Keep the roast warm while you put the vegetables and pan juices through a food mill. Defat and serve as gravy.

To carve a prime rib, place the roast so that the ribs are resting on the cutting board. Holding the knife perpendicular to the board, slice from either end. You will get two slices without a rib bone, then a third slice with a bone.

Rib Steaks

Rib steaks are usually cut from the seventh to the fifth rib, the large side of the ribs. The short ribs and deckle, an extra piece of meat on top, are removed before the lower three ribs are sliced into rib steaks. When boned out, this is the rib eye roast, also called a Newport roast.

Rib steaks differ from club steaks, which are cut from the eighth rib to the twelfth (the same as the prime rib), in that club steaks are a one-muscle meat while rib steaks are made of several muscles separated by a fine membrane and thin lines of fat. They are, therefore, a flavorful steak.

I have to admit that rib steak is my favorite kind of steak. The prestigious steaks we are used to here in this country—the sirloins, porterhouses, and T-bones—are almost never seen in Europe because their method of meat cutting is completely different from ours. But the rib steak is the same all over France, where it is called entrecote, and in Italy, where it is costata or contracoste. In Florence, rib steak is the meat for the famous Bistecca Fiorentina.

Rib steaks can be sautéed or broiled and served with many sauces. My own favorite is to sauté the steak quickly, then finish it in a marinara sauce.

We will discuss steaks in more detail in the section on the hindquarter.

Plate

The plate is the biggest part of the rib cage, a 20- to 25-pound piece that is the extension of the brisket from the fifth rib to the twelfth rib. The sixth, seventh, and eighth ribs are used for short ribs; the remaining ribs are too fatty. The bottom part of the plate is used to make pastrami, a delicatessen specialty: corned beef seasoned with pepper and other spices, smoked, and steamed.

Short Ribs

Short ribs for the following two recipes can be cut from the plate, the flanken (of the chuck), or the prime ribs. They should be cut into rectangles 2 inches by 3 inches, and most of the fat should be trimmed off before cooking. Serve the ribs with noodles, mashed potatoes, or mashed turnips.

3 pounds short ribs	2 carrots, peeled and chopped
2 tablespoons flour	1 cup wine, red or white
Salt, freshly ground pepper	1 cup beef stock
4 tablespoons oil or rendered suet	½ cup canned plum tomatoes or
fat (page 174)	1 cup fresh, peeled and
2 medium onions, chopped	chopped
2 tablespoons butter	1 tablespoon chopped parsley
2 celery stalks, chopped	

Roll the short ribs in flour seasoned with salt and pepper. Heat the oil or beef fat in a large skillet and brown the ribs on all sides in the hot oil.

Meanwhile, in a flameproof casserole, brown the chopped onions in the butter. When they are wilted, add the celery and carrots. Remove the browned ribs from the skillet and add them to the vegetables. Cook for about 10 minutes.

Add the wine and reduce by half. Add the beef stock and the tomatoes. Lower the heat, cover the casserole, and simmer for about 2 hours. Add the parsley 30 minutes before the end of the cooking.

SERVES 4

Short Ribs of Beef with Vodka and Caraway Seeds

6 pounds short ribs, cut into
   2-inch cubes
½ cup flour
½ teaspoon paprika
Salt, freshly ground pepper
1 cup finely chopped onions
1 cup diced carrots
¾ cup diced celery

1 garlic clove, chopped fine
2 sprigs of parsley
½ teaspoon thyme
1 bay leaf
½ cup vodka
1 tablespoon caraway seeds
2 cups beef broth
2 cups water

Dredge the pieces of beef in a mixture of flour, paprika, salt, and pepper. Arrange the pieces in one layer in the bottom of a roasting pan, meat side down.

Bake the meat in a preheated 450° oven for 30 minutes. Remove the pan from the oven and pour off the fat. Distribute the onions, carrots, celery, and garlic over the meat. Sprinkle the parsley, thyme, and bay leaf over the meat.

Return the pan to the oven and bake another 10 minutes. Remove the pan from the oven and sprinkle the vodka and caraway seeds over the meat. Add the beef broth and water and bring to a boil on top of the stove.

Cover the pan with foil, reduce the oven heat to 350°, and return the pan to the oven for 1 hour more. Remove the foil cover and continue baking for another 15 minutes, basting once or twice.

SERVES 6

Hindquarter

The two hindquarters, the back half of the steer, are each divided into a loin and a round. With the exception of the heel and the hind shin, all hindquarter meat can be oven-roasted. We are working our way from the front of the animal to the back, so let's take the loin first.

The Loin

The loin is the tenderest part of the beef. With the ribs, it is the body of the animal; all the best steaks and roasts come from the loin and the ribs. If you like to barbecue steaks on the grill, or if you serve your guests filet mignon, you buy meat from the loin. Needless to say, it is the most expensive part of the animal.

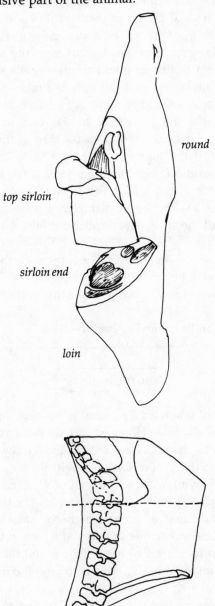

round

top sirloin

sirloin end

loin

The major cuts of the loin are the short hip, short loin, and flank. Just as we found that there are different ways of cutting the chuck in the forequarter, so there are different ways of handling the loin.

One Way

With the bone in, a whole hip is about 25 pounds. "Nature's way," that is, treating the individual pieces of meat as they are arranged in the animal without cutting out any of the bones, gives us steaks.

The first are Delmonico, club steaks, cut from the small end of the loin; they contain practically no fillet and are usually sold boneless. A T-bone steak is a little larger steak cut from the middle of the loin. The fillet on a T-bone steak should be from ¼ to 1 inch in diameter. After the T-bone steaks, the fillet increases in size to 1 to 1¼ inches and becomes a porterhouse steak. Sirloin steaks start at the end of porterhouse steaks, right at the hipbone. After the first slice, the pinbone, sirloin steaks are beautiful, big, flat-bone steaks, the largest steaks of the loin. When cut 1 inch thick, a sirloin steak will weigh at least 3 pounds; the fillet is 1¼ inches in diameter. Farther along, the bone begins to recede and the steaks get smaller until the short sirloin steaks at the end of the loin.

I suggest you avoid the first slice between the porterhouse and sirloin steaks. There is a bone between the upper part of the loin and the tail end with many attached tendons that make this particular steak a poor buy.

All these steaks can be broiled or pan-fried.

Broiling a Steak

It is very important when broiling meat to preheat the broiler at least 15 minutes ahead of time. Home stoves do not have fire bricks in them, which means the metal around the broiler absorbs the heat. If you don't preheat the broiler long enough, the meat will steam instead of broil and you will have a panful of juice and gray meat instead of meat that is juicy and pink inside. For the same reason, you should be sure that when you barbecue steaks on a grill, the coals have had time to become gray—that is, when they are at their hottest, not when they are flaming. I have found that a good way to cook steaks in a small domestic stove is to broil the meat on one side only.

A marinade, even a simple one like citrus or papaya juice, is a good tenderizer for steaks. Many people like to spread mustard or Worces-

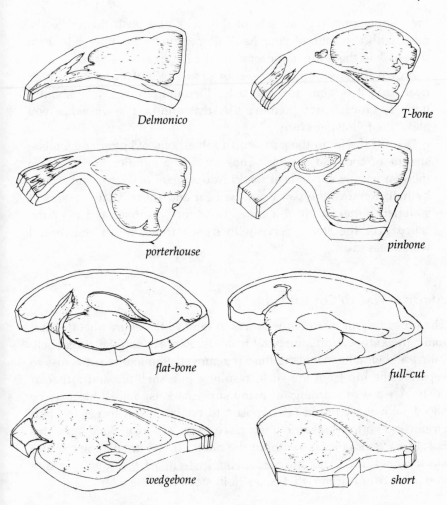

Delmonico

T-bone

porterhouse

pinbone

flat-bone

full-cut

wedgebone

short

tershire sauce on their steaks before cooking. My own preference is to cook one side of the steak, turn it over, and salt the already cooked side. Just before serving, I add a pat of butter and lemon juice.

Steak au Poivre

Steak that has been seasoned with crushed peppercorns makes a lovely dinner. The meat should be cut 1 inch thick, and you should allow about 12 ounces per serving. For a larger number of people, use a full cut of sirloin, for three people a porterhouse, for two a T-bone. For a single portion I suggest a shell steak (top of the loin.)

Crush fresh peppercorns of different types (black and white) with a mortar and pestle or a rolling pin over a paper towel. Place half of the peppercorns on one side of the steak and push them into the meat with the palm of your hand. Repeat with the other side. Rest the steak in the refrigerator for at least 2 hours.

Brown the steak on both sides in some hot butter and oil on high heat until it is done to your taste. Medium-rare will take about 4 minutes on each side. Remove the steak and keep warm while you make the following sauce.

Discard the fat in the pan. Add 1 tablespoon of butter and 2 tablespoons of chopped shallots. Cook for 1 or 2 minutes, then deglaze the pan with ½ cup of beef stock. Add a jigger of cognac and reduce by half. Remove the pan from the heat and stir in 3 tablespoons of softened butter, a bit at a time. Taste for seasoning and pour the sauce over the steak. Serve with french fries and an endive and watercress salad.

ANOTHER WAY TO CUT THE LOIN

The other way of treating the loin is to remove the entire fillet (tenderloin), the kidney, and kidney fat from the loin, leaving the outer shell, called a shell loin. After the fillet is removed, the loin is cut across to separate the hip from the shell, resulting in a shell hip and a regular shell. A word of warning: In many supermarkets, a shell hip may be sliced with the bone in (as opposed to boning it out to get top butt sirloin and bottom butt sirloin meat; see pages 192–194). Sometimes this is sold as "sirloin steaks without the fillet." If you are planning a nice steak dinner, this is not the cut for you. Instead, ask the butcher to slice you a full cut of sirloin, that is, a sirloin steak with the fillet.

Fillet of Beef

When you buy a fillet from the butcher, he will have trimmed off all the natural fat, a thick fat like suet that would give you a panful of grease if cooked with the fillet. The silver skin encasing the fillet must also be removed; it is like a rubber band, impossible to chew.

A perfectly trimmed fillet should be in the shape of a uniform cylinder. This means the butcher will have cut off the chain muscle that runs along the bottom of the fillet as well as the thick muscle attached to the fillet for about 3 inches at the large end. If you buy an untrimmed fillet at the supermarket and trim it yourself, you can use the large muscle at the end of the fillet for thin steaks or for kebabs; the chain muscle is rather fibrous and is best for ground meat.

Roast Fillet of Beef

The butcher will wrap this long, uniform piece of meat in a very thin blanket of fat cut from the flank or round (called cod fat) and tie it in many places with white string. This is called barding. If you are doing it yourself and do not have beef fat, wrap it with strips of bacon or, if you prefer not to have the smoky taste of bacon, with thin slices of fatback. The fat is important to keep the meat from shriveling while cooking.

Cook the fillet for about 1 hour to 1 hour and 15 minutes in a preheated, hot oven, 425°.

A fillet of beef is an elegant, expensive cut that deserves an attractive presentation. The aesthetics of the dish are as important as its taste. I like to serve it on a large platter, surrounded with vegetables that have been boiled until just tender, then quickly sautéed in butter. Green beans, cauliflower pieces, julienned carrots and turnips, potatoes cut into thin sticks, and fresh or frozen peas are all good.

SERVES 10 TO 12

Variation: Beef Wellington

Beef Wellington is an elaborate presentation. The fillet is garnished with truffles and pâté de foie gras (pâté of goose liver) and cooked in puff pastry or phyllo dough. Trim the fillet to a cylindrical shape and lard with 4 strips of salt pork. If you do not have a larding needle, make incisions with a small, sharp knife and poke the salt pork into the cuts. Insert 3 or 4 thinly sliced truffles into the meat at intervals. Tie the fillet lightly so it keeps its shape, season it with salt and pepper, and roast it for 20 minutes in an oiled pan. After it has cooled slightly, spread 6 ounces of pâté on top of the fillet and encase the meat in a sheet of pastry. Return to the oven and cook until the pastry is a nice brown color, about 25 minutes.

Steaks from the Fillet

Filet mignon and chateaubriand are center-cut fillet steaks. Chateau-briand steaks, the largest, are usually 2 inches thick, filet mignons, 1 to 1½ inches. Tournedos are 1½- to 2-inch-thick steaks cut on the bias from the small end of the fillet. If you are using a fillet for steaks, the meat from both ends can be trimmed off and cut into perfectly shaped cubes for kebabs or beef fondue. (This tender meat is perfect for these recipes, but you can also use more reasonably priced meat like top sirloin butt, the triangle and ball of the bottom butt.)

Filet Mignon with Cream Sauce

Stuffed mushrooms are a perfect accompaniment to this elegant dish.

6 fillet steaks, 1½ inches thick
Olive oil
Freshly ground pepper
2 tablespoons oil
4 tablespoons butter

Salt
4 tablespoons chopped shallots
¼ cup cognac or brandy
¼ cup heavy cream

Trim all fat off the steaks and rub with olive oil and pepper. Heat oil and 2 tablespoons of the butter in a large skillet. Cook the steaks in the hot fat for about 5 minutes on each side. Sprinkle the cooked side with salt.

Remove the steaks to a serving platter and keep warm. Discard the fat and add the remaining 2 tablespoons of butter to the pan. Cook the shallots in the butter for about 2 minutes. Add the cognac, reduce briefly, then add the cream and reduce further, scraping up all the bits in the pan into the sauce. Pour the sauce over the steaks and serve immediately.

SERVES 6

Stuffed Mushrooms

12 good-sized mushrooms,
   cleaned in acidulated water
   (page 8)
6 tablespoons melted butter
Salt, freshly ground pepper
3 tablespoons chopped onion
1 tablespoon oil
3 tablespoons finely chopped
   shallots

¼ cup Madeira
3 tablespoons fine bread crumbs
¼ cup grated Parmesan cheese
¼ cup grated Gruyère cheese
½ teaspoon tarragon
2 to 3 tablespoons heavy cream

Separate the mushroom caps from the stems; chop the stems fine. Brush the caps with 3 tablespoons of the melted butter and salt and pepper them lightly.

Sauté the chopped onion in the oil and 2 tablespoons of the butter for 4 to 5 minutes; do not brown. Add the shallots and mushroom stems. Cook for about 5 minutes. Add the Madeira and cook until the wine has evaporated.

Turn the onion mixture into a bowl and add the bread crumbs, Parmesan, Gruyère, tarragon, and cream. Thoroughly mix the stuffing ingredients and fill the mushroom caps, topping them with a bit of Gruyère and a few drops of melted butter.

Place the caps in a shallow, lightly buttered pan and cook for 20 minutes in a preheated 375° oven.

SERVES 6

Tournedos Rossini

Here is a traditional way to serve tournedos that is very rich and very haute cuisine.

4 fillet steaks, 1½ inches thick
4 medium baking potatoes, peeled and cut into balls with the large end of a melon baller
2 tablespoons oil
¼ pound (1 stick) butter
Salt, freshly ground pepper
¼ cup cognac
2 tablespoons port
⅔ cup veal stock
⅓ cup heavy cream or crème fraîche
4 round slices of foie gras, ¼ inch thick
1 black truffle, cut into 4 slices

Remove all the fat from the fillet steaks and tie them to hold them together. (If you are slicing the fillet yourself, tying the piece with string before slicing to the desired thickness will make your job easier.)

Clean the potatoes and scoop out little balls. Cook them for 4 minutes in boiling water, then drain. Heat the oil and 2 tablespoons of the butter in a flameproof casserole and add the potato balls. Brown them a bit, turning them once or twice, then put the casserole in a preheated 350° oven to finish cooking.

Heat 4 tablespoons of the butter in a skillet and brown the steaks on both sides in the hot butter. Season them with salt and pepper after they have cooked on the first side.

Discard the fat from the pan and add the remaining 2 tablespoons of butter. Add the cognac and ignite it. When the flame has died down, remove the steaks and keep them warm on a serving dish.

Add the port, veal stock, and cream to the pan and bring it to a boil. Cook until it has reduced by about half and is smooth.

Place a slice of foie gras and a slice of truffle on each steak. Ladle the sauce over the tournedos and surround them with the potatoes. Serve with endive and watercress salad on the side.

SERVES 4

Carpaccio

Carpaccio is an appetizer of raw beef sliced extremely thin and served with a sauce. Named for a fifteenth-century Venetian painter, it was made famous by Harry's American Bar in Venice. Filet mignon is the best cut for this dish, although if the meat is very good, you could use top round, boneless sirloin, or silver tip. The meat must be without any fat at all. The trick is to have the meat chilled, or slightly frozen, when it is sliced; in order to get it thin enough, it should be sliced on a slicing machine.

6 ounces filet mignon, sliced very thin
1 cup fresh mayonnaise (page 158)
2 tablespoons mustard powder
2 tablespoons cognac

4 drops Worcestershire sauce
6 tablespoons ketchup
4 tablespoons heavy cream
1 tablespoon chopped parsley

Keep the paper-thin slices of filet mignon in the freezer until ready to serve.

Mix the mayonnaise with the mustard, cognac, Worcestershire, ketchup, cream, and parsley and chill until needed.

Roll up each slice and secure with a toothpick. Serve on a platter with the sauce in a bowl in the center.

SERVES 6 TO 8 AS AN APPETIZER

Shell Loin

Now let's go back and see what is left of the loin when the tenderloin and kidney have been removed. The shell loin—that is, the outer shell of the loin—can be separated into two parts, the shell hip and the regular shell.

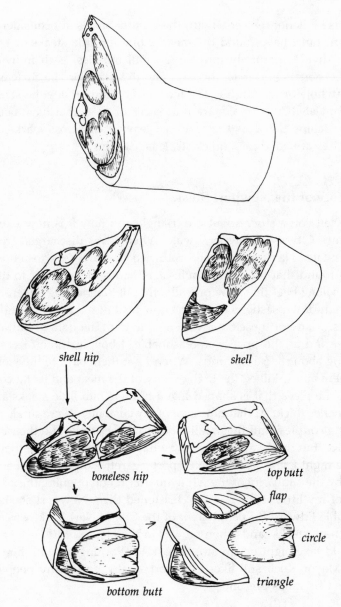

shell hip *shell*

boneless hip *top butt*

flap

circle

bottom butt *triangle*

The shell hip is usually boned out so that we have top butt sirloin and bottom butt sirloin. The top butt, the large muscle of the sirloin steak, can be divided into four boneless sirloin steaks (also called boneless rump steaks), each about 1½ inches thick. If you eat steaks at a restaurant, you may well be served part of one of these steaks, as each one is big enough for three portions.

Because it is not the center cut, the bottom butt is not considered the best part, but I have found the meat is fine for little steaks or London broil. It divides naturally into three small muscles, each individually shaped. There is the circle, the flap, and the triangle. The circle is good broiled whole or for fondue, the flap for London broil, cube steaks, or ground meat. (Cube steaks are thin slices of meat that have been put into a machine that cuts the tendons, leaving crisscross marks on the meat. They are good for a quick steak sandwich.)

The Story of the Newport Steak

Let me tell you a story about the triangle and how it is now known in New York City as a Newport steak. When I was discharged from the United States Navy in 1946 and returned to New York to reopen my store, I found that the meat wholesalers had switched over to the system of selling beef that now prevails, that of "fabricating" beef, that is, selling cut-down sections of the meat instead of forequarters and hindquarters. Many of these cuts were new to me. The bottom butt caught my eye, and as the price was reasonable, I bought three pieces, each weighing about 8 to 10 pounds. When I got them back to the store and took them apart, I liked the high quality of the meat and its fat content. I sliced the piece that is shaped like a triangle into little steaks about 1 to 1¼ inches thick. At that time a lot of my customers were single people or young couples, and they really took to these steaks and their reasonable price, but they wanted to know what to ask for next time they came in. One night I saw an ad for Newport cigarettes on television and was struck by the similarity of the white quarter moon opening the ad to the shape of my little steaks. So we christened them Newport steaks. The Honorable Edward I. Koch, Mayor of the City of New York, was a great fan of these steaks, and when he was in the House of Representatives, he would take eight or ten steaks back to Washington with him every week. Mayor Koch still likes Newport steaks, and many people give them as Christmas presents.

Shell Steaks

The other part of the boned-out loin is the regular shell. When the flank and chine bone are removed, it will yield 10 to 14 shell steaks (the number depends on how thickly they are cut), good for broiling, panbroiling, barbecuing, or steak au poivre. (See pages 186–187 for directions on cooking steaks.) They are sometimes called strip loin steaks and are sold with the bone in or boneless.

Flank Steak

Flank steak is the fibrous muscle located on the inside wall of the beef flank. The meat is tender and juicy. It is good butterflied and stuffed, for London broil or any other recipe calling for meat cut on the bias, and for meat cooked sliced—for example, for beef rolls or Chinese dishes. It weighs 2 to 2½ pounds (hamburgers can be made with the trimmings). In selecting a flank steak, be sure it is short and thick, with some white fat on it. The long, lean flank steaks are generally of poor quality and will be chewy, with not much flavor.

London Broil

Although many people now think London broil is a special cut of meat, it is actually a way of cooking meat. A boneless piece of meat is marinated, broiled, sliced into thin slices on the bias, and usually served with a mushroom sauce. Flank steak has traditionally been the best cut for London broil, but as beef has become more expensive, top round, sirloin tip, bottom round, chuck steak, and arm steak are now commonly used for this recipe. They are not all alike in tenderness or flavor, however, so my recommendation is still for flank steak.

It is important that the meat marinate for at least 2 hours or overnight. Any marinade may be used. I like this one with lemon juice because it tenderizes the meat.

1 flank steak, 2 to 2½ pounds
Paprika
Salt, freshly ground pepper
Juice of 1 lemon
1 garlic clove, chopped fine

1 tablespoon chopped parsley
½ teaspoon thyme or rosemary
* or marjoram (optional)*
Olive oil or other oil

Place the piece of steak in a deep dish and season it with paprika, salt, and pepper. Squeeze the lemon juice over it and sprinkle on the garlic, parsley, and herb of your choice. Wet the meat with the oil, turning it several times. Marinate the steak in the refrigerator for at least 2 hours or overnight. The longer it sits in the marinade, the more flavor it will absorb.

Broil the steak in a preheated broiler, first on one side, then the other, until it is done to your taste. I think it tastes best rare (about 6 minutes for each side).

Place the steak on a cutting board and with a sharp knife, cut thin slices on the bias. Serve plain or with a mushroom sauce.

SERVES 4

Butterflied and Stuffed Flank Steak Sicilian Style

I find flank steak is better for this than top round because the meat stays nice and moist.

1 flank steak, 2 to 2½ pounds
Salt, freshly ground pepper
½ pound veal, ground
½ pound pork, ground
2 eggs
6 slices of pancetta or bacon, cut
   into small pieces
1 tablespoon chopped parsley
3 tablespoons grated pecorino
   romano cheese
¼ pound salami, sliced

¼ pound provolone, sliced
4 hard-boiled eggs, split in half
   lengthwise
2 tablespoons oil
2 tablespoons butter
1 onion, sliced
1 cup dry red wine
1 16-ounce can peeled plum
   tomatoes with the juice
1 pound fresh shelled or frozen
   peas

Lay the flank steak on your workspace and butterfly it (page 13) with the knife running parallel to the fibers. Open it up like the leaves of a book. Flatten with a pounder and season it with salt and pepper.

Mix the ground meats, eggs, pancetta, parsley, and grated cheese together and season with pepper. Spread the meat mixture evenly all over the flank steak. Place the salami slices over the mixture, then the provolone. Place the hard-boiled eggs along the flank steak. Roll the flank up with the fiber of the meat so that you have a long roll.

In a flameproof casserole, heat the oil and butter. Heat the onion and the meat and let brown on all sides. Add the wine, reduce a bit, then add the tomatoes.

Cover the casserole and cook very slowly in a preheated 350° oven for 1 hour and 30 minutes. Add the peas and cook another few minutes until they are done. Serve the steak on a serving platter, covered with some of the sauce.

An alternate way to cook a stuffed flank steak is to wrap it in an extra-large piece of aluminum foil. Make a small hole at one end for the steam to escape. Place it in a roasting pan and cook in a preheated 350° oven for 1 hour. Open the foil and cook for another 10 minutes.

Carve the stuffed steak against the fibers.

SERVES 4

The Round

The round is the leanest part of the beef and has more meat without tendons than any other part of the animal. We usually divide a round

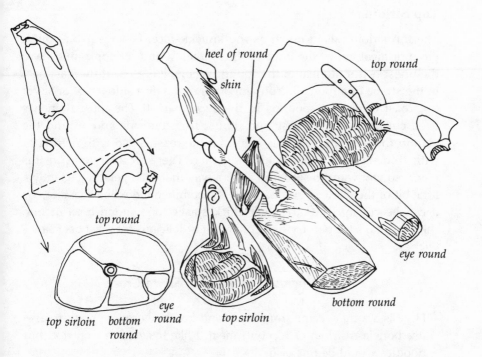

in the same manner as do the Europeans, into five different muscles, the top sirloin (also called sirloin tip or silver tip), top round, eye round, bottom round or rump, and heel of the round. Most dishes that call for sliced boneless beef come from the first four of these muscles. Only two or three slices of the top sirloin and the first few cuts of the top round are suitable for broiling, and I would suggest marinating them before broiling. Much of the meat in the round can be used in similar ways, but there are differences in the texture of the muscles that I will point out as we go along.

When the top sirloin is still attached to the round, the whole piece is called a Chicago round; with the top sirloin cut off, it is a New York round. In some large hotels a Chicago round, all 80 pounds of it, will be cooked whole in a special oven containing a holder for the shank bone. About 4 inches of the skin and meat are frenched off the end of the bone, and the round is inserted in the holder. The meat cooks evenly, and after 7 hours, it is pink all the way through. Cooked, it is a magnificent piece of meat called a steamship roast, resembling an upside-down Christmas tree. It is sliced by carving off thin slices around and around the femur bone in the center.

Top Sirloin

The top sirloin, also known as the knuckle-face, is a 12- to 14-pound piece of meat above the knee of the animal. It and the top round have the finest-textured meat of the round. Whole, it is a beautiful roast beef in the shape of a football. You will often find a nice sirloin tip, or silver tip, roast of about 6 pounds in the supermarket. The top sirloin has been cut in half lengthwise and the fat from the side and around the vein in the leg removed. It is helpful if the roast is tied with netting or with thin slices of fat to hold it together. There are two veins in this piece, so you want to slice it in such a way that each person gets only a little bit of the chewy vein. Barding is recommended when roasting. Or it can be cut into 1½- to 2-inch-thick steaks for London broil or into thinner steaks for pan-frying. Cooked, it is delicious for roast beef sandwiches.

Beef Stroganoff alla Leo in Santa Croce

Here is another recipe from my friend Leo in Florence. You can also use boneless sirloin or top butt meat. I like to serve this on rice, but noodles would be fine also.

1½ pounds boneless silver tip	1 jigger rum
5 tablespoons butter	1 jigger cognac
1 medium onion, chopped	2 tablespoons small dill pickles,
12 pearl onions, cleaned	cut in small pieces
½ pound fresh mushrooms,	1 teaspoon paprika
cleaned in acidulated water,	½ cup heavy cream
(page 8)	Salt, freshly ground pepper

Cut the meat into thin strips like french fries.

Heat 2 tablespoons of the butter in a large frying pan and cook the chopped onion until translucent. In another frying pan, brown the pearl onions in 2 tablespoons of the butter.

If your mushrooms are small button mushrooms, cook them whole; if they are larger, cut them into quarters. Partially sauté the mushrooms in a third pan in the remaining tablespoon of butter.

When the onion in the first pan is translucent, add the meat and brown on all sides. Add the rum and cognac and flame. When the flame has died out and the liquor has reduced a bit, add the pickles, paprika, mushrooms, and pearl onions. Add the cream, season with salt and pepper, lower the heat, and let simmer for 10 minutes.

Serve on a bed of rice pilaf.

SERVES 4

Top Round

The top round is the largest muscle in a leg of beef (18 to 22 pounds when the aitchbone has been removed) and the most versatile. Like the knuckle face, the texture of the meat is fine. When it is split in half lengthwise, you get two lovely roasts. You can cut two or three thick slices from the front of the round for London broil or beef fondue. Top round meat is excellent for minute steaks, cube steaks, beef rolls, pepper steak, and Chinese dishes calling for sliced meat. Lean top round meat is preferred for steak tartare, ground meat eaten raw and served with a selection of capers, raw egg, chopped onions, chopped parsley, salt, and pepper. It is not necessary to have prime steer meat; top cow round is very lean, sweet meat. Cut the meat into cubes just before serving and grind it quickly in a food processor, using on/off pulsing motions to grind the meat cleanly and prevent it from turning to mush.

Beef Scaloppine with Mushrooms

When you feel that veal scaloppine is beyond your budget, try this beef scaloppine. Cut thin slices from first-cut top round (or top sirloin or boneless sirloin) or ask your butcher to cut them for you.

1½ pounds top round, cut into
    thin slices and pounded
Flour
Salt, freshly ground pepper
¼ pound (1 stick) butter
1 garlic clove, crushed
¾ pound fresh mushrooms, sliced

Juice of half a lemon
2 tablespoons oil
½ cup dry white wine
½ cup beef stock
Chopped parsley

Dip the beef slices lightly in flour and season with salt and pepper.

Heat 4 tablespoons of the butter in a pan with the garlic clove. When it begins to sizzle, add the mushrooms, lemon juice, salt, and pepper to taste. Cook for about 8 minutes.

Meanwhile, heat the remaining 4 tablespoons of the butter with the oil in a heavy skillet. When they are hot, brown the meat quickly, first on one side, then the other, a few pieces at a time. Keep the browned cutlets warm until the other pieces are done. Discard the fat and return all the meat to the pan. Add the wine, deglaze the pan, and let the wine reduce a bit. Add the stock, salt, and pepper, and cook for 5 to 10 minutes, until the sauce is the correct consistency for your taste.

Sprinkle with chopped parsley before serving. Serve the mushrooms on the side as a garnish, or, if you wish, add them to the stock with the cutlets.

SERVES 4

Eye of the Round

The eye of the round, a 6-pound muscle attached to the bottom round, is a perfect cylinder. When you look closely at the meat, its texture is that of little circles next to each other. It is good trimmed and netted for roasting, for cube steaks or pepper steak.

Braised Beef Genoise Style

You can also use bottom round, boneless cross rib, or eye of the chuck for this dish. If the meat is lean, lard it by inserting small pieces of salt pork into it with a larding needle or small knife before you tie the roast.

Don't be put off by the fresh pork skins in the ingredient list; they are a flavorful addition. If you cannot find them at specialty markets or prime butcher shops, keep a supply in your freezer after you cook a fresh ham. (Do not use skin from a smoked ham.) Cut the skin off with as much fat as possible still attached to it and freeze. Scrape off the fat after defrosting. Or substitute cubed pancetta or salt pork.

1 piece of eye round, about 3½ pounds	4 ounces fresh pork skins, chopped into small pieces
¼ pound salt pork, cut into thin strips (optional)	1 onion, chopped
Flour	2 celery stalks, chopped
Salt, freshly ground pepper	2 carrots, peeled and chopped
½ ounce dried porcini mushrooms	1 tablespoon chopped parsley
1 tablespoon soft lard	1½ cups dry red wine
1 tablespoon olive oil	4 cups beef stock (page 173)
	1 teaspoon beef extract

Lard the eye round with salt pork if desired. Roll the meat in flour and season with salt and pepper. Soak the dried mushrooms in warm water for about 20 minutes.

Heat the lard and oil in a flameproof casserole. Add the pork skins and chopped onion and cook for several minutes. Add the celery, carrots, and parsley. Squeeze the water out of the mushrooms, chop them coarse, and add them to the casserole. Cook the vegetables together for 4 or 5 minutes.

Add the meat and brown on all sides. Add 1 cup of the wine and let it reduce to a third. Bring the beef stock to a boil in a saucepan. Add the rest of the wine to the casserole, reduce it a little, then add the boiling stock and the beef extract so that the beef is completely covered.

Lower the heat, cover the casserole, and simmer for about 1 hour and 30 minutes to 2 hours. Turn the meat occasionally. You will know that the meat is done when you can put a skewer through it easily.

Keep the meat warm while you defat the juices. Put the vegetables and juices through a food mill and serve over the meat as gravy (page 26).

SERVES 6

Bottom Round

The bottom round, also called the rump or the gooseneck, is a 14-pound piece of meat that needs to be cooked with liquid in recipes like pot roast, beef rolls, beef bourguignon, etc., although it can be used for cube steaks. It is more fibrous than the previous cuts of round; if you look at the meat carefully you will see the fibers running across the meat.

Old-Fashioned Boiled Dinner

I always associate this recipe with the great conductor Arturo Toscanini. When he was conducting the Symphony of the Air in the late 1940s and early 1950s, he liked to eat at Mama Marusi's restaurant on the Upper West Side of Manhattan. He loved boiled beef and especially loved to have the piece of rump that extends down into the sirloin. It was such a favorite with him that I sold every piece of rump I could get to Mama Marusi's. After Maestro Toscanini left New York, Sir John Barbiroli took over the Symphony of the Air, and he, too, loved a boiled beef dinner with rump and sirloin. It is a lovely piece of meat, which will slice like roast beef if not overdone; it is light and digestible.

It is nice to use more than one type of meat for a boiled beef dinner. Veal shanks are especially good because they provide gelatin. Hind shins and short ribs are good choices, as is brisket. You can also add chicken drumsticks and thighs to the beef meats. Serve with mustard, horseradish, or a green vinaigrette sauce with carrots and potatoes on the side.

1 piece of rump, 3 to 4 pounds	1 medium onion, peeled and cut
Salt, freshly ground pepper	in half with 1 clove pushed
2 knucklebones	into each half
2 celery stalks	1 bay leaf
4 carrots, peeled and cut into	4 potatoes, peeled
large pieces	

Season the meat with salt and pepper. Put the bones in a large pot with enough cold water to generously cover the bones. Bring the water to a boil, add the meat, and lower the heat.

Add the celery, carrots, onion, and bay leaf. Cook partially covered for 1 hour and 30 minutes to 2 hours. Half an hour before the meat is done, add the potatoes.

SERVES 4

Sauerbraten

Please notice that the meat should marinate at least 3 days in the refrigerator before cooking. Stewed red cabbage goes nicely with this.

1 piece of bottom round, 4 to 6	A few sprigs of parsley
pounds	Salt, freshly ground pepper
¼ pound salt pork, cut into thin	Flour
strips (optional)	¼ pound kidney suet fat,
½ cup dry red wine	shredded or 4 tablespoons oil
½ cup wine vinegar	4 tablespoons butter
1 cup water	½ cup chopped onion
1 onion, sliced	½ cup chopped celery
1 garlic clove, peeled and crushed	½ cup chopped carrots
2 bay leaves	

If the meat is well marbled with streaks of fat, you do not need to lard it, but if it is very lean, add thin strips of salt pork inside the beef. Place them in a pattern so that not only will you lubricate and flavor the meat, but it will look nice when you slice it.

Prepare a marinade with the red wine, vinegar, water, sliced onion, garlic, bay leaves, and parsley. Place the meat and the marinade in a clay crock, enamel pot, or deep Pyrex dish in the refrigerator for at least 3 days. Turn the meat once a day or more often.

Remove the meat from the marinade and pat dry with paper towels. Strain the marinade and reserve. Sprinkle the meat with salt and pepper and rub some flour on it.

Heat the beef fat in a heavy skillet and brown the meat. Meanwhile, heat the butter in a flameproof casserole and sauté the chopped onion, celery, and carrots in it. When the roast is completely browned, transfer it to the casserole with a cup of the strained marinade. Lower the heat, cover the casserole, and cook slowly for 2 hours. Keep adding the strained marinade throughout the cooking until you have used all the liquid.

SERVES 4

Braciole alla Bolognese

Bottom round is especially suitable for any kind of beef roll because it is a nice rectangular cut of meat that will give uniform slices about 4 by 6 inches. Beef rolls need to cook a long time, another reason top or bottom round is a good choice.

8 thin slices of bottom or top
   round
Salt, freshly ground pepper
½ pound shoulder of pork,
   chopped
½ pound veal, chopped
¼ teaspoon grated lemon zest
1 egg
½ cup stale bread, soaked in milk
   and squeezed
2 tablespoons grated pecorino
   romano cheese
2 tablespoons pignoli nuts
   (optional)

Flour
2 tablespoons butter
2 tablespoons olive oil
1 garlic clove, peeled and crushed
1 onion, chopped fine
2 celery stalks, chopped into
   small pieces
1 glass of good red wine, about ½
   cup
1 cup beef stock
2 fresh tomatoes, peeled, seeded,
   and chopped
1 bay leaf

Place the beef slices on your workspace and season with salt and pepper. Mix the pork, veal, lemon zest, egg, bread, cheese, pignoli nuts, salt, and pepper until the mixture adheres to itself. Spread about 1 tablespoon of the stuffing on each slice of beef. Tie the rolls in several places so that the stuffing will not come out. Roll the meat in flour.

In a large skillet, heat the butter and oil; when they are hot, brown the beef rolls a few at a time. Remove the meat from the pan and keep warm.

Add the garlic to the pan, and after it has cooked a little, add the chopped onion. Cook for a few minutes, until the onion becomes limp, then add the celery and cook another 5 minutes.

Return the meat to the pan and add the wine. Let it reduce by half. Add the beef stock, tomatoes, and bay leaf. Lower the heat to simmer, cover the pan, and cook slowly for 1 hour and 30 minutes. Taste for seasoning and serve on a bed of noodles or rice.

SERVES 4

Variation:

German-style rolladen are seasoned a little differently. Cover each beef slice with a coarsely chopped slice of bacon, 1 teaspoon of Dijon mustard, 1 tablespoon of chopped onions, and a slice of dill pickle. Brown the rolls in 4 tablespoons of beef suet or Crisco. After the beef is browned, sauté 2 coarsely chopped celery stalks, 1 finely chopped leek, 1 finely chopped onion, and 1 tablespoon of chopped parsley in the hot fat. Return the rolls to the pan, cover with 2 cups of beef stock, and cook as above. Strain the juices and serve over the rolladen.

Hind Shin and Shinbones

The heel and the shin are the toughest part of the round, good only for soups and stews or for ground meat. The shinbones are a source of marrow, the soft, fatty substance found in bone cavities that some chefs use as a condiment. To get marrow, ask the butcher to saw off the top of the bone on the femur side into a 3- to 4-inch piece, then crack the bone with the back of a cleaver. There will be a core of marrow in the bone ½ to ¾ inch in diameter.

Hungarian Goulash

Meat from the hind shin is the best choice for the Hungarian stew, goulash. The thin sinews become very tasty, juicy, and gelatinous when properly cooked, and the meat is not as expensive as round, cross rib, or brisket.

2 pounds shin of beef, boneless,
  cut into 2-inch cubes
Flour
Salt, freshly ground pepper
4 tablespoons butter
2 tablespoons oil
1 garlic clove, crushed
1 onion, chopped

½ teaspoon paprika
2 bay leaves
1 tablespoon chopped parsley
3 ripe tomatoes or 1 16-ounce
  can plum tomatoes, peeled,
  seeded, and chopped
1 cup beef stock or bouillon

Roll the beef cubes in flour and season with salt and pepper. Heat 2 tablespoons of the butter and the oil in a skillet or flameproof casserole. Add the garlic and let it brown a bit. Brown the meat on all sides in the hot fat in several batches so that you do not crowd the meat in the pan. Remove the last batch of meat from the pan and add the chopped onion. Cook the onion until it wilts.

Discard any extra fat and add the remaining 2 tablespoons of butter. Return the meat to the pan and cook for about 10 minutes, stirring constantly. Add the paprika, bay leaves, parsley, tomatoes, and stock.

Cover the pan and simmer for 3 hours. Serve with egg noodles.

SERVES 4

Oxtails

Only tails of pigs and beef are used for eating. Although a recipe calling for oxtail may not sound like filet mignon, there is something to the old saying, "The nearer the bone, the sweeter the meat." When buying oxtails, be sure to get the tail of a steer. Chunky pieces are meatier than long, thin ones; the fat should be white, not orange.

Oxtail Soup

4 to 5 pounds steer oxtails, cut at
  the joint
¼ cup olive oil
2 cups coarsely chopped onions,
  carrots, and celery
2 bay leaves

12 peppercorns, crushed
½ teaspoon marjoram
Salt, freshly ground pepper
1 cup white wine
1 pound egg noodles or 1 cup
  raw rice or barley

Place the oxtails in a fairly deep-sided roasting pan. Sprinkle with the oil, vegetables, bay leaves, peppercorns, marjoram, salt, pepper, and wine. Roast in a preheated 400° oven for 1 hour, stirring at intervals. The meat should be well browned.

Place meat, vegetables, seasonings, etc., in a tall stockpot and cover with warm water. Bring to a boil, lower the heat to simmer, and cook until the meat comes off the bones easily, probably about 3 hours.

Remove the meat and cut it off the bones. Strain the broth. Bring the broth to a boil and add noodles, rice, or barley, and/or mixed vegetables. Cook until tender. A few minutes before serving, return the meat to the soup.

SERVES 4 TO 6

Oxtails in a Casserole

When you go to the trouble of making a stew or a casserole, dishes that improve in flavor the day after they are made, be sure to make enough for several meals.

4 to 6 pounds steer oxtails, cut
   into sections
¼ cup oil
2 cups coarsely chopped onions,
   carrots, and celery
2 garlic cloves, peeled and
   crushed
A few sprigs of parsley
2 bay leaves

½ teaspoon rosemary
Salt, freshly ground pepper
1 cup dry red wine
2 cups tomatoes, peeled, seeded,
   and chopped
1 quart beef stock
16 small red potatoes
6 carrots, peeled and cut into
   large pieces

Place the oxtails in a fairly deep-sided roasting pan. Sprinkle them with the oil, chopped onions, carrots, celery, garlic, parsley, bay leaves, rosemary, salt, and pepper. Roast in a preheated 400° oven for 1 hour, stirring at intervals. The meat should be well browned.

Add the wine and cook for 5 minutes. Add the tomatoes and the beef stock and cover the pan with a sheet of aluminum foil. Lower the heat to 350° and cook for 1 hour and 30 minutes.

Remove the meat from the pan and pass all the juices and vegetables through a food mill. Return the meat and strained juices to the pan and add the potatoes and carrots. Cook until the vegetables are done, about 20 minutes. Adjust the seasoning if necessary and serve.

SERVES 4 TO 6

VARIETY MEATS

❧

AMERICANS DO NOT SHARE the European tradition of eating the heads, tails, and organs of animals. When western-raised beef plummeted meat prices in the late 1800s, we became a nation of muscle-meat eaters and could afford to throw out the innards and other exotica. It is a pity, because there are many delicious recipes for what we now call variety meats.

When I was a boy, ten cents would get you a lamb "pluck," that is, the liver, lungs, and heart of lamb; a calf pluck was twenty-five cents. No one ate kidneys in the thirties. I gave them to my customers for their pets.

It is only in the last forty or fifty years that we have begun to appreciate the value of liver and other organs. Calf liver became popular after the Byrd expedition to the South Pole because scientists found liver to be a good source of protein and iron. The price of calf liver shot up to about a dollar a pound in the middle twenties; now calf liver and veal kidneys have become luxury items in fancy restaurants and you must search them out at specialty butcher shops or supermarkets.

I hope you will let a sense of adventure tempt you into trying some of these little-appreciated delicacies.

Baby Lamb Head (Capuzella)

People may raise their eyebrows at the idea of eating a lamb's head, but like a calf's head, it is a popular appetizer or antipasto in French and northern Italian restaurants. Pig's head is edible also (see the recipe for Head Cheese, pages 249–250, in the Sausage chapter).

Roast Baby Lamb Head

Don't be aesthetically put off by this recipe. I promise you that it is as delicious as any rack of lamb. This is not knife-and-fork food; you have to break the heads apart as you do lobster shells and find the tender meat on the bones. The brain and tongue are easy to get at. Ask the butcher to split the heads in half from the nose to the neck with his saw.

2 hothouse baby lamb heads, split
   in half
2 garlic cloves, peeled and
   chopped very fine
2 teaspoons oregano
A small pinch of hot red pepper
   flakes

1 tablespoon chopped parsley
Salt, freshly ground pepper
½ cup bread crumbs
⅓ cup olive oil

Rinse the heads and pat dry. Lay all four pieces in a lightly oiled baking pan, cut side up. Sprinkle the garlic, oregano, red pepper flakes, parsley, salt, pepper, and bread crumbs over them and wet with the olive oil. Pour 1 cup of water into the bottom of the pan. Bake for 1 hour in a preheated 375° oven, basting now and then with the juices.

Serve with finger bowls.

SERVES 4

Calf Head

In Europe, you can buy half or a quarter of a head, but here calf heads are usually sold whole. When you buy the head, it will have been scalded, the hair removed, and completely cleaned. The head is not hard to bone out, but be sure to ask the butcher to saw it in half from the nose to the tongue. The tongue should be left intact.

TO BONE OUT A HEAD

Pull out the brains and reserve for other recipes (pages 211–212). Starting from the cut side, cut between the bones and the skin to separate the bones. As you cut and scrape, leave any meat with the skin. Keep the ears with the skin. Continue on both sides until you have removed all the bones, including those of the lower jaw. Remove the tongue, which is attached to the rear part of the neck, and cook as directed on pages 212–214 or in the recipe below for Calf Head in Aspic. The bones can be cooked with the head for enhanced flavor.

Calf Head Vinaigrette

1 calf head, boned

Bones from tongue and head, if available

Salt

Juice of 1 lemon

2 celery stalks, cut into large pieces

2 carrots, peeled and cut into large pieces

1 onion, halved, with 3 cloves stuck into the halves

A few peppercorns

2 bay leaves

1 cup virgin olive oil

2 tablespoons Dijon mustard

½ cup balsamic vinegar

½ cup chopped parsley

2 hard-boiled egg yolks, mashed

2 tablespoons capers, chopped

Rinse the boned head and roll it like a salami. Tie it in several places.

Put the calf head and the bones in a large pot and cover it with cold water so that there is at least 2 inches of water over the head. Add a small amount of salt, bring the water to a boil, reduce the heat, and skim off the scum that rises to the surface. Cook for 15 minutes.

Remove the head from the pot and rinse it under cold water. Rub it all over with lemon juice.

Return the head to the pot with the vegetables, peppercorns, bay leaves, and cold water to cover. Bring to a boil, reduce the heat, and simmer for 1 hour and 30 minutes to 2 hours. You do not want it to get too soft. If you can stick a fork into it, but not too easily, it is done.

Slice and serve hot with a vinaigrette sauce made by combining olive oil, mustard, vinegar, parsley, egg yolks, and capers. Or wrap it in a wet towel to prevent it from turning dark and serve cold with a vinaigrette sauce or in aspic, as below.

SERVES 12 AS AN APPETIZER

Variation: Calf Head in Aspic

Scald the tongue in boiling water for 5 minutes; when it is cool enough to handle, remove the skin. Place the bones and tongue in the pot with the head, vegetables, and seasonings, and cook according to directions above.

Remove the head and tongue from the liquid and shock them under cold water. Wrap in a wet towel and refrigerate overnight. Simmer the broth for another few hours, cool it to room temperature, and keep it in the refrigerator overnight.

The next day, remove any fat from the top of the broth. Mix 1 cup of the broth with 1 egg white and the eggshell, crushed; 1 cup of coarsely chopped carrots, onions, and celery; and ½ pound of lean beef. Whisk together. Pour the rest of the stock into a pot and mix the thickened broth with it. Bring the stock to a light boil and simmer for 30 minutes. The vegetable and meat mixture will slowly rise to the top, forming a crust covering the stock like a blanket. Carefully clear a space in the middle of the crust so that you can see the clarified stock beneath. Gently ladle the stock out and put it through a linen cloth to remove any further impurities. To see if the stock is strong enough for a good aspic, put a spoonful into the refrigerator. If it firmly gels within a few minutes, it is fine. If it is not strong enough, add a small envelope of unflavored gelatin.

Slice the tongue and head; layer them in a terrine with decorative vegetables of your choice on top of ½ inch of gelatin. (Let it firm in the refrigerator before you add the meat.) Continue to layer the meat and vegetables, surrounding them with ½ to ¼ inch of gelatin on the sides of the mold. Top with more gelatin (about ½ inch) and refrigerate. To serve, unmold upside down and slice.

Cut into slices, this is a lovely appetizer for a summer buffet, or it is nice cut into small pieces and served on crackers. It will keep 3 to 4 days in the refrigerator.

Brains

There is very little difference in taste between brains of pork, lamb, veal, and beef. All may be cooked in the same manner and need to be soaked and blanched before the final cooking. Handle brains gently so they do not mash. They are more attractive to eat if they are cut into cubes and presented as a firm meat.

Soak brains in cold water with a little salt for 10 to 15 minutes. Beef brains should soak for 1 to 2 hours. Remove any membranes with blood.

Blanch the brains in lightly salted boiling water with ½ tablespoon of lemon juice, a small onion, and a bay leaf, for about 15 minutes. Remove the brains from the liquid, shock in cold water, and remove any remaining membrane. Wrap in plastic wrap and keep in the refrigerator for up to 4 days or in the freezer until ready to use.

Veal Brains Oreganati

Veal brains are a delicate mass usually weighing about ¾ pound. If you are serving hearty eaters, double the recipe.

2 veal brains, blanched and
   shocked
1 teaspoon oregano
1 teaspoon finely chopped parsley
2 garlic cloves, peeled and
   chopped

½ cup bread crumbs
Salt, freshly ground pepper
1½ to 2 tablespoons butter
1 tablespoon olive oil

Cut the brains into 1-inch cubes and put them in a flameproof gratin dish. Sprinkle with the oregano, parsley, garlic, bread crumbs, salt, and pepper. Dot with the butter and oil.

Cook in a preheated 350° oven for 20 minutes, then run under the broiler until the bread crumbs are brown, about 5 minutes.

Serve immediately with sautéed spinach or a green salad.

SERVES 4

Brains Cooked in Batter

2 veal brains, blanched and
    shocked
Salt, freshly ground pepper
Flour

1 egg, lightly beaten
Vegetable oil for frying
Lemon wedges

Cut the brains into 1- or 2-inch cubes. Season them with salt and pepper and roll them in flour. Shake off any excess flour and dip into the beaten egg.

Fry the brains in hot oil until they are golden brown on all sides. Remove them from the oil and pat off any extra fat on paper towels.

Serve with lemon wedges and a salad made with strong-tasting lettuce like arugula.

SERVES 4

Brains Provençal

2 veal brains, blanched and
    shocked
Oil
Salt, freshly ground pepper
2 tablespoons chopped capers

24 pitted Gaeta olives
2 tablespoons pignoli nuts
4 tablespoons bread crumbs
2 tablespoons butter

Cut the brains into 1- or 2-inch cubes. Lightly oil a baking dish and arrange the brains in the dish. Season them with salt and pepper and sprinkle with the capers, olives, pignoli nuts, and bread crumbs. Dot with small pieces of butter.

Bake in a preheated 400° oven for 10 minutes.

SERVES 4

Tongue

Unlike most of the organs, which are soft and cook quickly, tongues and hearts are muscles and need longer cooking. Beef tongues are available fresh, pickled, smoked, or cooked and ready to eat. Unless they are fully cooked and ready to eat, they must be boiled and skinned before serving. Pork, lamb, and veal tongues are available fresh and fully cooked.

You will often find smoked beef tongue in the supermarket. Cook it for 2 hours in salted, boiling water. Let it cool, remove the skin, and slice as a cold cut.

Fresh beef tongue can be treated like veal tongue. Place it in a large pot filled with water, a carrot, an onion, and a celery stalk (all cut into large pieces), a bay leaf, and salt. Bring to a boil, lower the heat, and simmer for about 1 hour and 30 minutes to 2 hours. There are two little bones in the back of a tongue. When they pull out easily, the tongue is done. Remove the skin. A beef tongue will serve six, a veal tongue two.

The tongue may be served at this point with a green vinaigrette sauce, hot or cold, or with one of the following sauces.

Spicy Sauce for Boiled Tongue

This delicious sauce is also good served on other boiled items like boiled beef, pig's feet, and calf head.

5 tablespoons oil
6 anchovy fillets, chopped
1 tablespoon chopped parsley
2 green peppers, roasted, peeled, seeded, and chopped
1 tablespoon capers, chopped
A few basil leaves
1 cup chopped celery, the tender white part of the stalks

3 plum tomatoes, peeled, seeded, and chopped
3 slices of bread, crusts removed
Vinegar
1 boiled beef tongue or 3 veal tongues, cooked as directed above

Put 4 tablespoons of the oil in a small saucepan. Add the anchovies, parsley, green peppers, capers, basil, celery, and tomatoes. Cook gently for 15 minutes. Remove the pan from the heat and let the sauce cool a bit. Soak the slices of bread in vinegar, squeeze them out, and shred into the pan with the remaining tablespoon of oil. Stir the sauce and spoon it over the tongue slices.

SERVES 6

Braised Tongue

2 large red onions, sliced
2 celery stalks, chopped
1 carrot, chopped
2 garlic cloves, peeled and crushed
2 tablespoons butter
2 tablespoons olive oil

2 fresh tomatoes, peeled, seeded, and chopped
Salt, freshly ground pepper
1 boiled tongue, cooked as directed above, with 1 cup of liquid reserved

In a flameproof casserole, sauté the onions, celery, carrot, and garlic in the butter and oil. After they have cooked for about 10 minutes, add the tomatoes, season with salt and pepper, and cook for another 5 to 10 minutes.

After you have boiled the tongue, shock it under cold water, skin it, and add it to the casserole. Add about ½ to 1 cup of the liquid in which the tongue cooked, season with salt and pepper, and simmer for about 20 minutes. Remove the tongue, slice it, and serve with the sauce.

SERVES 6

Variation: Braised Tongue with Sweet and Sour Sauce

Add the following mixture to the tomatoes and onions just before you add the tongue: Dissolve 3 tablespoons of unsweetened cocoa in ½ cup of balsamic vinegar. Mix in 3 tablespoons of sugar, 1 tablespoon of pignoli nuts, ⅓ cup of raisins, and 2 tablespoons of candied citron cut into small pieces.

Sweetbreads

Sweetbreads, the thymus gland of animals, are a light, delicate meat that is firmer in texture than brains. The sweetbreads of veal are the best. Beef sweetbreads are rather fatty and coarse, but if well prepared, they will taste almost the same as veal. No one bothers with pork sweetbreads. When you buy a pair of sweetbreads, you will find that one is a nice smooth shape while the other half is a bit coarser. Sweetbreads vary from 1 to 1½ pounds a pair, depending on the size of the calf. Pairs may be cut and sold separately by weight.

Sweetbreads must be soaked and blanched before using. Soak them in cold water with a little salt for about 1 hour. Parboil them in lightly salted boiling water with 1 small onion, a quarter of a lemon, and a few

sprigs of parsley for 15 minutes. Shock them under cold water and remove any membrane (there is no blood on sweetbreads, unlike brains). Wrap in plastic wrap and place them between two dishes. This flattens the sweetbreads and squeezes out the water. They will keep in the refrigerator for a few days or in the freezer. (Unlike brains, which must be blanched before freezing, sweetbreads can be frozen fresh or blanched.)

Sweetbreads Fiorentina

1½ pounds veal sweetbreads
1 pound fresh spinach or 1 10-
    ounce package frozen spinach
1 onion, chopped
2 garlic cloves, peeled and
    chopped
5 tablespoons butter
3 tablespoons olive oil
¼ cup Marsala or dry sherry

1 tablespoon tomato paste
1 tablespoon water
Salt, freshly ground pepper
½ pound fresh mushrooms,
    cleaned in acidulated water,
    (page 8)
2 tablespoons chopped parsley
¼ cup heavy cream

Soak and parboil the sweetbreads. Wash the spinach and blanch it quickly in a very small amount of water. Shock under cold water, squeeze out some of the water, and chop coarse. If using frozen spinach, cook as directed.

Sauté the onion and 1 garlic clove in 2 tablespoons of the butter and 2 tablespoons of the oil in a large skillet for 3 or 4 minutes. Cut the sweetbreads into 1-inch squares and add to the pan. Cook for 10 minutes. Add the wine and reduce it for a few minutes. Dilute the tomato paste with the water and add it to the pan. Season with salt and pepper and simmer for 10 minutes.

If the mushrooms are the small button type, leave them whole. If they are larger, cut them into quarters. Sauté the mushrooms in 2 tablespoons of the butter. As soon as most of the liquid has evaporated, add them to the sweetbreads. Sprinkle parsley over the pan and cook another few minutes.

Quickly sauté the spinach and the last garlic clove in the remaining tablespoon of olive oil.

Remove the sweetbreads from the heat and stir in the remaining tablespoon of butter and the cream. Place the spinach on a serving dish and pour the sweetbreads over it.

SERVES 4

Veal Sweetbreads with Mushrooms

2 pounds veal sweetbreads
¼ pound (1 stick) butter
1 small onion, sliced
Salt, freshly ground pepper
½ cup dry sherry

1 garlic clove, peeled and crushed
1 pound fresh mushrooms,
   cleaned in acidulated water
   (page 8) and sliced
1 tablespoon fresh parsley

Soak and parboil the sweetbreads. Melt 4 tablespoons of the butter in a skillet and add the sliced onion. While it is cooking, slice the sweetbreads.

Add the sweetbreads to the pan, with salt and pepper to taste. Stir and cook for about 5 minutes. Add the sherry and cook for 2 or 3 minutes before stirring. If you think there is not enough liquid, add a little water.

Melt the remaining 4 tablespoons of butter in another skillet and add the garlic clove. When it has browned a bit, remove it, and add the mushrooms, parsley, salt, and pepper. Cook until some of the water that comes out of the mushrooms has evaporated.

Add the mushrooms to the sweetbreads, mix well, and cook for 5 more minutes.

SERVES 6

Sweetbreads Parmigiana

1½ pounds veal sweetbreads
Flour
1 egg, lightly beaten
1 cup bread crumbs

Vegetable oil for frying
4 tablespoons grated Parmesan
   cheese
¾ cup Tomato Sauce (see below)
4 slices of fontina cheese

Soak and parboil the sweetbreads. Cut them in half across to get 4 slices. Dip the slices in flour, then in the egg, then in bread crumbs. Press the bread crumbs onto the slices.

Fry the slices in hot vegetable oil until they are golden brown on all sides. Pat off any extra fat with paper towels.

Lay the slices in 4 individual baking dishes or a single dish that can hold all the slices in one layer. Sprinkle them with Parmesan cheese. Spoon tomato sauce over the cheese and top with a slice of fontina cheese to cover each slice completely.

Bake 15 minutes in a preheated 350° oven.

SERVES 4

Tomato Sauce

Unlike marinara sauce, this is a long-simmering sauce. It can be kept in the freezer until needed.

*1 garlic clove, peeled and finely
   chopped*
2 tablespoons olive oil
1 onion, minced

*1 16-ounce can ground tomatoes,
   with juice*
A pinch of hot red pepper flakes
Salt, freshly ground pepper

Sauté the garlic in the hot oil for 1 or 2 minutes. Add the onion and cook until it is translucent. Add the tomatoes, red pepper flakes, salt, and pepper. Cover and cook very slowly for 1 hour.

If you cannot buy ground tomatoes, buy peeled plum tomatoes and put them through a food mill.

YIELD: ABOUT 10 OUNCES

Heart

Like tongue, the heart is a muscle, not an organ, and requires longer cooking than the softer organ meats. Veal, pork, and lamb hearts are usually sliced thin and sautéed or cubed for stews. Beef hearts are much larger than those of the other animals; a stuffed and roasted beef heart will feed 4 people. Hearts should be completely trimmed of all outside fat before cooking.

Sautéed Veal Heart

Veal hearts are very tender but come in different sizes, so buy them by weight rather than by the number of hearts.

*1 pound fresh veal heart, cut into
   ½-inch slices*
1 tablespoon olive oil
1 teaspoon lemon juice
A pinch of marjoram or oregano
*A few drops of Worcestershire
   sauce*

Salt, freshly ground pepper
2 tablespoons butter
2 tablespoons oil
¼ cup sherry
Water or stock as needed
Chopped parsley

Place the heart slices in a dish with the olive oil, lemon juice, marjoram or oregano, Worcestershire sauce, salt, and pepper. Marinate for at least 1 hour.

Heat the butter and oil in a frying pan, and when hot, put in the heart slices. Cook on fairly high heat, turning often, for about 10 minutes.

Add the sherry, lower the heat, and cook for 5 minutes more. Sprinkle with chopped parsley and serve. You must be careful to cook the heart slices briefly; if they cook too long they will be like rubber.

SERVES 2 TO 3

Baked Stuffed Heart

1 whole beef heart
Salt, freshly ground pepper
4 tablespoons butter
6 slices of bacon, 2 of them
　chopped
1 small onion or 3 shallots,
　chopped
2 ounces cooked ham, chopped
　(see Note below)
6 mushrooms, chopped

2 slices of firm or stale bread,
　soaked in milk, squeezed, and
　shredded
1 egg, lightly beaten
1 tablespoon chopped parsley
1 cup beef stock or bouillon
2 cups coarsely chopped onions,
　carrots, and celery for gravy
　(pages 26–27)

Trim the heart of all the excess fat around the large side and remove the tubes attached there. With a boning knife, cut into the heart to make a pocket. Lightly sprinkle the heart with salt and pepper.

Prepare the stuffing: Heat 2 tablespoons of the butter in a skillet and sauté the 2 chopped bacon slices in it. When the bacon is brown, add the onion or shallots and the ham and cook for 2 or 3 minutes. Turn the bacon and onion into a bowl.

Sauté the mushrooms in the remaining 2 tablespoons of butter and add them to the bowl. Add the bread, egg, parsley, salt, and pepper. Mix well and spoon the stuffing into the heart.

Seal the heart with several skewers. Wrap the remaining bacon slices around the heart and hold them firm with twine.

Place the heart in a shallow roasting pan with some of the beef stock and the vegetables for gravy. Cook for 1 hour and 30 minutes in a preheated 350° oven, basting now and then with more beef stock. Put the juices and vegetables through a food mill and defat.

Note: You can substitute ½ pound of ground meat or sausage for the ham.

SERVES 4

Grilled Beef Heart

Cut the heart into ½-inch slices and marinate for a few hours before cooking. I like a simple marinade of 4 tablespoons of lemon juice, a finely chopped garlic clove, ½ teaspoon of Worcestershire sauce, chopped parsley, 2 tablespoons of olive oil, salt, and pepper.

Do not wipe the marinade off the heart slices. Place the slices on an oiled cookie sheet and preheat the broiler for at least 10 minutes before cooking. Cook the slices for about 10 minutes, 5 minutes on each side. (It is hard to be exact, as broilers differ in intensity.) Brush the marinade on the slices after you turn them over. Do not overcook or they will toughen.

SERVES 4

Liver

Liver is the organ with the highest quantity of iron and protein. The most delicate in taste is calf liver, followed by the liver from lamb, beef, and pork. Although beef liver is not as tender as calf liver, it will improve if you soak it in milk for an hour before cooking. Pork liver is shaped like a leaf with three lobes; it is often used to make pâtés.

Remove the thin membrane covering the liver and the tendon just in the center of the liver. If there are green spots on chicken livers, cut them out; bile has rested on these places and will make them bitter.

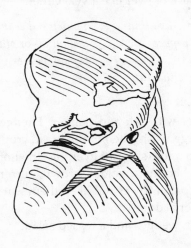

Calf Liver Veneziana

2 tablespoons butter
2 tablespoons oil
1 garlic clove, crushed
2 onions, sliced thin
1½ pounds calf liver, cut into
   thin julienne strips

Salt, freshly ground pepper
1 tablespoon chopped parsley
¼ cup balsamic vinegar

Heat the oil and butter in a skillet and add the garlic. When the garlic begins to sizzle, add the onions and cook them about 10 minutes. Do not let them burn.

Add the liver pieces, raise the heat, and toss the liver and onions together. Cook on this high heat for about 3 minutes. Season with salt, pepper, and the parsley. Add the vinegar, lower the heat, cover the pan, and simmer for 2 minutes. Serve immediately.

SERVES 4

Calf Liver Milanese

This is treating a slice of liver like a veal cutlet.

1½ pounds calf liver, sliced thin
Salt, freshly ground pepper
Flour
1 egg, lightly beaten with a little
   milk

1 cup bread crumbs
Peanut oil or other oil for frying
Lemon wedges

Sprinkle the liver with salt and pepper. Dredge the liver slices in flour, then in the egg wash, then in the bread crumbs.

Heat the oil. Slip a few slices of liver into the hot oil and cook until the bread crumbs become a golden brown, turning once. Place the cooked slices on a paper towel and keep them warm. Continue cooking until all the liver is done.

Serve with lemon wedges and a tossed salad.

SERVES 4

Chicken Livers or Pork Liver en Brochette

To cook pork liver on skewers, cut the liver into 1-inch squares and marinate. Wrap each piece in a piece of pork caul fat and alternate on the skewers with pieces of bread, pieces of thick bacon, and a bay leaf. Brush all the ingredients with melted butter before cooking.

1 pound fresh chicken livers or
  pork liver
Juice of 1 lemon

Salt, freshly ground pepper
½ pound sliced bacon
Sage leaves

Rinse livers and pat them dry with a paper towel. Cut them in half if they are large. Marinate the livers in the lemon juice, salt, and pepper for at least 1 hour. Cut the bacon strips in half, and wrap a piece of bacon around each chicken liver. Place on 6 skewers with sage leaves between each piece.

Rest the skewers on the sides of a roasting pan and place under a preheated broiler. Cook until the bacon is almost crisp, turning several times.

Serve as an appetizer or with sautéed mushrooms and rice pilaf.

SERVES 4

Risotto with Chicken Livers and Dried Mushrooms

Risotto is a delicate preparation. It requires constant stirring; if it is overcooked even by a few minutes, it is ruined. I suggest you read the Risotto recipe on page 163.

¼ ounce dried porcini
  mushrooms
2 cups chicken stock
6 tablespoons butter
1 medium onion, chopped fine
1 cup raw short-grain Italian rice

¼ cup dry sherry or *Marsala*
1 small pinch saffron threads
  (optional, see Note)
½ pound fresh chicken livers
Grated Parmesan cheese

Soak the mushrooms in warm water for 20 minutes.

Heat the stock to boiling. Meanwhile, heat 2 tablespoons of the butter in a flameproof casserole and add the chopped onion. Cook until the onion is just wilted. Add the rice, and stir to coat the rice with the butter. When the rice has absorbed all the fat, add the sherry. Cook a few minutes, until the wine evaporates. Ladle in some of the boiling stock, a little at a time, stirring between each addition and letting the rice absorb the liquid before you add more. Add the saffron and continue stirring.

In a separate pan, brown the chicken livers in 2 tablespoons of the butter for 3 to 4 minutes. Remove them from the pan, cut them into small pieces, and add them to the rice.

Squeeze out the mushrooms, cut them up, and add them to the rice. Continue adding stock to the rice, stirring constantly, until the rice is al dente. Taste for seasoning. The rice is usually salty enough to not need any further salt.

Remove from the heat and stir in the remaining 2 tablespoons of butter and a few handfuls of freshly grated Parmesan cheese. Sprinkle more cheese on top if desired.

Note: I like the taste of saffron and the lovely yellow color it gives to the risotto. If you prefer not to use saffron, add 1 tablespoon of tomato paste dissolved in a little stock. Do not use saffron powder.

SERVES 3 TO 4

Tripe

Tripe is the lining of the stomach of the meat animals. There are two different kinds of beef tripe available, honeycomb and smooth. When you buy tripe from your butcher, make sure it is scrubbed and partially cooked. If it is raw, it will need at least 6 hours' boiling to tenderize it.

Honeycomb Tripe Roman Style

4 pounds honeycomb tripe, partially cooked	¼ cup white wine
2 tablespoons oil	1 16-ounce can peeled plum tomatoes, with the juice
1 garlic clove, crushed	1 bay leaf
1 medium onion, sliced	A pinch of crushed red pepper
2 ounces prosciutto	Salt, freshly ground pepper
1 celery stalk, cut into pieces	1 tablespoon chopped parsley
2 medium carrots, peeled and sliced	Butter
	Grated Parmesan cheese

Cut the tripe into ½-inch slices. Put in a pot with enough water to cover, bring to a boil, lower the heat, and simmer for 10 minutes.

Meanwhile, heat the oil in the bottom of a flameproof casserole and sauté the garlic until it is just browned. Remove the garlic and add the onion and prosciutto. Cook for 5 minutes. Add the celery, carrots, and the wine. Let it reduce for a few minutes. Add the tomatoes and bay leaf and simmer 5 minutes.

Drain the tripe from the boiling water and add it to the casserole. Lower the heat, cover the casserole, and cook for 2 hours and 30 minutes. Half an hour before the end of the cooking, season with the crushed red pepper, salt, and pepper. Sprinkle with the chopped parsley just before serving.

Serve with butter and lots of grated cheese.

SERVES 4

Kidneys

Kidneys, especially veal kidneys, are considered a delicacy in Europe, where they are on the menus of some of the most expensive restaurants. In the United States, you will find them only at some ethnic restaurants. The most delicate kidneys are veal kidneys from milk-fed calves and spring lamb kidneys. Beef and pork kidneys are stronger in flavor. Lamb and pork kidneys are smooth and shaped like a kidney bean; veal and beef kidneys are a lot of pieces clustered around a center of fat. Although they are the same shape, veal kidneys are less than half the size of beef kidneys.

To remove some of the odor and bleach out the strong flavor of beef kidneys, parboil them, or cook the whole kidney very slowly in a pan with butter so that they give off some of their liquid. Rinse in cold water and cook as desired.

Sautéed Lamb Kidneys

Lamb kidneys can also be broiled on skewers like Chicken Livers en Brochette (page 221). Serve with lamb chops and sausages for a mixed grill, a good brunch dish.

¼ pound (1 stick) plus 1
  tablespoon butter
2 garlic cloves, peeled and
  crushed
½ pound mushrooms, cleaned in
  acidulated water (page 8) and
  sliced

2 onions, sliced
8 lamb kidneys, split and
  trimmed of center fat
Salt, freshly ground pepper
1 teaspoon rosemary
1 tablespoon chopped parsley
1 ounce cognac

Heat 2 tablespoons of the butter in a pan and add 1 of the garlic cloves. Cook for 1 or 2 minutes; add the mushrooms and cook for 5 minutes. Remove the mushrooms and keep warm.

Add 4 tablespoons of the butter to the pan and cook the remaining garlic clove and the onions in the hot butter until they are translucent. Remove and keep warm.

Add the 3 remaining tablespoons of butter to the pan and sauté the kidneys on fairly high heat. Season with salt, pepper, rosemary, and parsley. Cook 7 to 8 minutes in all.

Add the cognac and let it reduce. Return the mushrooms and the onions to the pan and cook for another 3 to 4 minutes.

Serve over steamed spinach that has been tossed in a pan with a few tablespoons of hot olive oil flavored with a lightly sautéed garlic clove.

SERVES 4

Broiled Veal Kidneys

Veal kidneys can be broiled or sautéed in butter. To broil, split the kidney down the side but do not cut all the way through. Wash the kidney in cold water and pat dry with a paper towel. Marinate in 2 tablespoons each of olive oil and lemon juice, a few leaves of rosemary and sage, and salt and pepper for at least 30 minutes in the refrigerator. Cook under a preheated broiler for about 5 minutes on each side.

Veal Kidneys with Sherry and Mushrooms

2 veal kidneys
6 tablespoons butter
1 garlic clove, crushed
1 medium onion or 4 shallots,
    peeled and chopped
1 tablespoon flour

Salt, freshly ground pepper
½ cup sherry
1 tablespoon chopped parsley
¼ pound fresh mushrooms,
    cleaned in acidulated water
    (page 8) and sliced

Slice the kidneys thin, as if you were cutting salami. Heat 4 table-spoons of the butter in a large frying pan. When the butter is sizzling, add the garlic and onion and cook briefly. Add the kidney slices and cook on high heat, stirring continuously. Sprinkle the flour over the kidneys and season with salt and pepper. Add the sherry and the parsley and simmer for about 5 minutes.

Meanwhile, in another pan, sauté the mushrooms in the remaining 2 tablespoons of butter. When the mushrooms have lost most of their liquid, add them to the kidneys and simmer together for another 2 or 3 minutes.

SERVES 2

Feet

We eat the skin and, therefore, the feet of pork, veal, and beef, but not of lamb. The feet of the front legs of a pig are called trotters; you can buy pickled trotters or cook them as suggested below. Split the trotters lengthwise between the toes.

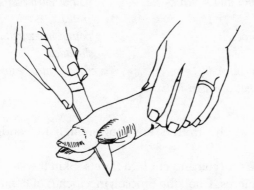

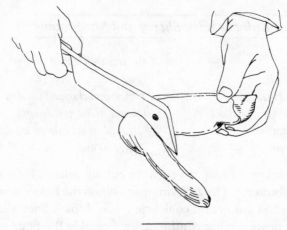

Trotters

Place split trotters in a large pot and cover them with cold water. Bring the water to a boil and skim off any froth that comes to the surface. Add a few coarsely chopped carrots and celery stalks, an onion cut in half and stuck with 3 whole cloves, a bay leaf, and a few peppercorns. Lower the heat and simmer for 2 hours, adding salt halfway through the cooking.

They are done when the bones can be removed easily.

Serve boiled trotters with a Dijon mustard or with a vinaigrette sauce. Or spread them with mustard, soft bread crumbs, and butter and grill them under the broiler until they begin to color. Allow 1 trotter per person.

Trotters Baked with Broccoli

4 trotters, split and boiled as
    above
1 bunch of broccoli
Salt
2 tablespoons olive oil
1½ pounds hot or sweet Italian
    sausages

¼ pound Parmesan cheese,
    grated
½ pound mozzarella cheese,
    shredded
2 eggs, lightly beaten

As soon as the trotters are cool enough to handle, remove the bones.

Clean the broccoli and cut into florets. Skin the stems and cut them into small pieces. Cook the broccoli in 2 inches of boiling, salted water until just done. Drain and shock under cold water.

Heat the oil in a skillet and cook the sausages; add a bit of water to prevent them from burning. When they are cooked and have cooled, cut them into thick slices.

Oil the bottom of a roasting pan (or put in a ladle of cooking water from the trotters). Place a layer of trotters, sausages, and broccoli in the bottom of the pan. Sprinkle with some of the Parmesan and mozzarella. Repeat with another layer, reserving some of the Parmesan for the top.

Add the reserved Parmesan to the eggs and pour over the top. Cook for 30 minutes in a preheated 350° oven.

SERVES 6

Calf Feet in Tomatoes with Parmesan

Calf feet are the best source of natural gelatin. When you get a calf's foot from the butcher, it will have been scalded and cleaned. Ask him to cut it crosswise and lengthwise so that you will have 3 or 4 pieces.

1 calf's foot, cut into 3 or 4
    pieces
1 cup coarsely chopped onions,
    carrots, and celery
1 large onion, chopped
¼ pound pancetta or salt pork,
    cubed

1 tablespoon oil
1 16-ounce can peeled plum
    tomatoes, with juice
Salt, freshly ground pepper
Grated Parmesan cheese

Place the pieces of foot in a large pot, cover with cold water, and bring to a boil. Skim off any scum that rises to the surface. Add the coarsely chopped vegetables, lower the heat, and simmer for 1 hour.

Meanwhile, prepare a tomato sauce: Sauté the onion and pancetta in the oil. When the salt pork has browned, add the tomatoes, salt, and pepper, and cook gently on low heat.

Cool the calf's foot under cold water and, with a small knife, remove the bones but keep the skin. (There is very little meat on the foot; the skin is the important part.) Add the foot pieces to the sauce and simmer for another 15 to 20 minutes. Serve with Parmesan cheese.

SERVES 4

PÂTÉS, SAUSAGES,
AND
PORK PRESERVING

P̂ÂTÉS AND SAUSAGES SOUND EXOTIC and beyond the reach of the home cook, but in reality they are simply a flavorful mixture of ground meats, herbs, spices, and other ingredients of your choice. Pâtés are baked in a terrine, earthenware dish, or other mold. Sausages are stuffed into a casing and cooked or cured.

Before refrigeration, sausage making was an important method of preserving meat. Different seasonings determine the taste of sausage, and almost every village and hamlet in Europe boasts its own special variety. One of the pleasures of making your own sausage is the fun of finding meat and seasoning combinations that appeal to your taste. Curing and smoking meat are other methods of preservation that we will discuss at the end of this chapter.

Grinding Meat

For most small jobs, a hand-operated meat grinder is sufficient. If you find a hand grinder too difficult, you can grind meat on the meat-grinding attachment of an electric mixer or in an electric grinder, or you can ask the butcher to grind the meat for you.

The grinder should have two or three plates of different-sized holes so that you can achieve a fine grind or a coarse grind. Holes run in size from ⅛ inch to 1 inch; holes of ⅛ inch and ⅜ inch will probably give you enough range. If the directions call for a finely ground sausage and you are worried your hole size is not small enough, put the meat through the grinder twice.

Pâté

Once you understand the basic rules on how to make pâté, you can take liberties with pâté recipes and have a great time creating your own concoctions. Pâtés are not at all difficult to make. They are wonderful for parties because they taste better when made a day or two ahead of time, and you can please your guests with pâtés that are new to them. Pork is an essential ingredient because it is juicy, soft, and flavorful.

Country Pâté

You can easily turn this recipe into a pheasant pâté. Grind the meat from the pheasant legs to substitute for the veal. Cut the breast meat into thin strips and marinate in cognac. Lay the strips of meat along the ground meat as you fill the terrine.

½ pound pork liver or chicken
    liver
1 pound pork, cut from the
    Boston butt, ground
1 pound veal, cut from the neck
    or shoulder, ground
2 eggs, lightly beaten
1½ teaspoons salt
½ teaspoon freshly ground
    pepper
A pinch of ground allspice
½ teaspoon thyme
½ cup finely chopped onions

2 tablespoons butter
½ cup Madeira
Wide, thin slices of fresh pork fat
Optional: ½ pound veal fillet,
    cut into julienne
    strips
¼ pound ham, cut
    into julienne strips
12 pistachio nuts,
    shelled
¼ cup dry sherry
1 tablespoon cognac
Salt, freshly ground pepper

Grind the livers and mix them with the ground pork and ground veal (or grind all three meats together).

Mix the meats in a bowl with the eggs, salt, pepper, allspice, and thyme.

Sauté the onions in the butter until they are soft but not brown. Pour the Madeira into the pan to deglaze it and cook it until it reduces by about half. Add the onions and Madeira to the meat in the bowl and mix it well.

If you wish to embellish the pâté by layering it with strips of meats and nuts, soak the strips of veal and ham in the sherry and cognac. Season with salt and freshly ground pepper.

Line a rectangular 9- by 4- by 5-inch pan (a metal or glass bread pan or an earthenware terrine with a cover) on the bottom and sides with the slices of pork fat. Leave enough fat overlapping the pan so that the fat will completely cover the top of the pâté.

Spoon some of the ground-meat mixture into the bottom of the pan. If you are adding the meat strips and nuts, lay half of the meat and nuts on the ground meat, then add more ground meat; add the remainder of the meat strips and top with the remainder of the ground meat. Fold the remaining pork fat over the meat.

Cover the pan with a piece of aluminum foil and, if you have it, a cover to fit the pan. (If you do not have a terrine cover, be sure the aluminum foil is tightly sealed around the top of the pan.) Set the pâté pan in a bain-marie, a pan of boiling water which comes three-quarters of the way up the bread pan.

Cook the pâté in a preheated 350° oven for 1 hour and 30 minutes to 2 hours. Add more boiling water to the bain-marie if necessary. Remove it from the oven and press a fork into the pâté. It is done if the juices that run out are yellow, not a rosy tinge.

Still leaving the foil on the pâté, place a 2- to 3-pound weight on the pâté and let it cool to room temperature. I keep a brick around for this, but cans will do. You may want to remove any excess juice and fat that comes to the top.

The pâté will keep 7 to 10 days in the refrigerator.

YIELD: 1 LOAF

Rabbit Pâté

1 cleaned, skinned rabbit, 3 to
   3½ pounds (pages 256–258)
½ pound veal, cut from shoulder
   or neck, ground (if needed)
½ pound pork, cut from Boston
   butt, ground
1 to 2 ounces cognac
½ cup chopped onion
2 tablespoons butter
¼ pound fresh back fat, cut into
   small cubes

1 egg, lightly beaten
½ teaspoon quatre épices (see
   recipe below)
½ teaspoon salt
¼ teaspoon freshly ground
   pepper
¾ pound fatback, sliced very thin
2 bay leaves

Cut the rabbit across at the end of the rib cage where the kidneys begin. Bone out the rib section and shoulders. You should have about 1½ cups or a little more. If you have less than that, add the veal. Grind the rabbit meat, veal, and pork together and put them in a bowl.

Remove the bones from the loin and legs of the rabbit and cut them into thin strips. Cover them with cognac and set aside.

Cook the chopped onion in the butter for about 5 minutes, until the onion is soft but not brown. Add the onion, back fat cubes, egg, quatre épices, salt, and pepper. Mix thoroughly.

Line two 9- by 4- by 5-inch terrines with the fatback slices and fill them halfway with the ground-meat mixture. Arrange the rabbit strips on the ground meat in an attractive pattern. Do not throw out the cognac. Fill the terrines with the remaining ground meat, place the bay leaves on top, and pour the cognac over all. Cover the terrines with overlapping slices of fatback and cover with aluminum foil and a cover, if you have them for your terrines.

Set in a pan of boiling water that comes halfway up the side of the terrines and cook in a preheated 350° oven for 2 hours to 2 hours and 30 minutes. The pâté is done when the juices come out clear, not pink, when the top is lightly pressed with a fork.

Take off the covers and place a brick or other weight on top of the foil covering the pâté. Refrigerate overnight.

YIELD: 2 LOAVES

Variation: Duck Pâté

Substitute a 5-pound duck for the rabbit. Remove all the skin and bones from the thighs and drumsticks of the duck and grind the meat with 1 pound of pork butt and 1 pound of shoulder of veal. Cut the breast meat into strips and marinate in brandy or cognac. Mix, season, and cook as above.

Chicken Liver Spread

This is different from the preceding pâtés in that the meat is cooked first, then mixed with the other ingredients and set in the refrigerator overnight.

¼ pound (1 stick) butter	3 hard-boiled eggs
2 cups finely chopped onions	1 tablespoon crushed juniper
1½ pounds fresh chicken livers	berries
¼ cup port wine	¾ teaspoon ground allspice
¼ cup gin	¾ teaspoon thyme
1 cup finely chopped parsley	Salt, freshly ground pepper

Heat the butter in a large, heavy skillet and cook the onions in the butter over moderate heat for about 10 minutes. Remove the onions with a slotted spoon and reserve.

Brown the chicken livers in the same butter over fairly high heat for 3 minutes. You want the livers to be brown on the outside, but pink on the inside. Transfer the livers to a bowl with the onions.

Add the port and the gin, deglazing the pan and scraping up all the brown particles. Pour the liquor into the bowl and add the parsley, hard-boiled eggs, juniper berries, allspice, thyme, 1 teaspoon of salt, and a grating of pepper.

Turn the mixture into either a food processor or a blender to smooth it out. Place it in a serving bowl, cover with plastic wrap, and refrigerate 6 hours or overnight. Let come to room temperature before serving with melba toast.

Quatre Épices

Quatre épices is a classic French combination of spices often used in pâtés and sausages. As you can see, in this recipe there are actually five spices. I highly recommend a small grinder to mix these spices. It is an inexpensive piece of equipment and extremely useful. You can also mix the spices in a good mortar and pestle or ask the spice shop to grind the spices together for you.

9 ounces white pepper
2 ounces ground ginger
2 ounces nutmeg, freshly grated

1 ounce cloves
1 ounce ground cinnamon

Mix in a grinder or mortar and pestle and store in a tightly closed jar.

YIELD: 15 OUNCES

Sausages

The sausages you buy at a store probably have been "extended" with permissible non-meat ingredients and other seasonings and preservatives. By making your own, you have absolute control of the ingredients. A group of Connecticut women became so enthused after reading an article I wrote on sausage making for the October 1981 issue of *The Cook's Magazine* that they formed a once-a-month sausage-making club. I hope I can tempt you into trying some of these easy recipes.

A hand-operated meat grinder is far superior to an electric machine for stuffing sausages because it is almost impossible to stuff the meat

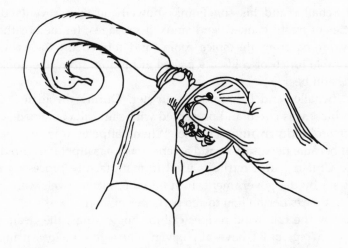

into the casings on an electric machine. If you do not have a grinder, you can stuff the casings by hand through a funnel.

Fresh pork is the key ingredient in most sausage recipes because it is the best of the domestic animals for salting, curing, and smoking. Pork butt, shoulder, trimmings of a pork bellie, ends of loin, and ends of fresh ham may be used in sausage, as may trimmings from other cuts. The ratio of fat to lean meat should be 30 percent to 70 percent. If the meat is too lean, the sausages will be hard and dry; if too fat, they will be too rich and shrivel up.

Salt has been used as a meat preservative for centuries. It is critical in sausage making. If you add too little salt, the taste will be flat; if there is too much salt, you will ruin the sausage. The basic rule of thumb is 1 ounce of salt to 3 pounds of meat. (If you do not have a scale, a scant 2 tablespoons of salt is approximately 1 ounce.) Use coarse salt (also sold as kosher salt); it spreads better than regular salt. Butcher's pepper is coarsely ground pepper.

In the old days, sausages were dried to keep them indefinitely. With the coming of refrigeration, drying is no longer necessary. Many people like the taste of dried sausage, however, so I have given you directions for drying. You will need saltpeter (potassium nitrate), a salt impurity formerly present in all salt. It is available at drugstores (See Saltpeter recipe, page 250.) As well as its preserving properties, saltpeter keeps the meat a nice pink color; without it, the meat would turn black and unappealing.

I recently had the pleasure of an illuminating tour of the spotless Schaller and Weber pork product plant in Astoria, Queens. Mr. Ferdinand Schaller and his son Frank showed me over seventy different varieties of fresh, cooked, and smoked sausages, let me breathe in the heady aroma from the spice room, and topped off the visit with a memorable lunch of cold cuts picked at random from tree hooks, dark bread, and beer.

Mr. Schaller and I discussed saltpeter. During the many centuries when meat was cured and preserved with salt, salt contained saltpeter, which broke down into a nitrite. When saltpeter was removed from salt, it became necessary to add a percentage of saltpeter to cured meats. In the United States nitrite is used to manufacture processed meat at levels set by the government. In June 1986, nitrite levels were reduced from 225 parts per million to 100 parts per million.

Most of the following recipes call for hog casings, the cleaned intestines of a pig, but I have also given you a few recipes using sheep casings (smaller) and beef casings (larger, known as beef bungs, middles, or rounds). All these casings and caul fat, used for the French version of breakfast sausage, are available from specialty meat or pork stores. The Standard Casing Company, Bergen Station, Jersey City, New Jersey 07304, (201) 434-6300 sells casings wholesale in 25 hank lots. They will provide information on where you may obtain smaller amounts, and they are a source of sausage-making equipment. You can usually buy casings by the pound packed in salt in a plastic container; a pound is about 50 feet of casings. A hank of casings will keep for a year this way in the refrigerator. You can return unused casings to the container after a sausage-making session; squeeze out the water and re-cover with salt.

Sausages will taste better if they rest overnight or even a day or two before cooking although they can be used immediately. Unless otherwise indicated, fry or broil them for about 20 minutes, turning several times. They keep well in the freezer (cooked or raw) or about 4 to 5 days in the refrigerator.

A few sausages such as Kielbasi (page 246), Sausages with Cumin (page 240), and Chorizos (page 239) taste better with a few hours' smoking. Home smokers are available from specialty houseware stores and catalogues. Some are electric, some use wood chunks or charcoal briquettes. All should be used on a porch or outdoors (see directions page 253), never inside. The alternative to a commercial home smoker is to build your own, see directions pages 253–254, or take your sausages to a commercial smokehouse.

I suggest you read the complete recipe for Italian Sausages Roman Style to get the process clear in your mind before you choose any of the other sausage recipes.

Italian Sausages Roman Style

This is the simplest of the sausage recipes, a very basic mix of meat, salt, pepper, garlic, and wine. It will yield about 6 pounds of sausages, about 18, depending on how long you want the sausages and how tightly you fill them.

About 12 feet of hog casings
4 pounds pork butt
2 pounds lean pork bellie
2 ounces coarse salt
1½ tablespoons black butcher
  pepper

2 garlic cloves, peeled and
  mashed very fine
½ cup dry red wine

Soak the casings in lukewarm water for about 5 minutes. Rinse the casings by runninng cold water through them, but do not squeeze out the water. They will slide onto the funnel much more easily when they are wet.

Cut the pork butt and bellie into small cubes. Grind the meat coarsely into a large bowl by using the ⅜-inch hole plate.

Add the salt, pepper, garlic, and red wine. Mix the ingredients together thoroughly with your hands so that the meat is no longer loose and has absorbed the moisture. You can almost knead the mixture like bread dough. It should take about 5 to 10 minutes, until the meat sticks together and also sticks to your hands.

Remove the grinding knife and plate from the grinder and replace them with a funnel, fastening it firmly onto the grinder with the tightening ring. Wet the funnel. Put the meat into the machine and let it protrude just a little bit out the end of the funnel (about ¼ to ½ inch). Carefully slip one end of the casing onto the funnel and pull the rest of the casing onto the funnel until you only have ½ inch left. Hold this end with your finger or tie it closed. Turn the handle of the grinder so that the meat pushes out into the casing. Be careful not to stuff the casing too tightly or it will rupture. (Casings are very strong lengthwise but not so strong on the sides.) When you have filled the casing, run your fingers along it to make sure there is a little give in it.

Let's assume you want your sausages to be about 4 to 5 inches long. When you have pushed all the meat into the casing, hold one end of the filled casing and with the other hand gently squeeze the casing 5 inches from the end you are holding. Spin the sausage around several times like a jumprope. Repeat the length of the filled

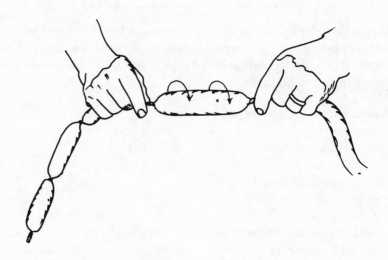

casing. If the meat has been well mixed, you will not need any further method of securing the sausage. (If you are nervous about them, you can tie them with string, but then you will have to remove the twine after cooking.)

Let the sausages rest in the refrigerator overnight or longer. Fry or broil for 20 minutes before serving.

YIELD: ABOUT 7 POUNDS

Variation: Dried Sausages

The proportions and the procedure are slightly different for dried sausages. Use the largest-size hog casings. There should be 80 percent lean meat to 20 percent fat, a substantially higher ratio of lean to fat than in cooked sausages. Do not grind the fatback or pork bellie with the lean meat. Instead, cut it up into minute pieces and mix it with the ground meat and seasonings.

Mix ¼ teaspoon of saltpeter with the 2 ounces of salt before you add salt to the meat. Or substitute the Master Saltpeter Mixture (page 250) for the salt in your recipe. After you have filled the casings, pinch the lengths you want and tie with string, leaving a loop on one end for easy hanging. Prick the casings with a pin to remove any air. Hang them in a cool, airy place (no more than 50° Fahrenheit) for at least a month, until they are hard to the touch.

Italian Sausages Neapolitan Style

This recipe will yield about 18 sausages. They are delicious grilled and served with sautéed green peppers and onions as a hero sandwich.

6 pounds pork shoulder or butt
and trimmings, cut into small
cubes
2 ounces coarse salt
1½ teaspoons black butcher
pepper
1 tablespoon fennel seeds

2 garlic cloves, peeled and finely
mashed or put through a garlic
press
1 tablespoon hot red pepper flakes
½ pound pork fatback (if
necessary)
About 12 feet of hog casings

Follow the directions in the preceding recipe. If you use loin of pork or ham trimmings instead of the shoulder or butt, the pork may be too lean. In that case, cut the fatback into very small cubes and add it to the pork after grinding. Use the ⅜-inch hole plate for grinding.

YIELD: ABOUT 7 POUNDS

Spanish Sausage—Chorizos

Like kielbasa, the Polish sausages, chorizos are usually smoked, but they can be eaten fresh.

3 pounds lean pork shoulder, cut
into cubes
2 pounds fatback or fresh pork
bellie, cut into small cubes
1 ounce salt
½ teaspoon freshly ground
pepper

1 scant tablespoon quatre épices
(page 234)
¼ teaspoon saltpeter
½ teaspoon cayenne pepper
1 teaspoon paprika
2 ounces Malaga raisins
About 12 feet of hog casings

Grind the pork using the ⅜-inch hole plate according to the directions on page 230. Add fatback or pork bellie to the meat with the salt and other ingredients.

Smoke for at least 2 hours to enhance the flavor; see pages 253–254.

YIELD: ABOUT 6 POUNDS

Sausages with Cumin

4¼ pounds beef, cut into cubes
6½ pounds pork shoulder or
butt, cut into cubes
2 pounds fresh fatback, cut into
cubes
4 ounces salt
½ teaspoon saltpeter (see Note)

1½ tablespoons freshly ground
pepper
7 ounces ground cumin
½ teaspoon cayenne pepper
10 garlic cloves, peeled and
mashed fine
About 24 feet of hog casings

Grind the beef on the ⅛-inch hole plate into a large bowl according to the directions on page 230. Using the same plate, grind the pork and fatback into the bowl. Add the salt and seasonings and mix thoroughly. Make links of 10 to 12 inches.

Lay the sausages on the rack of a home smoker and smoke for 2 to 4 hours until they reach the color you want. Turn them at least once during the smoking time. (They will gain some color from the saltpeter.) Do not let the sausages touch one another. If using a smoke house, string the sausages up on a wooden pole or broomstick and smoke for the same amount of time.

Cook in a pot with cold water to cover. Bring to a boil, lower the heat, and simmer gently for 5 minutes. Let the sausages cool in the water.

Note: Either mix the saltpeter with the salt or substitute the Master Saltpeter Mixture (page 250) for the salt and saltpeter in this recipe.

YIELD: ABOUT 14 POUNDS

Italian Sausages Siena Style

Grill these sausages on the barbecue and serve with Fettucini Capri.

3 pounds pork butt or shoulder,
cut into cubes
1½ pounds lean pork bellie
1½ pounds veal, cut from the
neck or shoulder
2 ounces coarse salt

1½ tablespoons black butcher
pepper
½ teaspoon marjoram
½ teaspoon coriander
½ cup dry white wine
About 12 feet of hog casings

Grind the meat using the ⅜-inch hole plate according to the directions on page 230. Regrind it, using the ⅛-inch plate. Add the salt and seasonings, making links of 5 or 6 inches.

YIELD: APPROXIMATELY 7 POUNDS

Fettuccine Capri

This is wonderful in summer when tomatoes are warm and fragrant from the garden and basil is plentiful. It is quick and easy. You make the sauce while the pasta water comes to a boil.

1 pound fettuccine, green or
   white or mixed
½ pound fresh plum tomatoes,
   peeled, seeded, and chopped
   coarse
½ cup fresh basil leaves, chopped
   coarse

2 garlic cloves, peeled and
   chopped fine
½ pound fresh mozzarella, cut
   into small pieces
4 tablespoons grated pecorino
   romano cheese

While the water for the pasta starts heating up, mix the tomatoes, basil, garlic, mozzarella, and pecorino romano cheese in a large serving bowl.

Cook the fettuccine according to the directions on the package; drain and turn the pasta in the bowl. Toss and serve immediately.

SERVES 4

Spiced Southern Sausage

3 pounds pork shoulder or butt,
   cut into cubes
1 ounce salt
¾ teaspoon freshly ground
   pepper
¾ teaspoon hot red pepper flakes

¼ teaspoon ground allspice
½ teaspoon rubbed sage
¼ teaspoon nutmeg
Pinch of ground cloves
½ cup cold water
About 6 feet of hog casings

Grind the meat with the ⅜-inch hole plate according to the directions on page 230. Change the plate to a smaller hole, ⅛ inch, and regrind. Mix the meat thoroughly with the salt, seasonings, and water.

Either stuff into casings or form into a long firm roll and wrap in aluminum foil. Refrigerate overnight. Slice off rounds and fry or broil for 20 minutes.

YIELD: ABOUT 4 POUNDS

French Sausage—Boudin Blanc de Toulouse

½ pound pork fillet, cut into
    cubes
1 pound fresh pork bellie, cut
    into cubes
½ pound veal fillet, cut into
    cubes
½ pound chicken breast, boned,
    skinned, and cubed
¾ pound onions, chopped
4 tablespoons clarified butter
1 cup milk
3 slices of white bread, crusts
    removed

1 goose or duck liver or ½ pound
    chicken livers
1 tablespoon salt, coarse or fine
1 teaspoon white pepper
1 teaspoon quatre épices
    (page 234)
½ cup heavy cream
3 eggs, lightly beaten
About 18 to 20 feet of hog
    casings

Grind the pork, pork bellie, veal, and chicken fine into a large bowl according to the directions on page 230. If the ⅛-inch hole plate is the smallest size on your grinder, put the meat through it twice. Sauté the onion until it is translucent (but not brown) in 2 tablespoons of the clarified butter; add it to the meat.

Heat the milk in a saucepan with the bread slices. When the milk comes to a boil, lower the heat and cook until it becomes like a soft dough. (You should have about ¾ cup of this panada.) Add to the meat.

Sauté the goose liver in the remaining 2 tablespoons of butter until nicely browned but not thoroughly cooked. Chop it into little pieces and add it to the meat.

Season the meat with the salt, pepper, quatre épices, cream, and eggs. Mix thoroughly and refrigerate for 1 hour.

This mixture is too loose to be stuffed into casings with a grinder. Use a hand funnel to fill the casings; tie them into 5- to 6-inch links. Place them in a wire basket and gently lower them into a large pot of boiling water. Cook gently for 20 minutes. Shock under cold water. Just before serving, grill them quickly.

YIELD: ABOUT 6 POUNDS

Duck Sausage—Saucisson de Canard

1 duck, boned and skinned
1 pound pork shoulder
1 pound veal shoulder
1 teaspoon quatre épices
  (page 234)
1 ounce salt

½ teaspoon freshly ground
  pepper
¼ teaspoon marjoram
¼ teaspoon rubbed sage
¾ cup cold water
6 to 8 feet of hog casings

Cut the duck breast meat into small cubes. Grind the remaining duck meat with the pork and veal with the ⅛-inch hole plate according to the directions on page 230.

Thoroughly mix the ground meat with the duck breast, seasonings, and water.

Stuff into casings. Fry or gently grill for 20 minutes.

YIELD: ABOUT 5 POUNDS

Breakfast Sausages

These sausages and the two following should be made with sheep casings, which are thinner than hog casings. The sausages will be narrow, the size of a finger. If you cannot get sheep casings, hog casings will do, or shape them into a roll and slice off rounds as in Spiced Southern Sausage (page 241).

3 pounds Boston butt or pork
  shoulder, cut into cubes
1 ounce coarse salt
½ teaspoon freshly ground
  pepper
¼ teaspoon nutmeg

¼ teaspoon marjoram
¼ teaspoon rubbed sage
Pinch of ground cinnamon
1 cup cold water
About 6 feet of sheep casings

Grind the meat with the ⅛-inch hole plate as directed on page 230. Add the salt, seasonings, and cold water.

YIELD: ABOUT 4 POUNDS

Variation: French Paupiettes

In this version, the Breakfast Sausages are wrapped in caul fat instead of stuffed into casings. Caul fat may be purchased at specialty meat or pork stores. The ingredients are the same, except use less cold water. Grind the meat with the large hole plate, ⅜ inch. Regrind the meat using the small hole plate, ⅛ inch. Soak the caul fat in cold water for about 5 minutes, then spread it on your workspace. Form flat triangles of meat of about 2 ounces each. Wrap each piece in caul fat and fry or broil. The sausages will look like little arrowheads.

Southern-Italian-Style Sausages with Cheese and Parsley

4 *pounds lean Boston butt, cut into cubes*
2 *pounds pork bellie trimmings, cut into cubes*
2 *ounces coarse salt*
1½ *tablespoons black butcher pepper*

3 *tablespoons chopped parsley*
½ *pound provolone cheese, crumbled*
1 *tablespoon fennel seeds*
1 *tablespoon hot red pepper flakes*
About 12 *feet of sheep casings*

Use the ⅜-inch hole plate as directed on page 230.

YIELD: ABOUT 7½ POUNDS

French Sausages—Chipolata

4 *pounds pork butt, cut into cubes*
2 *pounds fresh pork bellie, cut into cubes*
2 *pounds veal neck, cut into cubes*
1 *pound onions, chopped*
3 *ounces salt*

2½ *teaspoons butcher pepper*
2 *garlic cloves, mashed*
1⅓ *teaspoons quatre épices (page 234) or ½ teaspoon each of ground coriander, ginger, sage, and ⅛ teaspoon each of ground nutmeg and cloves*
About 15 *feet of sheep casings*

Grind the meat and onions together on the ⅛-inch hole plate as directed on page 230. If you cannot find sheep casings, use hog casings.

YIELD: ABOUT 10 POUNDS

Coteghini Milanese

These sausages are a northern Italian specialty. Unlike many of the previous sausages, they should be cooked in boiling water and are often served with lentils or other dried beans. Beef casings are used here, as they are in the next two recipes.

4 pounds pork shoulder or butt,
  cut into cubes
1 pound fresh pork bellie, cut
  into cubes
2 pounds pork skins, blanched,
  shocked in cold water, and cut
  into cubes
3 ounces coarse salt
¼ teaspoon saltpeter

1 tablespoon black butcher pepper
½ teaspoon peppercorns
2 garlic cloves, well mashed
¼ teaspoon thyme
¼ teaspoon ground sage
¼ teaspoon allspice
¼ teaspoon marjoram
1 teaspoon vanilla extract
About 6 to 8 feet of beef casings

Grind the meat and skins coarse with the largest hole plate. Thoroughly mix the meat and all the other ingredients and fill the casings as directed on pages 237–238. Beef casings are much larger than hog casings, so you will need a large funnel. Fill the casings tightly, avoiding air pockets, and tie them at 8-inch lengths with twine. The sausages must be tied on both ends. Leave a loop of string on one end. Hang them up in a cool, airy place for 5 to 7 days before cooking.

Place the coteghini in a large pot of cold water and bring to a boil. Lower the heat to simmer and cook for 1 hour and 30 minutes. After the first 30 minutes, prick the skin of the sausages with a pin or metal skewer. (Water will shoot out of the holes.)

If you are serving these with lentils, it is nice to cook the lentils in the coteghini water to give them flavor. Parboil the lentils briefly in fresh water, then drain them and continue cooking in the coteghini water. Slice the sausages and serve with the lentils.

YIELD: ABOUT 8 POUNDS

Kielbasa

Kielbasa is a Polish sausage that is stuffed into beef casings and shaped like a horseshoe. You will usually find them smoked, but they are fine fresh.

6 pounds pork shoulder or butt,
  cut into cubes
3 pounds fresh pork bellie, cut
  into cubes
1 pound lean tender beef, cut into
  cubes
2 tablespoons black butcher
  pepper
2 tablespoons crushed hot red
  pepper flakes

2 tablespoons paprika
3 ounces coarse salt
⅓ ounce saltpeter (if sausages are
  to be smoked or hung; see
  Note)
1½ pounds onions, chopped fine
2 large garlic cloves, peeled and
  mashed to a puree
About 12 feet of beef casings
  (rounds)

Grind the meat with the ⅜-inch hole plate into a large bowl as directed on page 230. Put the black pepper, red pepper flakes, and paprika into a small frying pan and toast over the flame, shaking the pan all the time. Do not let the spices burn. As soon as you get their smell to your nose and throat, pull it off the flame. Add the toasted spices to the meat with the salt, saltpeter, onions, and garlic and mix thoroughly.

Tie off one end of the casings before you start filling them, then tie the sausages at 12-inch lengths. Leave a loop at the end. Hang them in a cool, airy place or refrigerate overnight. Fry or broil for 10 minutes, then finish cooking for another 10 minutes in cooked sauerkraut.

Note: If you want to smoke the sausages, mix the saltpeter with the salt and diminish the coarse salt by ¼ ounce. Or substitute the Master Saltpeter Mixture (page 250) for the salt and saltpeter in the recipe. You must use saltpeter if you hang the sausages; if they are refrigerated before cooking, the saltpeter is not necessary. Smoke as directed on pages 253–254.

YIELD: ABOUT 12 POUNDS

Bologna Sausage

Bologna sausage is made of ground pork and beef mixed with enough water to give the sausage a fine, tenacious texture. Commercial concerns sometimes grind cracked ice with beef from freshly slaughtered cattle, because this method gives a finer grain to the finished product. Since commercially made sausage is full of fillers and extenders, you might like to make your own bologna in bulk. Here is a recipe for a large amount.

1¼ pounds coarse salt
1 ounce saltpeter
30 pounds beef, cut into cubes
20 pound pork trimmings, cut
    into cubes

2 ounces black butcher pepper
1 ounce coriander
1 ounce mace
5 quarts water or shaved ice
About 60 feet of beef casings

Mix the salt and saltpeter together or use the Master Saltpeter Mixture (page 250). Grind the beef coarsely with the ⅜-inch hole plate according to the directions on page 230. Mix 10 ounces of the salt with the beef and cure it in a cool place for 48 hours. Grind the pork with the same size plate, mix it with the remaining 10 ounces of salt, and cure for 12 hours. (It is not absolutely necessary to cure the pork; if not cured, add 6½ ounces of salt to the cubed pork before it is ground with the beef.)

Regrind the beef, using the ⅛-inch plate. Add the pork to the beef and regrind again with the ⅛-inch plate. Add the spices and water and mix vigorously until the mass is sticky. Thorough mixing may require 30 minutes.

Tightly stuff the sausage into beef casings and allow them to hang in a cool place overnight.

Cook the sausages in boiling water for 20 to 30 minutes. Shock in cold water and hang in a cool place for 24 hours. Refrigerate or freeze.

If you wish them smoked, hang in a well-ventilated smokehouse (heated 110° to 120°) for 2 hours until they become a rich mahogany color. Cook as directed.

YIELD: ABOUT 60 POUNDS

Venison Sausage

Venison sausages are an excellent way to use up the poorer cuts of the animal like the breast and neck. Be sure to remove any blood clots. You can make sausage with any of the other furry animals, like moose, reindeer, bear, or buffalo. Be sure to remove the fat from the game; it is too strong to enjoy.

7 pounds venison meat, cut into
  cubes
3 pounds fresh pork bellie, cut
  into cubes
3 ounces coarse salt
1 teaspoon black butcher pepper
1 teaspoon rubbed sage

½ teaspoon coriander
½ teaspoon thyme
3 garlic cloves, peeled and
  mashed
1 teaspoon hot red pepper flakes
  (optional)
20 feet of hog casings

Grind the meat with the ⅜-inch hole plate into a large bowl as directed on page 230. Thoroughly mix the meat and all the other ingredients and fill the casings as directed on pages 237–238. If casings are not available, make patties and wrap them in caul fat. Fry or broil.

YIELD: ABOUT 11 POUNDS

Blood Sausage

Traditionally, blood sausage is made with pork blood, but only beef blood is allowed for sale in the United States.

1 pound fatback
6½ ounces onions, chopped
Lard for frying
2 eggs
⅓ cup heavy cream
2 ounces salt

A pinch of freshly ground pepper
A pinch of thyme
1 bay leaf, crushed
1 pint beef blood
About 12 feet of hog casings

Cut half the fatback into small cubes and melt the other half. Sauté the onions in lard until translucent. Mix the pork, onions, eggs, cream, salt, and seasonings. Carefully mix in the blood.

Fill the casings as directed on pages 237–238; tie the sausages with twine every 6 inches.

Place the sausages in a wire basket and plunge them into boiling water; cook at a simmer for 20 minutes. Drain and cool. To serve, cut a couple of gashes across them and grill lightly.

YIELD: ABOUT 3 POUNDS

Variation: Roman Style

Use ½ pound of fatback, 1 pint of blood, 1 orange peel cut into julienne strips, ¼ pound of raisins soaked in water and drained, 2 ounces of salt, a pinch of pepper, ½ pound of sugar, ½ teaspoon of cinnamon, and ¼ teaspoon of nutmeg.

Variation: Flammande

Add to the ingredients in the first recipe 3 ounces of moist sugar, 2 ounces of raisins, and 2 ounces of currants soaked in warm water and drained.

Head Cheese

Be sure to ask the butcher to saw the head into quarters before you take it home. (Sawing prevents bone splinters that may result from cracking the head with a cleaver.) Pull out the brains and reserve for other recipes (pages 211–212).

1 pig's head, cut into quarters	3 tablespoons pignoli nuts
1 pound pork skins	1 teaspoon slivered lemon zest
1 onion, cut in half and studded with 3 cloves	Freshly ground pepper
	½ teaspoon nutmeg
2 carrots, peeled and chopped coarse	¼ teaspoon cinnamon
	¼ teaspoon coriander
2 celery stalks, chopped coarse	Beef bung casings (optional, see
Salt	Note)
2 cloves garlic, peeled and chopped fine	

Rinse the head pieces under cold water and place them in a large stockpot with the pork skins. Cover with cold water, bring to a boil, and lower the heat to simmer. Skim the scum off the top, add the onion, carrots, and celery and 1 teaspoon of salt. Cook for 1 hour and 30 minutes. The meat is done when it comes off the bones easily. You do not want to overcook it.

When the pieces are cool enough to handle, remove the meat from the bones; cut the meat and skin into small pieces and place them in a large bowl. Add the garlic, nuts, lemon zest, 1 teaspoon of pepper, and other seasonings and toss well.

Fill beef casings as directed on pages 237–238 and place in the refrigerator to chill. It will be ready the following day and will keep for a week.

If casings are not available, place the mixture in a colander and cover it with a dish with a small weight on top. Cool, then chill overnight. Unmold. It will keep for about 1 week.

Note: Beef bungs are the largest intestines of beef; beef rounds and beef middles are smaller in width and are used mostly for salamis and other semi-soft sausages. If you cannot find beef bungs, follow directions for weighting the Head Cheese in a colander.

Home Preserving of Pork

Just as making your own sausages is a simple process that is worthwhile for home cooks, curing meat can also be easily done at home. While it is probably not worth your while to make pastrami—curing, seasoning, smoking, and steaming a large piece of beef breast is more than most people want to take on—curing and smoking meats need not be complicated. You may like prosciutto ham but have trouble finding one that is not too salty. I will tell you how to air-dry a fresh leg of pork so you attain a prosciutto to your taste.

Curing is the process whereby meat is preserved by salting, either in a dry mixture or in a wet brine, both are called a pickling cure. If it is going to be smoked, a further preserving process which adds a distinct flavor, a wet brine is used. If it is to be air-dried, it is cured dry. American Indians cured venison by salting it, then hanging the meat up to dry at the top of the tepee above the fire.

Here are a few simple guidelines for the preserving of pork at home. You can use the same process using the wet brine solution to make corned beef from the beef brisket, bottom round, or rump. Top sirloin or silver tip of beef can be dry-cured and treated like prosciutto.

Salt, saltpeter, and sugar are the necessary ingredients for curing meat. Saltpeter, like nitrite, is a preservative agent that maintains the color of the meat and prolongs shelf life. I prefer using saltpeter to nitrite (unless you have a good knowledge of the chemical); if the meat is to be used in a short period of time, coarse salt alone will do the trick.

For every 100 pounds of pork, double the master recipe below. Mix the curing ingredients together thoroughly, being especially careful to incorporate the finely powdered saltpeter completely into the salt.

Master Saltpeter Mixture

4 *pounds salt*   1¼ *ounces saltpeter*
1 *pound sugar*

Mix together well and keep in a labeled jar. It will be good for years.

DRY-CURING

Weigh the trimmed meat, allowing 100 pounds of meat for the above amount of curing ingredients. The skin should be left on the meat. Divide the curing mixture into two equal parts, one part to use at once, the other half saved for resalting. Bacon does not need resalting, so allow only half the amount of the curing mixture.

Rub the first half of the curing mixture on all surfaces of the meat, poking some into the shank ends. Pat a thin covering on the shoulders; pat about a ½-inch layer on the lean face of hams and bacon.

Fit the salted meat into a flat box, being careful not to shake off the curing mixture. Place the box in a cold place, 36° to 40° Fahrenheit. Allow 2 days to the pound for hams and shoulders, 1½ days to the pound for bacon.

Six to 8 days after the meat has been placed in the cure, resalt it with the other half of the curing mixture (except for bacon). If the weather is warm, the salt will melt and run off; keep an eye on it and resalt if necessary.

TO PREPARE A HAM FOR CURING

Remove the aitchbone from the ham without scoring the meat. With the back of a dull knife, squeeze out the few drops of blood that may still be in the vein along the femur bone.

Prosciutto

Here is how to air-dry a fresh leg of pork into prosciutto, a delicious Italian ham that is lovely as an appetizer with melon or figs, to flavor meat and pasta dishes, or simply as a cold cut.

4 pounds coarse salt
1 pound sugar
1 teaspoon saltpeter
1 firm leg of fresh pork, skin on
A glass of white or *red wine*
2 tablespoons garlic mashed into
*   a paste*

Freshly ground pepper
¼ pound fresh pork fat
1 tablespoon flour
Salt
2 to 3 tablespoons water

Mix the salt, sugar, and saltpeter thoroughly and rub on all the exposed meat, especially around the ball of the femur. Place the ham in a large box and store in a cool place at a temperature between 36° and 40° Fahrenheit for 2 days per pound of ham.

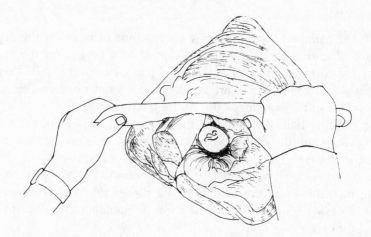

Check the ham once a week; if the salt has melted and run off, resalt it.

Remove the ham from the box and rinse it well under cold water, then with a glass of wine. Tie a cord to the shank and hang the ham up for 2 days. After 2 days, rub the mashed garlic over the exposed meat. Cover the garlic paste with pepper.

Hang up the ham again, this time for a week. Render the pork fat. Make a paste with the fat, the flour, salt, pepper, and water. Spread this paste over the exposed meat and the fat.

Wrap a sheet of cheesecloth around the ham and place it in a large brown bag. This keeps the ham clean but allows the ham sufficient air. Hang the ham in a cool, dry, airy place for at least 3 months.

Sweet pickle curing in brine

Dissolve the salt, sugar, and saltpeter in 4½ gallons of cold water. The temperature of the solution should be 36° to 40° Fahrenheit. You can add a packet of pickling spices for added flavor if you wish. Fit the cold, smoothly trimmed cuts into a clean barrel or crock and cover them with the solution. Weight the meat down to keep it from floating to the top. The meat should be completely submerged.

Keep the container in a cold place for a minimum of 28 days. Allow 3½ to 4 days per pound for hams and shoulders. Thus, a 6-pound shoulder would need 28 days, a 15-pound ham, 60.

On the seventh day of the cure, remove all the meat and stir the pickle mixture strongly. Repack the meat into the solution and recover with weights. Move the meat around again on the fourteenth and twenty-eighth days.

If you are not planning to smoke the meat, bone it out and tie it; boil it 30 minutes to the pound for boiled ham.

SMOKING

When the curing time is up, remove the pieces of meat from the pickling solution. Soak the fully cured meat in cold, fresh water for about 15 to 30 minutes to remove some of the surface salt.

Scrub the meat clean with a sharp brush and hot water (110° to 125°) so that it will keep a bright color during the smoking.

Thread strong twine through the shanks of hams and shoulders to hold them in place for smoking. Reinforce the flank end of bacon with a hardwood skewer or a clean, galvanized wire.

Smokehouses range from the temporary "one-hog" variety made from a 50-gallon barrel to permanent structures suitable for both smoking and storing meat. They need to be of tight construction to permit easy regulation of temperature and flow of smoke and air.

A rapid flow of air past the meat is needed at the beginning of the smoking operation to drive off surplus moisture. Near the end of the smoking period, a less rapid air movement prevents excessive shrinkage in the weight of the meat.

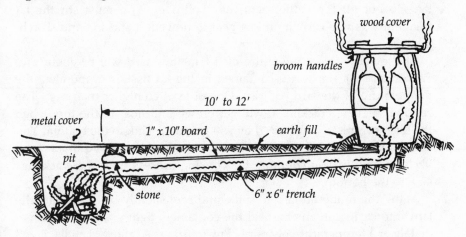

The temperature in the smokehouse should be 90° Fahrenheit, although some smokehouses get up to 120°. The best woods to use are hickory, apple, and cherry. Do not use pine because the pitch and rosin will give off sooty smoke and an unappealing smell.

Here is how to smoke small quantities of meat in a 50-gallon barrel with both ends removed or in a box with tight sides. Set the barrel over the upper end of a shallow, sloping covered trench. Dig a pit at the lower end for the fire. Control the heat of the fire by covering the pit with a piece of sheet metal and mounding the earth around the edges to cut off almost all draft. Hang clean muslin or burlap over the top of the barrel to protect the 1-inch opening between the barrel and the cleated top. The meat is tied to broomsticks resting across the top of the barrel.

Hams that have been cured and smoked need further boiling, about 20 minutes to the pound. A whole ham of 15 pounds will take about 5 hours. Allow about 30 minutes to the pound for half a ham. Cover with a glaze and finish in a hot oven for 30 minutes, page 90.

Rendering Pork Lard at Home

Pork lard is a great all-purpose shortening, especially for pie crusts.

Leaf lard is the best fat; it will render 95 percent of its weight. Cut it into small pieces. Back fat and fat trimmings should be ground. All can be cooked together.

Put small quantities of fat into a large, heavy kettle (like cast iron) on low heat. Stir constantly; when it has begun to melt, add the rest of the fat. Do not fill the kettle, or it may boil over. You must stir the fat frequently as you cook it on low heat to prevent it sticking and scorching.

At the start, the temperature of the melting lard will be about 212° Fahrenheit. As the water contained in the fat tissues evaporates, the temperature of the lard will rise. Do not let it go higher than 255°. The residual tissues, cracklings, will get brown and float to the top; when the fat is completely melted, they will gradually sink to the bottom. You will get lard with the greatest amount of moisture removed that is least likely to spoil if you continue the cooking process until the cracklings sink to the bottom.

Allow the rendered lard to settle and cool slightly before ladling the lard into clean containers. Seal the containers tightly and store immediately at a temperature near or below freezing. As the lard chills, it will produce a fine grain.

Strain the lard at the bottom of the kettle through a press or a screen of two or three thicknesses of cheesecloth. Cracklings can be used to flavor homemade bread.

GAME

W ILD GAME HAS ALWAYS BEEN APPRECIATED by Europeans and Asians, who have created beautiful recipes to enhance the presentation of the game. It is somewhat different in the United States. Colonial Americans depended on game for their daily meat, but they prepared it very simply. By the mid-1800s, professional hunters were shooting huge numbers of wildfowl and other game to sell in the marketplace. (In the 1880s you could buy a dozen mallard ducks for $3.00, a dozen quail for $1.25.) Open season all year, a complete lack of regulations to control the indiscriminate hunting, and a continually increasing human population that encroached on the feeding and mating grounds of game all served to decimate our natural stock of game almost to extinction.

In the early 1900s the United States signed a treaty with Great Britain (and later with Canada and Mexico) to help preserve migratory wildlife. Hunting was limited to certain times of the year in designated areas, and the amount of the catch was regulated. Hunters can no longer sell their catch for profit, although they can give it away. That is why the only game you can buy in the markets today has been raised on game preserves.

Recently there has been a swing back to game in this country. You can now buy farm-raised game in supermarkets as well as in specialty meat markets. Even if you have not had any previous experience cooking game, I hope some of the following recipes will introduce you to these delicious foods that have been the delight of kings and gourmets for centuries.

Precautions for New Hunters of Small Game

Every precaution should be taken by the hunter to make sure the game he shoots is fit to eat when he gets it home. Often there may be warm days during the first few weeks of the hunting season; if so, clean out the entrails of game birds when you shoot them or soon thereafter. It is not good practice to keep warm, undrawn birds (quail, dove, pheasant, etc.) in the pocket of your hunting coat or bag. Clots of blood caused by the gunshot or partly digested food will taint the meat.

To draw game birds, cut down lengthwise at the back of the neck and pull out the windpipe and crop. Make an incision between the tail and the legs. Put your fingers into the incision and follow the roof of the breast until you come to the liver, gizzard, and entrails. Pull them out.

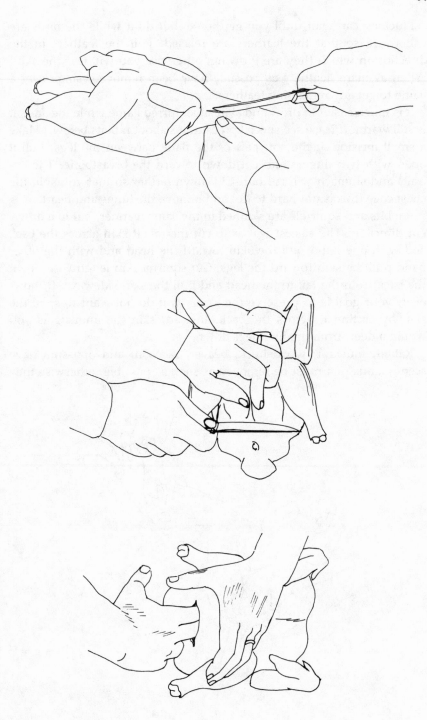

Plucking can wait until you get home, but do it while the birds are still warm so that the feathers are relaxed. Pull the feathers in the direction in which they are growing; otherwise you will tear the skin. When as many feathers as possible have been removed, singe over a flame to get any remaining feathers.

It is much easier to draw and skin small furred game while the animal is still warm. (Please see special precautions about rabbits below.) Make a small incision at the soft part of the flank between the legs. Pull it open with two fingers and cut down toward the breastbone. The entrails and stomach will fall out. Cut down farther so that you split the chest cage (this is not hard to do) and remove the lungs and heart.

Rabbits and squirrels are skinned in the same manner, but in a different direction. The easiest way is to cut the rabbit skin across the back and with one hand pull the skin toward the head and with the other hand pull the skin toward the legs. Cut squirrel skin lengthwise down the back from the tail to the head and pull the skin sideways. If, however, your goal is to preserve the skins, you do not want to spoil the skin by cutting it across the back. Instead, skin the animals as you would a deer, from the hind legs down.

Rabbit, muskrat, woodchuck, beaver, raccoon, and opossum have scent glands that must be removed as soon as possible, otherwise they

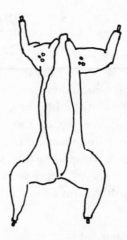

will taint the meat. These pea-shaped, waxy red nodules are easy to see; during the breeding season, the glands have a strong odor. When you remove them, be careful not to cut them or bring them in contact with the meat. In rabbits the glands are found under the forelegs where the forelegs join the body; in raccoons, beaver, and other small animals, they are under the forelegs and also along the spine in the loin area.

Shoot only lively game. If the animal was acting in a sluggish manner before it was killed or if the liver looks diseased, it is an indication of sickness. Wild rabbits need special care because tularemia, a rabbit disease, is transmissible to humans.

SPECIAL PRECAUTIONS AGAINST TULAREMIA FROM RABBITS

Do not hunt rabbits until two or three weeks after a heavy frost. Carry with you a pair of gloves and a bottle of Lysol. Wear the gloves when you are handling the rabbit, and rinse your hands with Lysol when you are finished. As soon as the rabbit is killed, split it from the crotch to the breastbone. Holding it by the head and forefeet, let all the entrails fall to the ground. Using a stick, locate the liver and look it over carefully. If there are no cystlike white spots the size of peas, it is safe. If the spots are present, bury the rabbit, being extremely careful not to let the rabbit touch any scratch you may have.

Most game animals are healthy and clean. They live in uncrowded conditions and are mostly vegetarians, eating berries, plants, fruits, and seeds. The dressing and cooking of an animal are equally important, the dressing to preserve the quality of the meat, the cooking to bring out its natural flavor.

Braised Quail

Quail is the best-known game bird in the United States, appreciated both for its cleverness in the art of camouflage and for its delicious taste. It is abundant in western states that raise fruit and in the South, where hunting rights for quail have come to represent a good cash crop. Quail are about 4 to 5 ounces cleaned; allow two per person. Farm-raised quail come frozen in a box with two packages of four birds each; the quail will be split down the back.

Wild rice goes nicely with game. I like to cook wild rice and white rice together to give the wild rice some texture.

8 quail
4 tablespoons butter
Salt, freshly ground pepper

¼ to ½ cup Madeira or other
   sherry
1½ cups chicken stock

Sauté the quail in hot butter on fairly high heat in a heavy frying pan. Turn, season with salt and pepper, and cook until they are brown on all sides.

Remove them with a slotted spoon and keep warm. Discard any excess fat. Pour in the Madeira and deglaze the pan, picking up any brown bits. Add some of the chicken stock and reduce by a third.

Return the birds to the pan, partially cover the skillet, and cook in a preheated 325° oven for 15 minutes. Remove the cover and cook another 10 minutes, adding more stock if necessary.

Serve on a bed of wild rice (see below) with the juice spooned over the quail.

SERVES 4

Wild Rice

¾ cup wild rice
1 onion, chopped fine
6 tablespoons butter
2 cups chicken stock (page 25) or
   water

Salt, freshly ground pepper
¼ cup raw white rice
2 tablespoons grated Parmesan
   cheese

Soak the wild rice in water for about 20 minutes. Drain, reserving the water. Sauté the onion in 4 tablespoons of hot butter in a flame-proof casserole or a saucepan. When the onion is translucent, add the rice. Cook for a few minutes and season with salt and pepper. Add the stock or water, lower the heat, cover the pan, and cook for 45 minutes.

Add the white rice and cook another 18 minutes.

Cream the rice with 2 tablespoons of butter and grated Parmesan before serving.

SERVES 4

Broiled Quail with Grape Sauce

This recipe and the following one are quick and easy. Prepare the sauce first, then broil the quail, finishing the sauce while the quail crisp under the broiler.

8 quail
1 tablespoon olive oil
Salt, freshly ground pepper
1 tablespoon butter
½ cup chopped onions
¼ cup chopped carrots
1 cup white or red grapes,
    seedless if possible

½ teaspoon thyme
½ bay leaf
½ cup dry red wine
1 cup chicken stock
2 teaspoons Dijon mustard

Split the quail down the back and flatten them out. Remove the backbones and necks, chop into large pieces, and reserve. Season the quail with a little olive oil, salt, and pepper and place them on a broiler tray cut side up.

In a large saucepan, sauté the bones and necks in oil on moderate heat until they are well browned. Add the butter, onions, and carrots and cook for 5 minutes. Add ½ cup of the grapes, chopped, the thyme, bay leaf, red wine, and chicken stock.

Bring the mixture to a boil, lower the heat, and simmer for 10 minutes. Strain the sauce into a clean saucepan and simmer for another 20 minutes.

Halfway through the sauce reduction, broil the quail in a thoroughly preheated broiler for about 10 minutes on each side, until they are crisp. Watch them carefully.

Cut the remaining grapes in half and stir them into the sauce for 2 to 3 minutes. Whisk in the mustard, season with salt and pepper, and serve over the broiled quail.

SERVES 4

Quail en Brochette

8 quail
Juice of 1 lemon
¼ cup olive oil
½ teaspoon marjoram
½ teaspoon rosemary
Salt, freshly ground pepper

8 thin slices of salt pork or bacon
5 slices of firm white bread, cut
  into quarters
5 slices of bacon, cut into squares
Fresh sage leaves

Wash the quail and pat them dry. Marinate them in a bowl with the lemon juice, olive oil, marjoram, rosemary, salt, and pepper for about 30 minutes.

Wrap each quail in a thin slice of salt pork or bacon. Take three long skewers. Spear a slice of bread, then a square of bacon, a few sage leaves, and a quail. Repeat to the end of the skewer and for the next two skewers.

Place the skewers across a roasting pan and put in a 450° oven. Baste with any remaining marinade or some olive oil. Cook for about 25 minutes, basting and turning occasionally.

SERVES 4

Boneless Quail Stuffed with Wild Rice

This is a little more work than the preceding recipe, but it makes a fine presentation when you are entertaining. It is not hard to bone quail; you will find that after the first one or two, you can do it quickly.

8 quail
Salt, freshly ground pepper
1 cup chopped onions, carrot,
  and celery
12 juniper berries
¼ cup cognac
¼ cup wild rice
¼ pound (1 stick) butter
1 small onion, chopped
2 cups chicken stock (page 25) or
  water

¼ cup raw white rice
1 egg, beaten
2 tablespoons grated Parmesan
  cheese
4 slices of fatty prosciutto,
  chopped
Flour
½ cup veal or chicken stock
8 slices of white bread
Watercress for garnish

With a small paring knife, cut the quail down the back. Remove the breastbone, wishbone, and rib cage. Leave the wings and the drumsticks intact; remove the thighbone. Wash the quail and pat them dry. Sprinkle them with salt and pepper.

Make a quick stock with the quail bones and giblets, a few chicken backs or necks if you have them (cut into small pieces), and the chopped vegetables. Use 3 to 4 cups of water in order to get 1 cup of stock for cooking the quail.

Crush the juniper berries and soak them in the cognac for at least 2 hours.

Soak the wild rice in water for about 20 minutes. Drain.

Heat 4 tablespoons of the butter in a saucepan and sauté the onion in the hot butter until it is translucent. Add the rice and cook a few minutes. Add the chicken stock, cover the pan, lower the heat, and simmer for 45 minutes. Add the white rice and cook until it is tender but not mushy, about 18 minutes.

When the rice is cool, turn it into a bowl. Add the egg, Parmesan cheese, and prosciutto. Mix well.

Fill the quail with the wild rice mixture and tie each one with white string. Roll them lightly in flour.

Brown the quail in the remaining 4 tablespoons of butter, turning them several times. Strain the cognac into the pan a little at a time. When it has evaporated, add ½ cup of the quail stock and the veal stock; cover the pan and cook for about 10 minutes.

Remove the quail and keep warm while you reduce the sauce to the density you like. Toast the bread and cut the slices into ovals. Place the toast ovals on a serving platter with the quail on them and cover with the sauce. Garnish with watercress.

SERVES 4

Squab Perugina

Squabs are young pigeons, 21 to 30 days old, that have never flown. They are specially bred for food and are considered game because their flavor has a gamier taste than that of most pheasant or quail on the market. You can find them at specialty butcher shops or Chinese markets.

6 squabs	¾ cup Marsala or any dry sherry
Salt, freshly ground pepper	¾ cup white wine
6 slices of prosciutto	12 lemon slices
Fresh or dried sage leaves	½ cup water
12 slices of bacon	

Clean the squabs and singe off any fine hairs left on the skin. Rinse and pat dry. Season the cavities with a very little salt and pepper and place in each cavity a slice of prosciutto and a few sage leaves. Use 2 fresh or 3 dried leaves for each cavity. (Do not use powdered sage.) Truss the birds with white string and set aside.

Cook the bacon in a large skillet until nicely browned. Remove the bacon and reserve. Brown the squabs on all sides in the hot bacon fat. Pour off all the fat and add the Marsala. Reduce for a minute or two. Add the wine and reduce by half.

Add the lemon slices and water. Cover the skillet, lower the heat, and simmer for about 1 hour.

Reheat the bacon. Split the squabs lengthwise down the backbone and arrange them on a serving platter. Place a slice of bacon and a slice of lemon on each squab half and serve with a bit of the sauce from the pan.

SERVES 6

Pheasant Saint Buge

Although the story goes that pheasants were first imported into the United States from England by George Washington for his Mount Vernon estate, it was not until 1880 that they received their start in this country as a game bird. Judge O. N. Denny, then U.S. consul in Shanghai, shipped Chinese ring-necked pheasants to Oregon, where they were set free on the Willamette River. Since then they have been introduced into nearly every state, thriving especially well in the northern half of the United States.

Like many game birds, pheasants are lean and the breast is the driest part of the meat. Slipping a slice of salt pork, bacon, or fatback between the skin and the flesh of the breast adds flavor and keeps the breast meat juicy. Or you can wrap the slices around the bird and secure them with a string.

Although I have not given you a special recipe for wild turkeys, the largest upland game bird in the United States that has been successfully reintroduced into some New England states, they are cooked exactly as you would a domestic turkey. Like many game birds, they are good on the rare side. Wild turkeys are lean and need the extra help of two strips of salt pork, bacon, or fatback inserted between the skin and the breast.

Pheasants weigh between 2½ and 3½ pounds; the cock and the smaller hen are sometimes sold together as a brace; allow 1 pheasant for 3 or 4 people.

1 pheasant	*¼ cup calvados*
Salt, freshly ground pepper	*Juice of half a lemon*
4 thin slices of salt pork or bacon	*½ cup heavy cream*
4 tablespoons butter	*Optional: bread slices fried in*
1 onion, chopped coarse	*butter, spread*
1 carrot, chopped coarse	*with orange marmalade*

Wash the pheasant, pat dry, and season with salt and pepper. Make an incision at the V of the neck between the skin and the flesh of the breast on both sides of the breast and slip a slice of salt pork or bacon into each side. Wrap the remaining 2 slices of salt pork around the body of the pheasant. Truss the bird so the wings, legs, and salt pork are tied together.

Heat the butter in a flameproof casserole large enough to hold the pheasant and add the chopped onion and carrot to the hot butter. After they have cooked for 3 or 4 minutes, add the pheasant and brown it on all sides. Cover the casserole and place it in a preheated 450° oven for 35 minutes. Reduce the heat to 350°.

Remove the pheasant, cut it into serving pieces, and keep warm. Drain any excess fat from the pan. Add the calvados and flame it carefully. Add the lemon juice and cream and stir well, scraping up any little bits in the pan.

Return the pheasant to the casserole and cook it in the oven for another 15 minutes.

Arrange the pheasant pieces on your serving platter and strain the sauce through a strainer or food mill over the pheasant. Serve with butter-fried triangles of bread and orange marmalade.

SERVES 3 TO 4

Variation: Pheasant with Mushrooms

Macerate 12 crushed juniper berries in 1 cup of white wine for 30 minutes. Rub olive oil on the pheasant, season with salt and pepper, and insert salt pork between the skin and meat of the breast as above. (Do not wrap the bird in salt pork.)

Cook the vegetables in butter (add 1 chopped celery stalk if desired), brown the pheasant, and pour in ½ cup of the white wine you have strained from the juniper berries. Cook, covered, at 425° for 45 minutes, turning the pheasant and basting it with the remainder of the wine.

Meanwhile, sauté 1 chopped onion in 4 tablespoons of butter; add ¾ pound of cleaned mushroom caps and cook, covered, for 15 minutes.

Cut the pheasant into serving pieces and keep warm. Add the cognac and flame; add the cream diluted with 2 tablespoons of currant jelly. Return the pheasants to the casserole, add the mushrooms, and cook another 15 minutes in a 325° oven.

Pheasant Andalusian Style

This recipe and the preceding recipes for pheasant would also be good with quail or squab.

1 pheasant, about 3½ pounds	3 slices of bacon
1 teaspoon dried rosemary	¼ cup olive oil
Salt, freshly ground pepper	1 small onion, chopped fine
3 small white onions, peeled	1 cup dry white wine
2 wild mushrooms, sliced	1 cup chicken stock
6 green Spanish olives, pitted	1 small glass of cognac or brandy
1 bay leaf	¼ cup heavy cream

Wash the pheasant and pat dry inside and out with a paper towel. Season the inside and outside of the bird with rosemary, salt, and pepper. Place the white onions, mushrooms, olives, and bay leaf in the cavity; close with a skewer or truss with white string. Wrap the bacon around the outside of the breast.

Heat the olive oil in a large flameproof casserole. Cook the chopped onion in the oil for a few minutes; add the pheasant and gently brown on all sides. Add the wine and let it reduce; add the stock, partially cover the casserole, and simmer on moderately low heat for about 45 minutes.

Remove the pheasant and cut it into portions. Keep the pieces warm on a serving platter. Deglaze the pan with the cognac; add the cream and heat through. Pour the sauce over the pheasant and serve.

SERVES 3 TO 4

Roast Wild Duck

Canvasback, mallard, black, teal, and pintail are only a few of the many wild duck varieties shot by hunters in the United States and Canada. They range from 1½ pounds to 3 pounds in weight and are distinguishable by their plumage. Wild ducks should be plucked dry, the pinfeathers removed, and the fine hairs singed over a flame. Remove the entrails and wipe down with a wet cloth inside and outside. Remove the fat duct on top of the tail.

Wild ducks are usually lean; like pheasant and wild turkeys, they need a slice of salt pork, bacon, or fatback slipped between the skin and the flesh of the breast or wrapped around the outside of the duck.

Unlike domestic duck, wild duck should always be served rare. You may be a little put off by the almost bloody look of the meat, but you will find the taste is far better rare than well done.

2 wild ducks	*1 apple, peeled and cored*
Salt, freshly ground pepper	*2 thin slices of salt pork* or *bacon*
2 small white onions, peeled	

Clean and dry the ducks and rub with salt and pepper inside and outside. Place an onion and half an apple in the cavity of each duck. Wrap with the salt pork slices or slip them under the skin of the breast meat.

Roast the ducks in a preheated 450° oven, basting every few minutes according to the following schedule (the larger ducks need the longer time):

Mallards, canvasbacks, blacks	18 to 20 minutes per pound
Pintails, blues	15 to 18 minutes per pound
Teals	12 to 15 minutes per pound

SERVES 4

Variation: Southern Style

Season two mallards or canvasback ducks with salt and pepper inside and outside. Stuff the cavities with a cooked veal sweetbread cut into small pieces, ½ cup of chopped salt pork, a few thyme leaves, and a small amount of mace. Sew openings closed and baste with 1 cup of port wine during roasting.

Roast Goose Italian Style

If you are shooting your own geese, take careful aim to be sure you get a goose and not a gander. The flesh of the young goose is delicious and tender, but that of an old wild gander is tougher than leather. The plumage on the gander is coarse and heavy, and there is a large wingspur at the elbow of its wing.

These two recipes are suitable for domestic geese and wild geese with this one very important difference: The domestic goose is very fatty. It should be cooked on a rack and the fat poured out halfway through the cooking; see the procedure for Roast Goose English Style (below). Although a goose has a large frame, it does not have a lot of meat. An 8-pound goose will serve 6 people; for 10 people you need a 14-pound goose.

1 wild goose, about 10 pounds
Salt, freshly ground pepper
1½ pounds Italian Sausages
    Roman Style (pages 237–238)
15 to 20 pitted green olives,
    sliced
2 dozen chestnuts, peeled, lightly
    roasted, and chopped coarse
    (see Note, page 139)
1½ cups butter-fried croutons
2 eggs, lightly beaten
¼ teaspoon marjoram
A few gratings of fresh nutmeg

1 to 2 black truffles, sliced
    (optional)
3 tablespoons olive oil
2 to 3 onions, chopped coarse
2 celery stalks, chopped coarse
2 to 3 carrots, peeled and
    chopped coarse
A small bunch of parsley
1½ tablespoons flour (optional)
½ cup chicken stock
½ glass dry Marsala or any
    other dry sherry

Wash and dry the goose inside and out and season with salt and pepper. Cut the gizzard, heart, and neck into small pieces.

Discard the sausage skins and mash the meat into a bowl. (If using sausages with marjoram or nutmeg seasoning, omit those ingredients from the stuffing.) Add the olives, chestnuts, fried croutons, and eggs. Add the marjoram, nutmeg, some salt and pepper and mix well. Spoon the stuffing into the cavity. If using truffles, lay thin slices of the truffles on top of the stuffing along the length of the goose. Truss the bird so the stuffing will be firmly held inside the cavity and the wings and legs are tied close to the body (see page 15).

Cover the bottom of a large oval flameproof casserole with the oil; add the onions, celery, carrots, parsley, and the chopped gizzard, heart, and neck of the goose. Lay the goose on top of this fragrant bed. Sprinkle flour over the vegetables if you wish a thicker gravy. Pour in the chicken stock. Butter or oil a piece of parchment or waxed paper cut the shape of the casserole and place it over the goose, butter side down. Cut a hole in the center so steam can escape.

Cover the casserole and cook in a preheated 350° oven for 2 hours and 30 minutes to 3 hours. Stir the vegetables and turn the goose from time to time, always being sure to replace the paper and the cover.

Remove the goose and keep it warm. Add the Marsala to the juices in the pan on moderate heat and deglaze the pan. When the wine has almost evaporated, strain the vegetables and juices through a strainer or a food mill. Remove as much fat as possible from the juices and serve with the goose.

SERVES 8

Variation: Roast Goose English Style

4 cups water
Goose giblets, chopped
2 cups coarsely chopped onions,
   carrots, and celery for gravy
   (pages 26–27)
4 large onions, unpeeled
1 cup chopped celery
2 cups bread, soaked in milk,
   squeezed, and shredded
1 egg, lightly beaten

¼ teaspoon marjoram
A few gratings of fresh nutmeg
1 tablespoon crushed sage leaves
1½ teaspoons salt
½ teaspoon freshly ground
   pepper
1 to 1½ tablespoons flour
½ glass dry Marsala or other
   sherry

Make a stock with 4 cups of water, the chopped giblets of the goose, and ½ cup of the coarsely chopped vegetables. Cook until it is reduced to about 2 cups.

Bake the onions (unpeeled) in a preheated 350° oven for 20 minutes. When they are cool enough to handle, peel and chop them. In a large bowl, mix the onions, celery, bread, egg, marjoram, nutmeg, sage, salt, and pepper. Stuff the goose and truss it.

If you are cooking a domestic goose, place it on a rack in a preheated 350° oven and cook for 1 hour. Remove the goose from the pan and pour out all the fat. Return the goose to the rack and place around it the remaining 1½ cups of coarsely chopped carrots, onions, and celery. Sprinkle with the flour and cook for 10 minutes. Add the stock and cook slowly for another 1 hour and 30 minutes, basting often with the stock. Deglaze the pan with the Marsala and make gravy.

Rabbit Hunter's Style

You can use rabbit bought in the supermarket or wild rabbit or hare shot in the woods for this or any of the following recipes. If you want more sauce to serve with polenta or rice, use the large-size can of tomatoes.

3 tablespoons oil
1 garlic clove, crushed
1 rabbit cut into pieces, about 3½
  pounds
1 large onion, chopped
1 teaspoon rosemary leaves

Pinch of marjoram
1 tablespoon chopped parsley
1 cup dry wine, red or white
1 16-ounce can peeled plum
  tomatoes
Salt, freshly ground pepper

Heat the oil in a flameproof casserole and color the garlic in the hot oil. Add the rabbit, onion, rosemary, marjoram, and parsley and brown on all sides.

When the rabbit is thoroughly browned, add the wine and reduce. Add the tomatoes and season with salt and pepper. Cover the casserole, reduce the heat, and simmer for 2 hours or longer, stirring frequently to prevent the meat sticking on the bottom of the casserole.

SERVES 4

Variation: With Wild Mushrooms

Sauté 1 pound of fresh porcini or shiitake mushrooms in 2 tablespoons of butter. Add to the rabbit halfway through the cooking. You can use regular mushrooms, but the wild ones have more flavor.

Rabbit Provençal

In this recipe you immerse the rabbit a day ahead of time in a fragrant marinade, which then becomes the cooking liquid.

2 cups dry white wine
1 cup chopped carrots
1 cup chopped onions
1 cup chopped celery
2 bay leaves
1 teaspoon rosemary
Salt, freshly ground pepper
2 rabbits, about 3½ pounds each,
  cut into neat pieces
½ pound salt pork

¼ pound fat prosciutto or bacon
  or pancetta
2 garlic cloves, chopped
1 tablespoon chopped parsley
1 large onion, chopped
Chopped celery and carrots
  (optional)
1 8-ounce can peeled plum
  tomatoes, with the juice
1 cup strong beef stock

Boil the wine, vegetables, bay leaves, rosemary, and some salt and pepper for 5 minutes. Cool.

Wash the rabbit pieces and pat dry. Place in a terrine or earthenware bowl and cover with the cold marinade. Refrigerate for 12 to 24 hours.

Chop the salt pork with the prosciutto, garlic, and parsley. Brown in a large heavy casserole. Add the chopped onion, celery, and carrots if desired, and cook for 3 or 4 minutes.

Remove the rabbit pieces from the marinade and pat them dry. Brown them in the casserole. Strain the wine from the marinade into the casserole and reduce. Add the tomatoes with the juice and the beef stock. Cover the casserole and simmer gently for 2 hours to 2 hours and 30 minutes. Taste for seasoning.

SERVES 8

Variation:

Roll the rabbit pieces in flour before browning in 4 tablespoons of butter and 4 tablespoons of hot oil. Remove the vegetables from the marinade and add to the casserole. Cook as above with the wine from the marinade. Serve with polenta with the gravy from the casserole poured over it.

Hare St. Hubert

1 *hare, 4 pounds, or 2 small*	1 *bay leaf*
rabbits	*Pinch of rosemary*
1 *cup chopped carrots*	2 *cups red wine*
1 *cup chopped onions*	1/4 *cup vinegar*
1 *cup chopped celery*	1 *tablespoon flour*
6 *tablespoons olive oil*	1/2 *cup veal stock*
1 *garlic clove, sliced thin*	2 *tablespoons currant jelly*
2 *whole cloves*	1/2 *teaspoon orange zest, cut into*
1/2 *teaspoon sage*	*julienne slivers*

Cut the rabbit into neat pieces. Sauté the chopped carrots, onions, and celery in 3 tablespoons of the olive oil for 15 minutes without browning. Add the garlic, cloves, sage, bay leaf, and rosemary. Cook for 2 or 3 minutes. Add the red wine and vinegar. Bring to a boil, remove from heat, and let cool. Marinate the rabbit pieces overnight in the refrigerator.

Dry the rabbit pieces and brown them in the remaining 3 tablespoons of hot oil in a large casserole. Strain the marinated vegetables, saving the liquid. Add the vegetables to the casserole and cook until nicely browned. Sprinkle with flour; stir and cook for 1 or 2 minutes. Add the wine from the marinade a little at a time until it has all been absorbed. Add the veal stock, lower the heat, cover the casserole, and simmer until the meat is tender, about 2 hours to 2 hours and 30 minutes.

Remove the meat from the casserole with a slotted spoon. Add ½ cup of warm water to the casserole to deglaze. Remove any excess fat. Add the currant jelly and orange zest; stir the sauce and serve over the rabbit.

SERVES 4

TO BONE A RABBIT

Lay it on its back on your workspace with the hind legs away from you. Split the pelvic bone in two so the two legs come apart and the bone is open. Start cutting around the pelvic bone on one side. Cut around the ball and socket of the pelvic bone and the femur bone. Sever the nerve holding the femur bone to the socket. Continue cutting until you come almost to the back where the spine is. There is not much meat between the skin and the bone, so be very careful not to inadvertently poke holes in the skin. (If there are holes, sew them up after stuffing.) Repeat on the other side.

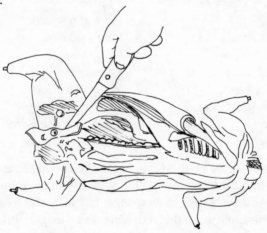

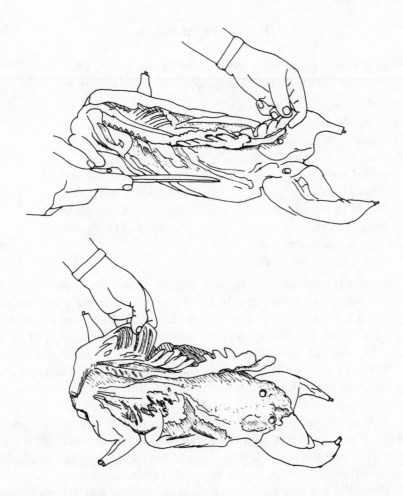

Cut across where the tail is attached and pull the pelvic bone up a little bit to loosen it. Scrape and pull the two fillets on either side of the spine away from the backbone and five or six finger bones, but do not detach them. Cut underneath the finger bones, being careful not to cut the eye of the chop. As you work toward the back, there is no meat, just skin, and you can gently pull the bones off by pulling and scraping. When you reach the rib cage, snap off the backbone you have worked on so far.

Cut along the bones of the ribs and pull away whatever meat you can. Leave the shoulders attached. Break the backbone off at the neck. The femur bones in the back legs can be removed or left as is.

Note: A farm-raised rabbit may have globs of fat in the rib-cage area. These should be removed.

Boned Stuffed Rabbit

You can be creative with the stuffing for this rabbit. I first tasted this particular version in the Champagne country of France in the 1970s.

1 fresh rabbit, about 4 pounds	1 egg, lightly beaten
Salt, freshly ground pepper	Pinch of sage
1½ pounds beef, ground	1 tablespoon chopped parsley
½ pound veal, ground	6 slices mortadella
½ pound pork, ground	1 carrot, peeled and chopped
4 slices of bacon	1 celery stalk, chopped
2 onions, 1 chopped fine, 1	A small glass of white wine
chopped coarse	A small glass of Slivovich
½ cup bread soaked in milk,	
squeezed, and shredded	

Season the rabbit with salt and pepper. Grind the beef, veal, and pork together in a meat grinder or food processor or ask your butcher to do it for you. Finely chop 2 slices of the bacon and mix with the ground meat, the finely chopped onion, bread, egg, sage, and parsley. Season with salt and pepper.

Place a layer of the stuffing in the rabbit. Arrange 3 slices of the mortadella rolled into cones on top of the stuffing, add another layer of stuffing, and the remaining 3 slices of mortadella.

Sew up the rabbit with a large needle, or tie it as you would a roast beef. Place the rabbit on a large sheet of heavy-duty aluminum foil. Cover it with the remaining 2 slices of bacon and surround it with the chopped onion, carrot, and celery. Add the white wine.

Close the foil and place it in a shallow roasting pan in a preheated 350° oven for 1 hour and 20 minutes. Open the foil, baste the rabbit with the juices, and cook with the foil open for another 25 minutes. Make gravy from the vegetables and juices and flavor with the Slivovich liqueur.

SERVES 6

Stuffed Roast Squirrel

Squirrel can be cooked like rabbit, as can woodchuck and beaver. The beaver is a strict vegetarian who feeds on bark, twigs, tree buds, berries, and lily roots, all eaten underwater. Beaver meat is dark in color but fine in texture, and tender. The fat should be cut off and discarded. Here is a recipe for squirrel that is good for any of the small furred animals.

4 squirrels
12 juniper berries, crushed
Salt, freshly ground pepper
1/4 cup lemon juice
1 tablespoon lemon zest, cut into
  julienne slices
1/2 cup olive oil or peanut oil
1 garlic clove, peeled and chopped
1 medium onion, chopped
2 tablespoons butter or oil
1 pound mushrooms, chopped

1 1/2 cups stale bread soaked in
  milk, squeezed, and shredded
1 egg, lightly beaten
8 slices of bacon
1/2 cup white wine
Optional: 1/2 cup beef stock or
  bouillon
1 tablespoon butter
1 tablespoon flour
2 tablespoons
  currant jelly

Spread the squirrels in a roasting pan. Rub the meat with juniper berries, salt, and pepper. Pour the lemon juice, lemon zest, and olive or peanut oil over them and let rest for at least 2 hours.

Brown the garlic and onion in the 2 tablespoons of butter or oil. Add the mushrooms and cook until they give up their liquid. Turn the garlic, onion, and mushrooms into a bowl and add the soaked bread and egg. Season with salt and pepper and mix well.

Divide the stuffing into four parts and fill the cavity of each squirrel with stuffing. Close the openings with skewers.

Place the squirrels breast down in a shallow roasting pan and place 2 slices of bacon on each squirrel. Pour the remaining oil from the marinade over them and cook in a preheated 350° oven for 1 hour and 30 minutes, turning them and basting them with the white wine from time to time.

Serve with mashed turnips and potatoes.

If you wish a gravy, keep the squirrels warm on a serving platter while you deglaze the pan with the stock. Make a roux of butter and flour and whisk it into the hot stock. Add the currant jelly at the end.

SERVES 4 TO 6

Large Game

If you bag a deer, open it up from the neck down to the crotch and eviscerate it as soon as possible. Hang it on the branch of a tree (away from the sun) so that all the blood will drain away; this will take about 30 minutes. If you cannot tie the animal to a tree, prop up the head. Be sure to keep the liver; it is delicious.

Hunters who take their deer home tied to the hood or front fender of a car are letting their vanity outweigh their common sense. The animal should be kept as cool as possible; the heat of the motor is detrimental to the meat.

Venison should age in a cool place (like a butcher's refrigerator) at 34° to 36° for at least a week before skinning.

TO DRESS A DEER

If you are going to skin the deer yourself and cut the meat into pieces suitable for the freezer, here is how to do it.

You will need a saw, a skinning knife (a boning knife with a rounded point), a butcher (steak) knife, a boning knife, a steel, and a cleaver. If you do not have a pulley with which to hang up the deer, lay it on a large table with the back side down.

A deer will weigh between 80 and 100 pounds, similar to a small calf. The cutting procedures are the same as for veal, with the difference that the shoulders of a deer are smaller than those of veal, the legs larger.

On one side of the incision, cut with the skinning knife between the skin and the flesh from the lower part of the abdomen. Holding the skin with one hand, cut and scrape between the skin and the flesh in a scraping movement, being careful not to cut the flesh or the skin. Start pulling the skin across to the outside of the body. Cut right up the hind legs to the feet, pulling the skin toward the outside. Continue down to the neck, still on the same side of the incision.

When one side is complete, start on the other side of the incision, pulling the skin over to the outside as before. When you reach the neck, pull the skin off the shoulders.

Turn the deer over so the stomach is down. Grab hold of the skin at the hind legs and pull the skin entirely off the deer in one piece. Cut the skin off at the neck. Dry the skin and rub salt on the inside of it. (If the raw hide is folded and rolled before it is cool and dry, it will spoil quickly. You can send it to a tanning house for processing to make into beautiful gloves and jackets. If you plan to use the hide in this manner, you should take special care to prevent abrasions on the skin from dragging the carcass on the ground.)

Saw off the head. Divide the meat into primary cuts; you will get a neck, two shoulders, a rack, a loin, and a pair of legs, just as we did with veal. Then you break these cuts down into usable parts that you can cook right away, freeze, or preserve in a marinade. Be sure to cut away and discard any part of the meat that is bloodied from the gunshot, usually in the shoulder.

The hind legs are heavy and bulky, so get them out of the way first by cutting them off the body at the hip. Cut through the meat with the butcher knife. When you come to the bone, change to the saw and saw through the bone. Finish cutting the meat with the knife. You do not want to cut through meat with a saw; it will tear the meat.

Count the first two ribs and cut across to separate the loin from the body. Count eight more ribs and cut across again; this is the rack. You are left with the neck and shoulders, which are connected by a lot of membrane. You can pull the membrane off to separate the three pieces.

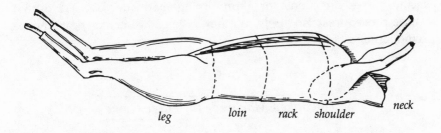

leg   loin   rack   shoulder   neck

Now you are ready to cut these primary cuts into usable parts. The neck weighs about 12 to 15 pounds. It can be boned out for sausage or ground meat or cut across in 2-inch-thick slices for braising and stews.

The shoulders are about 11 to 15 pounds apiece and are good boned out, seasoned, rolled, and roasted. The shanks are like the neck, good for sausage or stews.

The better cuts of the animal are left. The rack is about 6 to 9 pounds. With the breast attached, it is like the bracelet of lamb or veal. Remove the breast 4 inches from the eye of the chops and use it for stews or, boned, for ground meat or sausage. Split the rack down the spine lengthwise with the saw. Now you can cut rib chops of any thickness you desire.

The loin is also about 6 to 9 pounds. Cut off the flanks that cover the front of the animal so that about 3 inches remains attached to the eye of the chop. The flank meat you have cut off is not suitable for flank steak because it is thin and full of membranes; grind it for sausage or ground meat. Cut the remainder of the loin in half lengthwise. You can either cut it into chops or you can bone out the two pieces for 3- to 4-pound saddle roasts. (If you have shot a very large, 400-pound deer, the chops will be steaks.) Be sure to remove the kidney.

The two hind legs, about 25 to 30 pounds, offer a wealth of possibilities. By following the aitchbone directly down, you can cut off the rump to make a rump roast of 3 to 4 pounds, then continue slicing diagonally up the leg to get three to four round bone steaks (similar to ham steaks). Or you can separate the muscles at the seam too get three small roasts or meat for cutlets. If you want to have a hunting party for about 20 people, remove the aitchbone; the top round, sirloin, and bottom round can be cooked as a large roast of 15 to 18 pounds. (This roast should be barded, covered with strips of fatback, before roasting.)

Any meat you are not intending to freeze can wait in the refrigerator, loosely wrapped in clean paper with air circulation, for 2 to 4 days. It should marinate for another 24 to 48 hours in the refrigerator (below) to tenderize the meat and further flavor it. If you do not have freezing facilities, see directions for a preserving marinade (pages 279–280). These procedures also apply to other large game such as bear, moose, reindeer, and buffalo.

Uncooked Marinade for Large Game

Like salad dressings in French families, marinade recipes are carefully guarded and handed down from one generation to another. The soaking of meat in brines and pickles to enhance the flavor and tenderize the meat has been a common practice in Europe and Russia for centuries. It is useful to soften the flavor of game meat from an old animal; when the meat is fresh from a young animal, however, you may not want to lose the flavor by marinating it very long. This recipe is for meat you plan to use within 48 hours.

1 onion, chopped coarse
2 carrots, peeled and chopped
   coarse
2 celery stalks, chopped coarse
12 peppercorns, crushed
3 garlic cloves, peeled and
   crushed
6 sprigs of parsley
1 teaspoon basil

1 teaspoon thyme
2 bay leaves
Salt, freshly ground pepper
2 cups dry red wine (or more; see
   Note)
½ cup peanut oil
½ cup vinegar
Water to cover the meat, if
   necessary

Place the vegetables and seasonings in a crock or large enamel pot. Season the pieces of meat with salt and pepper. Place them on the vegetables and pour the liquids over them. Add water if necessary to cover the meat. Marinate in the refrigerator 24 to 48 hours, turning the meat at least twice a day.

Note: If you are marinating a large piece of meat like a leg of venison or bear, use almost a bottle of wine.

YIELD: ABOUT 4½ CUPS

Preserving Marinade

This cooked marinade is for hunters who have bagged some big game and are without freezer space to preserve it. If kept in a large crock in a cool place, this marinade should preserve your game for months.

Double this recipe for large quantities of meat.

½ pound lard or Crisco
1 pound onions, chopped coarse
1 pound carrots, peeled and
   chopped coarse
1 pound celery, peeled and
   chopped coarse
Small bunch of parsley, chopped
   coarse
2 bay leaves

¼ cup chopped fresh basil leaves
   or 2 tablespoons dried basil
1 whole head garlic, crushed but
   not peeled
3 tablespoons dried thyme
1 teaspoon whole cloves
1 tablespoon salt
2 quarts wine vinegar
1 quart red wine

In a large casserole, heat the lard and add the onions, carrots, and celery. Cook until soft but not brown.

Add all the remaining ingredients, let come to a boil, lower the heat, and simmer for 45 minutes. Remove from the heat and cool completely.

Place the meat in a large crock and cover with the marinade, adding water if necessary. Cover the crock tightly. Keep in a cool place.

This marinade may be reused by reboiling it and storing it in sterilized jars.

YIELD: ABOUT 6 QUARTS

Noisettes of Venison with Fruit

Because venison gets tough if it is overcooked, these noisettes should be browned quickly in hot butter. Seasoning the meat with a dry marinade of juniper berries and lemon zest gives the meat a little extra flavor. The elegance of prunes in Madeira complements the meat.

12 large dried prunes, pitted	Olive oil or peanut oil
Madeira wine to cover the prunes	Flour (optional)
1 boneless saddle of venison, cut into 12 noisettes 1½ inches thick, about 3 to 4 pounds	¼ pound (1 stick) butter or clarified buter
12 juniper berries, crushed	1 cup dry white wine
1 lemon zest cut into julienne strips	1 cup veal stock
Salt, freshly ground pepper	1 cup game stock
	Bread slices fried in butter (optional)

Cover the prunes with Madeira and marinate them for at least 24 hours.

Place the noisettes in an open pan and season them with the juniper berries, lemon zest, salt, and pepper. Sprinkle with oil and set aside for at least 2 hours.

Lightly flour the noisettes if desired. Heat the butter in a large heavy skillet and brown the noisettes quickly on all sides, being careful not to burn the butter. Turn them several times. Remove the meat to a serving platter and keep warm.

Meanwhile, bring the prunes and Madeira to a boil, lower the heat, and simmer for 10 minutes.

Discard the fat in the pan and deglaze the pan with white wine. Let the wine reduce to less than half; add the veal stock and game stock. Simmer on low heat to reduce for at least 5 minutes.

When the stock has reduced by half, add the prunes and the wine and cook for another 5 minutes, stirring gently and continuously.

Return the noisettes and juices to the pan and heat through so the meat absorbs the flavors.

With a slotted spoon, set the prunes around the noisettes, alternating them with triangles of fried bread. Ladle the sauce over the meat.

SERVES 6

Variation: With Pears

Poach peeled pears in a sugar syrup. Deglaze the pan with ¼ cup of cognac and ¼ cup of Madeira. Add the stock and cook until the stock has reduced by half. Add the pears, cut into eighths, to the sauce for a few minutes to let them absorb the flavor.

Braised Leg of Venison

Chestnut Puree (below) is a lovely seasonal accompaniment to any game roast.

Half a leg of venison, about 6 pounds
A few strips of fatback
Uncooked Marinade for Large Game (pages 278–279)
½ pound salt pork, diced
2 cups coarsely chopped onions, carrots, and celery

Salt, freshly ground pepper
1 cup dry red wine
1 cup beef stock (pages 278–279)
Optional: 1 tablespoon flour
1 tablespoon butter

Marinate the venison leg in the uncooked marinade for 24 to 48 hours before cooking. Tie a few strips of fatback around the venison before marinating.

Remove the meat from the marinade and pat it dry. Reserve the marinade.

In a large flameproof casserole, brown the diced salt pork. When it has browned, add the vegetables and the venison, lower the heat, and brown gently on all sides. Season with salt and pepper. Add the wine, a cup of the liquid from the marinade, and the beef stock. Partially cover the casserole and simmer for 1 hour and 30 minutes to 2 hours. Do not overcook the meat or it will get tough. An old deer will take longer than a young one.

When the meat is done, pass the vegetables and juices through a food mill. If the gravy is too thin, thicken it with a roux of flour and butter whisked into the strained gravy.

SERVES 8 TO 10

Chestnut Puree

Either peel the chestnuts according to directions in Note on page 139, or buy canned, unsweetened chestnuts at the store.

1 pound chestnuts, skinned
2 celery stalks, cut into large
　pieces
½ fennel root, sliced or 1
　teaspoon fennel seeds
1 bouquet garni

1½ to 2 cups chicken stock
5 tablespoons butter
A few gratings of fresh nutmeg
Salt, freshly ground pepper
3 to 4 tablespoons warm milk

Place the chestnuts in a saucepan with the celery, fennel, and the bouquet garni. Cover with chicken stock and bring to a boil. Simmer for 40 to 50 minutes, adding more stock if necessary.

Drain the chestnuts and reserve the liquid. Discard the celery, fennel slices, and bouquet garni. Mash the chestnuts with a potato masher or put them through a food mill. Beat in the butter and a little of the cooking liquid. Season with nutmeg, salt, and pepper.

Heat the puree over moderate heat or in a double boiler and beat in enough warm milk to achieve the consistency of mashed potatoes.

Braised Leg of Wild Boar with Sweet and Sour Sauce

I always think of wild boar in the mountains of Umbria where I was born, but boar can also be hunted in the United States in game preserves in Tennessee. Boar is cooked in exactly the same manner as venison, but the marination time, 7 or 8 days, is considerably longer. The sweet and sour sauce complements the taste of the meat.

1 leg of wild boar, 8 to 10 pounds
Preserving Marinade (pages 279–
　280)
4 tablespoons butter
4 tablespoons oil
2 onions, sliced thin
2 carrots, peeled and sliced
2 celery stalks, sliced
Salt, freshly ground pepper
1 cup dry red wine
2 cups veal stock
6 tablespoons sugar
2 garlic cloves, peeled and crushed

1 bay leaf
¼ cup vinegar
4 tablespoons grated unsweetened
　chocolate
1 tablespoon potato starch or a
　roux of 1 tablespoon flour, 1
　tablespoon butter (optional)
¼ cup white raisins
15 dried prunes soaked in
　Madeira
Candied citron
Candied orange peel

Remove the skin from the ham, score it, and place in a large terrine or crock. Cover with the cooked, cooled marinade and place in the refrigerator for 7 to 8 days, turning the ham at least twice a day.

Heat the butter and oil in the bottom of a large flameproof casserole and add the sliced vegetables. Cook for 5 minutes, then add the boar and brown it on all sides with the vegetables. Sprinkle with salt and paper and add the wine. Reduce to half and add the veal stock. Partially cover the casserole and place it in a preheated 350° oven for about 3 hours, or until a meat thermometer registers 170°.

Remove the meat to a serving platter and keep warm; defat the juices from the roast.

Make the sweet and sour sauce: Dissolve the sugar in a saucepan with the garlic and bay leaf. When it has turned a golden color, add the vinegar. The sugar will congeal, but keep stirring it with a wooden spoon until it dissolves again. Add the chocolate, bring it to a boil, lower the heat, and cook until the chocolate is completely melted. Add 1 cup of the juices from the roast and stir well. Strain into a clean saucepan.

If you feel that the sauce is too thin, thicken with potato starch or a roux of flour and butter. Simmer the sauce until it is the correct density. Add the raisins and prunes, then the candied citron and orange peel. Slice the boar and serve the sauce on the side.

SERVES 14 TO 16

MEAT
PACKAGING

THE LAST TEN YEARS have seen tremendous changes in the meat industry. In this chapter I will show professional chefs and stewards who buy meat in quantity for their restaurants, hotels, clubs, etc., what they should know about some of the new ways in which meat is processed and packaged.

The major innovation is that, with a few exceptions, meat is no longer delivered in carcass form. About twenty years ago slaughterhouses began experimenting with vacuum-sealed bags called cry-o-vac. Instead of shipping a whole carcass of beef to the wholesaler, who then sold it to the butcher, slaughterhouse workers broke the beef down into individual muscles (work formerly done by butchers in their stores) and delivered the broken down beef parts to the butchers. At first, there was a good bit of resistance on the part of butchers and chefs. Many butchers felt cheated by not having the opportunity to select the meat themselves. A box of meat weighing 70 to 80 pounds contains cry-o-vac bags with meat parts that may come from five different animals. The butcher cannot always be sure of getting meat of the same quality in the same bag. Under this system, bones and fat no longer come to the butcher with the carcass, rather, they are sold separately by the slaughterhouse. If a butcher wants to get marrow bones or neck bones, he must buy a whole bag, which may be more than he can sell. Also, in the early days of cry-o-vac packed meat, there was a strong ammonia-like smell when the bag was opened.

The technology improved (the slight odor on opening the bag now disappears within fifteen minutes) and butchers and chefs began to see the advantages of meat with a long shelf life. Instead of going to the market every other day, stewards, chefs, and butchers can now buy every few weeks and order specific cuts to suit their business needs. The unions like cry-o-vac packaging because 70-pound boxes of meat are considerably less heavy than carcasses and therefore less dangerous to their men. Supermarkets are enthusiastic because the boxes stack easily and can be transferred into their stores by forklifts. Supermarkets no longer need to hire experienced butchers who know how to break down a leg of veal or bone out a shell; anyone who has a steady hand can operate a slicing machine or a band saw. In some instances, the supermarket can buy the meat "case ready"; all the butcher has to do is put the meat into the refrigerated cases.

The use of cry-o-vac packaging has extended to pork, lamb, and veal. Today less than ten percent of meat is delivered in carcass form and that is to prime butcher shops and kosher shops.

Some years ago the National Association of Meat Purveyors, in conjunction with the United States Department of Agriculture, developed lists of cuts of meat by number. The most up-to-date book of these lists, with color pictures of the different cuts of all meats, was published in 1981 and is available from the Superintendent of Documents, U.S. Printing Office, Washington, D.C. 20402, or from the National Association of Meat Purveyors, 8365 Greensboro Drive, McLean, Virginia 22102, telephone: (703) 827-5754. The book costs approximately $35.00. Beef cuts run from numbers 100 to 193, lamb cuts 200 to 238, veal cuts 300 to 343, and pork from 400 to 423. Due to a continuing reliance on cry-o-vac packaging, there are more and smaller cuts available today than in 1981.

The other two major changes in the meat industry are in grading and inspection. Grading meat has always been voluntary, paid for by the processor; it is perfectly legal to sell ungraded meat (see page 168). Grading was marked into the fat with blueberry "ink." But now that the meat is broken down at the slaughterhouse, there is no longer any fat on which to mark the grade, so purchasers cannot be sure what grade of meat they have received. There is a high potential for abuse.

When I was working as a butcher, the United States Department of Agriculture inspected every animal and certified it healthy and safe for human consumption. As of this writing, in December 1990, legislation is under consideration for the USDA to get out of the meat inspecting business entirely, and turn all the inspecting over to the meat producing companies. It seems to me this is another situation that does not benefit the consumer.

Poultry

There has been a terrific change in the way poultry is sold over the last sixty to seventy years. In the 1920s consumers expected their chickens to be alive when they bought them. Butchers, however, were not allowed to sell live poultry in their stores; only licensed live chicken markets could sell live chickens.

It took a lot of educating and the closing of many live chicken markets before butcher shops selling poultry would be accepted by the public. Until 1940, New York dressed chickens were sold with head, feet, and entrails. The next step was a law prohibiting poultry to be shipped interstate unless it was eviscerated; crates filled with chickens and cracked ice were then trucked into the cities.

Meat rationing during World War II meant long lines at butcher shops. Smart entrepreneurs bought crates of chickens, cut them into parts, and opened store fronts to sell chicken parts to customers who did not have time to wait in line for a few chops. By the end of the War in 1945 when rationing and price ceilings ended and meat became available again, chicken in parts was a booming business. Processors cut up the chickens and packed the parts in 15-pound bags (five bags to a crate) with cracked ice. Today cases of iced chicken, whole and already cut up, arrive at butcher shops and supermarkets in refrigerated trailers. Whole oven roasters may be vacuum packed, and fully cooked chickens packaged by the producer are also available in some supermarkets.

Chicken parts are sold as:

Breast, bone-in
Breast, boned and skinned
Cutlets (a cutlet is half a breast)
Nuggets (a nugget is the small filet of the breast)
Drumsticks
Thighs
Wings
Livers, gizzards, and hearts
Feet (often only available in Chinese markets)

Turkeys are no longer sold just for the Thanksgiving and Christmas holidays. In the 1960s turkey breeders, faced with the problems of raising an entire flock for a once-a-year sale, used the advent of strong plastic bags and the efficiency of the new vacuum-packing machines and quick-freezing machines to freeze and package whole turkeys when they were in their prime. However, turkeys are big birds and it required a lot of freezer space to store the turkeys until the market demand made it profitable to sell them.

The most recent evolution in turkey marketing is selling turkey parts directly to the consumer, an experiment that started in the 1970s. It was slow going at first but thanks to a growing realization that turkey is a fine tasting protein with a minimum fat content, turkey parts have become acceptable as year-around food. Producers have added turkey cold cuts and sausages to their line of turkey products.

When fresh turkeys are vacuum packed and shipped in cartons, they do not need icing as long as they are refrigerated. They will last in good condition in the refrigerator for eight to twelve days. Fresh case-ready packages of turkey parts for retail use are vacuum packed at the processing plant and will only last four to five days in the refrigerator.

Turkey parts are packaged as:

Breast, bone-in
Breast, boned
Breast, boned and cooked (roasted)
Cutlets (sliced breast meat)
Drumsticks
Wings
Ground meat

Cooking a breast of turkey is no different than cooking a roast chicken and the result is all white meat. Or you can do as I do and bone out a whole turkey and make four roasts, one from each breast half, and one from each leg/thigh combination. I bone out the legs and thighs, remove all the tendons from the drumsticks, stuff the leg/thigh, tie it, and roast it to feed four people. Once you have removed the bone and tendons from the drumstick, it can be easily sliced just like any other roast. Oddly enough, you do not see turkey thighs for sale separately.

Pork

The meat packing industry began in the United States in the northeast colonies in the 1650s when pigs were cut into pieces, salted, and shipped in barrels to the West Indies. When Cincinnati was the pork capital of the country, the meat was shipped down the Ohio River.

Refrigeration replaced salting in the 1880s, making it possible for meat to be shipped across the country to the West Coast. Pork packaging is essentially the same today as it was a hundred years ago. Pork is not packed in cry-o-vac bags; it is wrapped in parchment paper and shipped in boxes.

The new developments in pork are the continuing efforts to cross-breed pigs to produce lean pork with less fat, a far cry from earlier days when farmers bred their pigs for their lard. (see page 65).

Pork is seldom sold whole, except as baby suckling pigs for roasting, spit roasting, or wrapping in ti leaves and cooking in hot rocks for a luau. It is also shipped in sides, as some ethnic groups like the Chinese prefer fresh cut pork.

Older pigs can be dry and on the tough side so I advise that you look for animals under one year old. A light pink colored loin of about 12 to 14 pounds will be more tender and more flavorful than an 18- to 22-pound loin from an older pig whose meat will be darker and tougher.

Pork is available in the following traditional cuts:

Head, jowls on or jowls off
Shoulder, whole or Boston butt off
Trotters (toes) and hocks
Boston butt, bone-in or bladeless
Full loin, center cut loin, and boneless center cut loin
Bellie, skin on, skin off (bacon), back fat
Spare ribs (with sternum bone on)
Barbecue style spareribs (sternum bone off)
Baby back ribs
Country style ribs
Hams (hind legs)

Cured and processed pork is available as the following:

Picnic hams, smoked or ready to eat (from the shoulder)
Smoked Boston butt, bladeless
Smoked hocks
Smoked loin, uncooked or ready to eat
Cured boneless loin (Canadian bacon)
Smoked ham (hind leg), commercially produced—fully cooked and
    ready to eat
Prosciutto dry cured ham, ready to eat because of its long aging
Smithfield ham, farm raised; dry cured, it needs soaking, boiling, and
    baking
Boiled and steamed hams, cooked and shaped
Boned ham shaped into a cylinder for cutting into round ham steaks,
    cooked or uncooked
Lean and fat trimmings for sausages

Lamb

New methods of producing lamb include staggering the conception
times so that young lambs will be born at all times of the year, and
giving lamb grain in the holding pens as a supplement to their diet of
mother's milk and grass. Some lamb is still available in carcass form,
but less and less every year.

The four major parts of lamb—chuck, rack, loin, and leg—are available in cry-o-vac packaging as follows:

Shoulder (chuck) with neck, shanks, and brisket
Square cut shoulder

Neck
Hotel rack
Split rack, chined
Loin
Split loin with kidney fat removed
Leg, bone-in, singly or doubles
Leg, boned and netted

New Zealand lamb pieces are smaller than ours and are well packaged as:

Shoulder chop, blade bone
Shoulder chop, round bone
Fore shank
Split rack: six ribs, chine bone removed
Rib chop, cut individually
Loin chop, cut individually
Loin, split vertically
Trimmed leg, short cut, ready to cook
Sirloin steak, cut off the leg

Veal

Veal is the most delicate meat. It does not have a thick coat of fat to protect it, nor does it have a fel, the parchmentlike skin that covers lamb meat. Most veal is shipped with the hide still on, then skinned, cut, and packaged at its destination point. All of the portions are available in cry-o-vac. It can only be kept for a short period of time.

During the last few years there has been a tremendous controversy concerning the raising of veal. (To understand the difference between the three kinds of veal—bob veal, nature veal, and conventional veal—please read the introduction to the veal chapter on page 130.) To get true nature veal, male calves are restricted to a diet of milk and milk replacers from the time of their weaning until they are ready for market in twelve to fourteen weeks. The meat is a lovely light pink color and is very delicate. Some animal activists object to the necessity of restricting the young calves in barns so that the only food they receive is the milk formula. They claim that the calves should be raised "naturally," that is, allowed to graze and eat grass. The problem is that once a calf starts to eat solid food like grass or hay, it produces three more stomachs to digest that food and thus becomes a ruminating animal. Its meat gets dark and it is no longer true veal, rather, it is baby beef.

I firmly believe that nature veal raised the European way on milk and milk extenders produces the most delicious and the most delicate meat. I do not think veal raised this way is inhumane because my experience is that barns where nature veal calves are raised are clean, airy, and well lighted. The stalls are washed every morning and the animals are treated very gently to prevent bruising the flesh. No farmer is going to mistreat the very animal on whom his livelihood depends.

Veal is available in the following parts:

Leg, bone-in
Tbs (one piece: top sirloin, top round, bottom round)
Top round
Bottom round
Shoulder, bone-in
Shoulder clod
Loin
Loin, split and trimmed
Breast, bone-in
Rack, whole
Rack, split
Shank
Cutlets, sliced from the leg
Cutlets, sliced from the shoulder clod
Loin chops
Rib chops
Cubed, cut from the neck or shoulder

Beef

In an effort to produce lean meat, breeders are working hard to grow an animal that will not have much fat externally but whose meat will still be palatable, tender, and flavorful. It takes years of breeding and cross-breeding to get results but the determination of cattle ranchers, private breeders, and university research programs will eventually yield fine leaner meat. The Black Angus Association has come up with very fine choice cattle but only a small amount is available to a limited number of restaurants and hotels.

My own feeling is that in an effort to get less fatty meat to the consumer, the meat industry is pushing fourth and fifth grade beef that does not have the flavor, tenderness, and texture of prime beef. (See page 168 for definitions of the seven grades of beef.)

I am dubious about the claims of "organic meat." I thoroughly approve of raising meat without the addition of steroids or hormones but it seems to me that in order to be truly organic, the cattle must graze on grass from soil that has not been fertilized with chemical fertilizers, eat grain and corn that have had no contact with chemical fertilizers, and drink water from a pure, clear spring. A tall order.

The way we buy beef now, by separate individual muscles in cry-o-vac bags, is the same system the Europeans have been using for years. Instead of buying a chuck steak to be potted, braised, etc., we are now offered four individual muscles from the same piece of meat: top blade meat, mock tender, under blade meat, and a chuck eye roast. We need to understand how best to use each of these individual muscles.

Top blade meat weighs three to four pounds and looks like an oval slice with a thin tendon across the center; at one time it was called a chicken steak. It may be broiled, sautéed, or braised whole. The mock tender looks like a cone; it may be braised or potted whole, or sliced and stir fried or sautéed for pepper steak. Under blade meat is a flat, solid piece of meat weighing about four pounds. If marinated, it may be grilled, or it may be sliced for beef stroganoff or for stir-frying. The chuck eye roast is not a solid muscle, but a number of muscles that are connected by lines of fat and membrane. It may be potted for slow roasting or cut into cubes for a fine beef stew.

Short ribs come from three different places. First, and most common, are the three ribs from the thick side of the prime rib; second are three ribs cut from the plate. Both of these are cut from the sixth to the ninth rib. Finally, we have the short ribs cut from the first to the fifth rib under the chuck; these are called flanken. All of these short ribs may be braised, used for boiled beef, or cut into cubes and potted. If marinated overnight, they can be grilled.

A prime rib consists of the seven ribs from the fifth to the twelfth. When we use the expression prime rib, we are not designating the grade of the meat, but rather the best or choicest part of the rib section. If you ask for a prime grade rib roast, then it should be graded prime.

A skirt steak is the diaphragm from the rib cage of cattle. It is narrow, with the fibers running crosswise. It makes a wonderful, juicy steak and is usually broiled.

A flank steak is the inner muscle of the cattle's abdomen. It is twice as wide as a skirt steak and its fibers run lengthwise. It can be used for a London broil, butterflied for a braciola, or sliced thin for stir-frying.

The neck is the very end piece, from the end of the shoulder blade to the Atlas bone from which the square cut chuck has been removed. It is used mainly for hamburgers or cut into cubes for stew; it also may be used for boiled beef.

A brisket is the very front piece of the breast, from the first rib through the fifth. Boned out and trimmed of its fat, it is used for braising or potting. It makes a terrific boiled dinner, a beef bourguignon, or beef flammande. Most briskets are cured for corned beef.

The fore shank is normally a poor piece of meat, tough, with very strong tendons. Its best use is cut crosswise with the bone and cooked for a good beef stock. It can be ground for hamburger but I do not recommend this as no matter how finely it is chopped, small pieces of tendon will remain in the meat.

A forequarter of beef is available in the following cuts, most of which require braising or some other method of cooking in liquid:

Square cut chuck, bone-in (sometimes called the neck)
Square cut chuck, boneless
Neck, bone in
Neck, boneless
Shoulder clod (also called cross rib), boneless
Top blade meat, boneless
Mock tender, boneless
Under blade meat, boneless
Chuck eye roast, boneless
Brisket, bone-in
Brisket, boneless, deckle on (the deckle is a covering, an extra upper
    muscle over the eye of the main cut)
Brisket, boneless, deckle off
Whole prime rib, seven-rib cut
Prime rib, seven-inch cut, oven ready
Prime rib, boned and tied
Boneless rib eye
Short ribs from the plate
Short ribs from the chuck, i.e., the flanken

A hindquarter of beef is available in the following cuts, all of which may be used for roasting or broiling:

Loin (whole)
Short loin
Short hip
Shelled loin
Regular shell, bone-in
Shell chined and partly trimmed
Shell chined, boned, and totally trimmed

Shell hip, bone in
Shell hip, boneless
Top sirloin butt
Bottom sirloin butt
Bottom sirloin flap
Bottom sirloin triangle
Full tenderloin
Full tenderloin, defatted, side muscle on
Full tenderloin, defatted, membrane removed
Butt end tenderloin
Flank steak, regular, skinned
Skirt steak
Round (whole)
Round, boneless
Round, shankless, partially boneless
Knuckle face (also called sirloin tip or top sirloin)
Top round (also called inside round)
Bottom round (gooseneck)
Bottom round (gooseneck), heel off
Eye round
Hind shank, bone-in
Hind shank, boneless

Variety Meats

Here is a list of organ meats, also called variety meats or offal, that are available either in cry-o-vac or in five- to fifty-pound plastic containers.

PORK	LAMB
Brains	Brains
Tongues	Tongues
Hearts	Hearts
Livers	Livers
Kidneys	Kidneys
Tripe	Tripe
Heads	Heads
Casings, wide and narrow	Casings
Caulfat	
Leaf lard	
Chitterlings (large intestines)	
Sows' ears	
Fresh skins	

VEAL	BEEF
Brains	Brains
Tongues	Tongues
Hearts	Hearts
Livers	Livers
Kidneys	Kidneys
Livers	Tripe, plain or honeycomb
Kidneys	Pancreas
Sweetbreads	Scalded feet
Scalded heads	Blood
Scalded feet	Cheek meat
	Casings: rounds, middles, and bungs

Wild Game

Wild game has become more popular in recent years, but in this country it is against the law for a hunter to sell what he kills. He may give it away, but he may not sell it. Much of our game, therefore, comes from commercial game farms or it is imported. Here is a list of what is available:

FEATHERED GAME	FURRED GAME
Scotch grouse	Scotch venison
Wildwood pigeon	New Zealand venison
Wild turkey	Native venison
Chukea partridge	Reindeer
Ringneck pheasant	Wild boar
Bob white quail	Wild hare
Mallard duck	Native buffalo
Guinea hen	Raccoon
Jumbo squab (pigeon)	

Some restaurants like to feature the meat of exotic animals and there are entrepreneurs in the business of supplying lion meat, bear meat, llama meat, hippopotamus meat, giraffe meat, alligator meat, and rattlesnake meat.

INDEX

Note: Capital letters indicate recipes.